ADDIE BRAVER

ADDIE
BRAVER

ERIC T. BERGMAN

Polk Place Publishing
Minneapolis, MN

ISBN: 978-0-578-43695-1

Printed in the United States of America

Cover art by Dan Perry. More of Dan's work can be found at www.stcroixart.com.

For Maggie and Drew

TABLE OF CONTENTS

SUMMER, 1977

JUNE

S	M	T	W	T	F	S
			1	2	3	4
5	6	7	8	9	10	11
12	13	14	15	16	17	18
19	20	21	22	23	24	25
26	27	28	29	30		

JULY

S	M	T	W	T	F	S
					1	2
3	4	5	6	7	8	9
10	11	12	13	14	15	16
17	18	19	20	21	22	23
24	25	26	27	28	29	30
31						

AUGUST

S	M	T	W	T	F	S
	1	2	3	4	5	6
7	8	9	10	11	12	13
14	15	16	17	18	19	20
21	22	23	24	25	26	27
28	29	30	31			

SEPTEMBER

S	M	T	W	T	F	S
				1	2	3
4	5	6	7	8	9	10
11	12	13	14	15	16	17
18	19	20	21	22	23	24
25	26	27	28	29	30	

Prologue
April 8, 1965

The little girl was terrified. Everything around her was harsh and unfamiliar. And when an airplane—bigger than anything she'd ever seen before—roared to life nearby, she clung fearfully to her father's camouflaged pants. Someone hollered, "*Cheeeese*," but she never took her eyes off the man she adored.

A strange feeling for this little girl—fear. Though only three and a half years old, she wasn't used to being afraid of anything. She was now—they all were. But not her father. He smiled down at her with the glow of unconditional love and a reassurance that they would see each other again.

"It's going to be your job to keep this safe, honey," he said, handing her the Polaroid photograph that had just been taken of them. "Put it somewhere you won't forget, okay?"

She cradled the picture in her hands and nodded gravely as a lump formed in her throat. The shapes in the Polaroid began to appear—first her and her father, then next to them her mother holding her baby brother. The girl studied her parents' faces in the photograph. His displayed a contemplative, confident smile. Hers was a portrait of sorrow and confusion.

The little family huddled close together until an official-looking man in an olive-green service uniform approached them and announced, "Corpsman, it's time."

"Why do you have to go, Daddy?!" the little girl wailed.

"We talked about this, Addie. Remember?" he explained, kneeling in front of her. "There are men far away that need my help. But I won't be gone forever. We'll be together again—I promise."

His vow was too much for the girl's mother to hear. She wept uncontrollably while her son squirmed in her arms. The young family embraced again until the uniformed man reminded him—more insistently this time—that the plane was about to take off and that he had better be on it.

"I love you," he told his sobbing wife. "All of you." His smile faltered momentarily as he kissed each of them goodbye.

But the little girl wouldn't let go of his hand as he turned toward the aircraft. "Please don't go, Daddy!" she cried over and over again, pleading with him to stay until he finally scooped her up in his arms.

"Can you do one more thing for me, honey—while I'm gone?" he asked her tenderly. "Take care of your brother for me. Watch over him. It's a big job, but I know you can do it." Through fresh tears the girl agreed and he set her down next to her mother.

"We're going to be okay," he insisted. "Everything's going to work out just like I planned." And with that final promise he jogged up the stairs and disappeared inside the aircraft.

The little girl squeezed her mother's hand, never taking her eyes off the airplane as it taxied down the runway, lifted gently off the ground and climbed high into the western sky. "Mommy," she asked sadly as they walked across the runway tarmac, "What's Vietnam?"

1

HALVERSON ROAD

"Come on, Shorty! JUST LET GO!"

Adeline Pearson stood impatiently with her hands on her hips in the gravel valley of Halverson Road. High on the crest of the hill, her 13 year-old brother Billy sat uneasily on his too small, too battered Huffy bicycle, and soaked in her words.

The last day of school—Friday, June 3, 1977—was over but Addie wasn't looking forward to another summer vacation. Instead, she was trying to delay its start for as long as she could. For 15 year-old Addie, summers meant one thing—three long months tiptoeing around her alcoholic step-father.

"Shut up, Addie!" Billy yelled down at her. "And stop calling me Shorty!"

"When have I ever called you *Billy*?!" she hollered back. Billy shrugged, answering that he didn't know. "Exactly! So let's go already, Shorty!"

"Knock it off, Addie! How come everything hasta be a fight with you?!"

Addie was a hard person to like and she knew it. Her instincts had been finely honed to push back against everything and everyone in her life. Addie had her reasons, but if her brother simply saw her as his angry, impatient sister, then so be it. It wasn't like she was going to tell Billy what really drove her, what had driven her for years—protecting him.

"Don't blame me!" she replied, ignoring his question. "You were the one who said riding your bike no-handed was a big deal!" Addie blew a strand of straw-blonde hair away from her pale, freckled face. "I'm just making sure you put your money where your mouth is!"

A boyhood rite of passage or not, Billy wouldn't be rushed, and had said as much thirty minutes earlier. Addie didn't listen then either, telling him to get his bike and meet her on Halverson Road the moment they stepped off the school bus.

"What's her problem?" he muttered, squeezing the cracked rubber grips on the bike's handlebars. As was his habit when he was nervous, Billy chewed on his lower lip. It was shaping up to be a long, prickly summer.

He looked over at nearby Carson Hill, then to the interstate a mile further, ready to surrender to Addie's stubborn demand. But his focus and

3

her attention were quickly drawn to a familiar, unwelcome rust-orange Ford Comet turning off of Halverson Road and onto Pine Circle. Addie's hands left her hips and her scowl faded.

"Come on, Shorty!" she implored, her eyes blazing with a renewed intensity. "You can do this!" Billy didn't feel any of Addie's confidence, but he lifted his foot off the pedal anyway. The bike quickly gained speed, the tires kicking up small rocks that had been loosened by a road grader the day before. Slowly, his hands rose off the handlebars.

For an instant Billy believed his sister—*I can do this!* But his belief vanished when the bike's front tire struck an unyielding rock and twisted hard to the right. Leading with his left shoulder, Billy slammed onto the gravel, slid past Addie and tumbled headlong into the ditch. The bike followed, coming to rest at his feet like a dog napping near its master.

Addie stepped casually into the ditch and examined the bike for damage before returning her hands to her hips. "You're fine," she said matter-of-factly. "So you fell, so what? You're not hurt that bad, Shorty."

"My name's not Shorty!" Billy yelled, his eyes wet with tears. "And this," he gestured to his ripped t-shirt. "This is all your fault!" One sleeve was gone, ripped free by a piece of clear glass that had buried itself in his shoulder.

"Hold still," Addie ordered as blood trickled down Billy's arm. "This is gonna hurt." Billy grunted as she yanked the shard free. He scanned the ditch for his torn sleeve, hoping to use it to stanch the flow of blood, but found a faded red bandana instead. Hidden beneath it was more broken glass.

"Is that a bottle?" Billy asked, pressing the bandana into his shoulder.

"It used to be," Addie answered. "Before your shoulder smashed it to pieces." She didn't have to guess whose bottle it was—she knew. "Let me do that," she said, snatching the bandana from his hand. Billy grimaced while Addie searched the cloth for a set of embroidered initials. After finding them—*JRP*—she tied the bandana around the wound, then picked up his bike.

"Thanks, Ad."

"So what are you going to tell Mom?" she asked, pointing to his torn shirt.

"That you talked me into it, and as usual I was the only one who got hurt." Billy smiled despite his misery.

4

"But you're gonna try again, right? You'll regret it if you don't. I'm serious."

"Serious about what? It's just Halverson Road," he replied. "It's not like I'm not crossing the Atlantic in a hot air balloon." But Billy's failure embarrassed him—he had practically grown up on two wheels. Adding to his humiliation was the fact that he was still riding a bike more suited for a boy half his age.

"It's not just Halverson Road," Addie murmured, looking in the direction of Pine Circle where the Comet was most likely parked. "Some things you just have to face."

"Some things *I* have to face?!" Billy snarled in disbelief. "You're one to talk."

For a moment Addie's eyes flashed with a familiar anger before softening. "I know, Shorty," she admitted. "I guess we both have things we need to work on this summer."

"Come on," he said, calling a truce. "Let's go home. But how many times do I have to ask you? Stop calling me Shorty."

*

They climbed out of the ditch and away from Halverson Road towards the only other house on Pine Circle. The sprawling rambler, like most of the half-mile *Loop*—no one called it Pine Circle—was home to the Farelli family. It bordered the lower field of nearby Carson Farm.

"What happened to you, Billy?"

Renny Farelli always seemed to appear out of thin air whenever Billy was within shouting distance of his house. A year younger and much shorter than Billy, with a shock of unruly black hair, Renny was easy company, constantly chattering on about whatever was on his mind.

"Whaddya think happened?" Addie said accusingly.

Renny's cheerful expression disappeared. That Addie's irritation with him wasn't personal was beyond Renny's comprehension.

"Knock it off, Addie," Billy interjected. "Renny didn't do anything." He waved his friend over. "Come on, Ren. Grab my bike."

Renny wheeled the bike around to Billy as the trio passed through the Farellis' front yard. As Addie had feared, a hundred feet ahead of them and across the Loop, the Comet was parked in the Pearson's driveway—

just two shallow trenches of dirt on a thin patch of grass. Next to it sat their modest trailer home.

"Hey, Billy—I thought your dad was out of town?" Renny said.

"He's not our dad!" Addie barked.

Calling the man in the trailer, *Dad*, made sense to Billy, even if it felt wrong sometimes. But not to Addie. She still remembered another man. That man's face lived on in her brother's smile, another reason she protected Billy so fiercely. To protect Billy was to protect her father's memory. The only name Addie ever used for the other man was *Jake*.

*

Jacob Ronald Pearson had brought Billy, Addie and their mother Anna to Halverson Road almost ten years earlier, in the fall of 1967. He was somewhat shocked when she had agreed to his hasty marriage proposal that same summer. Friends since childhood, Anna was everything Jake wasn't—quiet, self-disciplined and organized. In the beginning, her calm demeanor rubbed off on Jake. He drank less and worked more. His usual stubble was gone and his stained clothes were swapped out for clean ones.

But as Jake's luck ebbed and flowed over the course of time, his destructive habits resurfaced. At first, Anna did her best to encourage him. When Jake was jobless, she combed through the want ads, leaving phone numbers on their small kitchen table for him to call when he *"felt like it."* And she constantly bargained with him to drink only beer. Anything stronger, Anna knew, revealed an ugliness in Jake that she couldn't hide from Billy and Addie. But as the hopelessness of her efforts eventually became clear, Anna's thoughts often escaped to the past.

*

Anna Pearson had once been Anna Travers, marrying her high school sweetheart eight months after graduation. Will Travers, possessing a poet's soul and a warrior's heart, was a conflicted young man at the dawn of a conflicted decade. Military service, he decided, would give him the answers he needed. So, against Anna's wishes, he enlisted in the U.S. Navy in December 1960.

Stationed in San Diego, Will was joined the following spring by a pregnant Anna. Little Addie, born in late September, was a handful from the start. But Anna employed the same patience with her feisty daughter that she used to soothe her idealistic husband. By the time Billy was born in November of '63, Anna had already begun planning for life after Will's six-year enlistment was up. She wanted to bring her family home.

But in the spring of '65 the Navy gave Will a choice. Complete his enlistment stateside as a Navy Corpsman instructor or serve one year in Vietnam attached to a Marine unit in America's rapidly escalating war in Southeast Asia. Discharge nine months early would be Will's reward.

Anna was unyielding in her opinion. *Stay in San Diego*, she begged him. *Stay with us!* But she knew of Will's need to be tested—how the Navy's offer pulled at him. So, when Corpsman Travers boarded a DC-10 heading halfway around the world, Anna could only wave goodbye. Addie, speaking for her mother and brother, cried over and over, "Don't go Daddy!"

After a few months in-country, the battle that had previously warred within Will fused together. Corpsman Travers instinctively knew the rhythms of the boys in his unit. So attuned to their cries for help, he knew where he was needed on the battlefield whenever his squad was dropped into a combat zone. Consequently, he was able to tend to the emotional and physical wounds of his comrades and carve out a level of independence for himself within the military's rigid chain of command.

Like Anna before him, Will began thinking about life after Vietnam—college on the G.I. Bill, maybe a career in medicine—as his tour of duty ground on. His decision to serve overseas had hurt her deeply, but they managed to find their way back to each other in daily letters. He wrote of his safe, easy duty. She told him how well they were getting along in his absence. But between the lines of these little white lies, Will and Anna rebuilt their love.

The opposing parts of Will that had merged together in war eventually unraveled. He questioned the wisdom of orders from superiors who didn't understand the enemy or the terrain they fought on. One by one, friends began filling body bags. And all the time he thought of Anna.

Will's war ended in late November 1965, three weeks after Billy's 2nd birthday when he jumped out of a hovering helicopter and into a rice paddy, fifty yards away from a jungle clearing. Without thinking, he picked a lotus flower that lay at his feet and put it in the left breast pocket of his faded fatigues. Suddenly, the jungle erupted with enemy rifle and mortar fire. Will turned toward the chaos—scanning the landing zone for fallen comrades—and was struck by a single bullet through his heart. The small hole reddened and grew, staining the flower's fragile white petals. Corpsman William Travers, 23 year-old husband and father, was gone before he hit the ground.

The next twelve months were an unending nightmare for Anna. Will appeared to her every night in her sleep. Sometimes he was dressed in the combat uniform he had died in, but more often he sported the crisp Navy whites he'd worn the day they were married.

The last time Anna dreamed of Will was the same day Jake Pearson re-entered her life. Jake was untroubled by thoughts Will had struggled to reconcile. Ethical dilemmas never bothered him. Grief-stricken and numb, Anna accepted Jake's clumsy marriage proposal, even giving in to his demand that Billy and Addie take *Pearson* as their last name. Not stopping there, he insisted that Will's name never be spoken in his presence, nor could she ask questions about Jake's mother, gone since he was 17. Anna Travers, a single mother with an uncertain future, meekly agreed.

*

"You wanna go around the Loop a few times?" Renny suggested hopefully. "I can get my bike." The idea was a grateful distraction to Billy and Addie, pulling their attention away from the hostility and history inside the trailer in the form of their step-father.

"I'm game," Billy replied, taking his bike from Renny.

"Sure," Addie agreed. "But Shorty's bled enough for one day. Let's walk instead." Billy scowled at her use of his nickname in front of Renny but yielded, laying his bike in the grass.

Laid out before them was the lower field of Carson Farm. Beyond it, up a long hill, stood a big white house in front of a narrow strip of tall pine trees that separated the farm's two fields of hay. Addie had admired the house when she was younger but her appreciation hardened into resentment as year piled on top of year, like some cruel joke compared to the cramped trailer home they lived in. Inspired by her bitterness, Addie took out a small notepad from the back pocket of her faded denim shorts. She wrote quickly, hiding her words from Billy and Renny.

A field of shimmering gold,
Rises up a gentle slope.
Mocking me all the way,
Choking off any ray of hope.

Addie's notepad went wherever she did, one of only two places she ever revealed her true feelings. Words came easily to her—they always had—but remained hidden from prying eyes. She couldn't bear to be found out, have her heart exploited.

"He's gonna do it this year, Billy!" Renny sputtered as Addie tucked the new poem into her pocket.

"No one has hit .400 in the majors in over 30 years, Renny," Billy countered with an eye roll. "Besides, he's not even close. Last Sunday's paper said he was hitting .366. It's NOT gonna happen."

Addie groaned. For the last four summers the two boys had carried on a running argument about the only thing that mattered to Renny Farelli—the Minnesota Twins' Rod Carew hitting .400 in a single baseball season.

".376," Renny corrected him. "He was 4 for 5 yesterday. This is the year, Billy. I can feel it!"

Billy was almost as excited as Renny about Rod Carew's incredible start to the 1977 season, even if he occasionally dampened his friend's wild enthusiasm. He pored over box scores too, though he never cataloged the slugger's batting average the way Renny fanatically did.

Addie's hastily scribbled rhyme and one more Rod Carew debate brought them halfway around the Loop, parallel to the state highway. She stopped their procession and looked wistfully at a familiar mailbox across the blacktop. Attached to its metal post was a twirling wrought iron sculpture rising ten feet in the air. It had been an inviting target for Addie and Billy ever since they were strong enough to lob rocks across the road.

"Whaddya say, Shorty?" Addie asked him. "It's been a long time."

Billy looked at her with an expression that shouted, *Knock it off with Shorty, already!* He glanced over at Renny, but his friend was too distracted by a baseball card he'd fished from his back pocket to hear Addie. No harm done, but Billy realized his sister was stalling. He

9

couldn't remember the last time they had thrown rocks at the mailbox, clear proof that she didn't want to go anywhere near the trailer until their mom got home from work. Addie may have protected him from Jake for years, but Billy was no fool.

"Okay," he finally agreed. "But what's the bet?"

"Mom made chocolate chip cookies last night," Addie said with a sly grin. "Winner gets the loser's cookies for a week."

"Why'd ya hafta pick that?" Billy groaned, his shoulder still burning from his tumble into the ditch. "You don't even like chocolate chip."

Addie ignored him and scoured the road for rocks. She glanced over at Renny, who had been silent for some time. "Whaddya say, Carew? You want in on this? The mailbox is only a hundred feet away." But a hundred feet may as well have been a hundred miles to Renny. As nimble as his brain was with numbers, he was just as clumsy when it came to anything athletic.

"How 'bout I be the umpire," Renny offered innocently.

The game was simple. Taking turns, they threw rocks at the mailbox. The first person to hit it won. Addie's first attempt was a near miss— Billy's too, though Renny considered each throw with all the seriousness he could muster.

"Did you hear that?" he asked, furrowing his brow. "I thought I heard a little ping. Did you hear a ping, Billy?"

Addie stared at Renny, who was crouching awkwardly in the ditch between the Loop and the highway. "I didn't hear a thing, twerp. And neither did you. But you'll hear this." On *this*, she grunted and fired. The rock came in fast and low, clanging hard against the mailbox door, knocking it open. She spun around, a wide grin spreading across her face.

"Nice throw," Billy said coolly.

"Nice throw?!" Addie ran across the highway and closed the mailbox door. "Shorty, you couldn't do that in a million years!" she crowed triumphantly.

"Like a Twins' double play," Renny said, happy to agree with Addie for a change. "Like Thompson to Carew to Kusick—right on target. She's gonna win for sure, Shorty."

"Your turn," she said, pointing to the mailbox. "If you miss, you lose."

"You miss, you lose, Shorty," Renny repeated.

Billy scowled at Addie but spoke to his friend instead. "Renny, you don't know squat. Carew hasn't played 2nd base in two years and Craig Kusick's just a designated hitter now, not a first baseman. And Thompson . . . well, Danny Thompson's dead." Besides Rod Carew, shortstop Danny Thompson had been Renny's favorite Minnesota Twin. He had died of leukemia a few months after the 1976 season.

"You didn't have to say that!" Addie hissed, her hands digging into her hips.

"Neither did you!" Billy shot back. "And you know what I'm talking about!" He let the rock drop from his hand. "You win. I'm going home." Billy began walking across the Loop to the trailer, but before he took two steps Addie grabbed his wrist. Her eyes were unblinking, but betrayed a trace of compassion as well.

"I'm sorry," she whispered, letting go of his arm.

"How long have I asked you not to call me that?!" he replied angrily. Addie tried to say more but Billy waved her off after seeing Renny rocking back and forth in the ditch, unsure what he'd done wrong.

"Hey Ren, I'm sorry. I just don't like when Addie calls me that."

"I won't say it again, Billy. I promise."

Billy smiled. He knew Renny was a lot of things—smart, awkward, obsessive—but more than anything else, he was a loyal friend. "I liked Danny Thompson too, Ren," he said, changing the conversation to something Renny could understand. "I'll make you a deal. If I get Thompson's baseball card this summer you can have it." Renny's face brightened and, just like that, his hurt feelings disappeared.

They cut their lap short. The way home would go through the Loop's interior—a mixture of lawn, prairie grass and Norway pines, but dominated by *Pete's Woods*.

Pete's Woods, with its mixture of poplar and pine trees, hazelnut bushes and blueberry patches, covered nearly an acre inside the Loop. It wasn't named for anyone called Pete, though Pete had certainly existed.

*

Years earlier, Billy and Renny had been playing catch with a tennis ball in the Pearsons' yard. Spotting a gopher near the edge of the unnamed

11

woods, Billy lobbed the ball at it. To the boys' great surprise, the ball struck the gopher in the head. Blood quickly oozed from its ears.

They both agreed that some sort of burial was in order. Billy ran home and returned with an empty shoebox to put the gopher in while Renny found two paint sticks and some string in his dad's garage. As Billy dug a shallow pit at the edge of the woods, Billy fashioned a crude cross with the flat sticks.

"Shouldn't we put a name on the cross?" Renny wondered.

"Gophers don't have names, Ren," Billy replied.

"How about Pete," Renny suggested.

"Why Pete?"

"Cause if I had a dog I'd call him Pete. But we can't get one since my sister's 'lergic to 'em."

Billy smiled. "Fine by me." He reached into his back pocket and pulled out a pocket knife.

"Where'd you get that?" Renny asked, his eyes widening.

"Jake, er, my dad gave it to me," Billy answered uncertainly. He pulled out the blade and braced the cross with his left hand and began carving a *P* with his right. On the first down stroke the blade buried itself deep into Billy's palm. Dark red blood quickly pooled around the gash. He didn't cry out, but his face paled immediately. Five stitches at the emergency room followed an hour later.

After that, Billy wanted nothing to do with Jake's gift. Addie would find the knife a few years later, hidden in his dresser, and keep it as her own. Meanwhile, the gopher's grave remain unmarked, but Pete's Woods was born.

*

The most impressive stand of trees wasn't in Pete's Woods, however. Springing from one root system, five trees that Billy and Addie called *The Pines* rose forty feet in the air behind the Pearson's trailer, a few feet from the gravel Loop. They had often climbed to the top of each tree when they were younger, straddling the sturdy branches for long stretches of time. Now, after Renny ran home ahead of them, Addie got another idea.

"Let's climb the Pines."

"Really?" Billy asked doubtfully. "I can't remember the last time we did."

"All the more reason to," Addie replied, eyeing the Comet still in the driveway.

"Okay, but if I say yes, the bet's off."

"Fine. You can keep Mom's cookies, but I'm calling it a forfeit."

Addie could have told Billy the truth—that his spectacular fall on Halverson Road and the kindness he'd shown Renny had softened her heart. But Addie had decided long ago that her job wasn't to share her burden with Billy, it was to spare him—as best she could—from the life they were living. Whatever softness remained within her she kept to herself, carefully hidden in her poems and diary.

*

Billy and Addie's Halverson Road was one mile of rolling gravel that ended abruptly against the smooth pavement of the state highway. Nestled next to this juncture was their half-mile Loop, adjacent to the familiar fields of Carson Farm and Carson Hill.

A short mile west of this intersection was I-35, the interstate freeway that meandered non-stop all the way to Texas. To the east, the highway curved gently for a few miles before melting into the small village of Lost Elm, Minnesota. Its population, at least according to a sign at the town's limits (862), hadn't changed in generations. Neither had the water tower in the center of town. The supporting iron framework and gray tank, topped by a red teapot dome, belonged to a bygone era.

Billy loved Lost Elm. He and Renny regularly biked into town on the shoulder of the highway, a warm feeling washing over him whenever the old water tower came into view. During the summer their destination was usually the same, Ervin's Filling Station at the south end of town.

Mr. Ervin—tall, gaunt and well over 70 years old—would nod to Billy and Renny, routinely inquiring, "What'll it be today, gentlemen?" They went straight for the *Topps* baseball cards, ceremoniously dividing ten packs between them. Along with two cans of orange pop and one large bag of M&M's, Billy and Renny would be on their way.

"Next Saturday, boys?" Mr. Ervin always asked them after placing their money in the register. The boys typically nodded, mouths already full of chocolate.

Billy usually insisted on taking the service road home. It ran parallel to a set of railroad tracks, past Lost Elm's long-abandoned train depot. Billy loved wandering through the empty rail yard, often wondering why there were so many tracks but so few trains.

*

Forsaken like so many other small towns after the completion of the interstate freeway, Lost Elm had once been a rowdy railroad junction. Commemorating this, halfway between Halverson Road and the faded population sign, a modest billboard stated:

AT THIS POINT
ON FEBRUARY 15, 1870
THE CONSTRUCTION OF THE
NORTHERN PACIFIC RAILROAD
WAS COMMENCED

Tentatively christened *Northern Pacific Junction* after construction of the railroad began, the town quickly became a transportation hub for a booming local lumber industry, as well as a thoroughfare for iron ore mined in northern Minnesota bound for steel mills back east. At its peak, half a dozen tracks hugged the southern edge of the compact village, whose population peaked at 1,200 in 1914.

Progress and growth, it turned out, led the town to drop its original name. Between 1881 and 1911, Northern Pacific Junction managed to burn through three different schools. After the last blaze, town council members—pressured by civic-minded mothers—passed a bill to construct a fireproof, three-story brick school building. But snuck into the funding bill was a passage that read: *After the school's completion, water and sewer pipes will be installed within village limits with all deliberate speed*. Recent arrivals had pressed for the improvements, referring to the annual summer stench from hundreds of outhouses as "*God-awful*." Besides, they argued, putting the town on a modern water system would prevent the bucket brigade sort of firefighting that had doomed the three previous schools in the first place. Approval was nearly unanimous, but where to place the water tower was not.

The *Fight of '14*, as local historians came to call it, fell into two camps. Local business leaders demanded that a water tower be erected near the intersection of Chestnut Avenue and 3rd Street—the center of town. They stressed that it would be a symbol of strength and civic pride. Naturally, an opposition movement—dubbed *The Elmers*—quickly sprang up. "We're not opposed to progress," they argued. "Just don't destroy our park." The land they were fighting to save, Junction Park, occupied the same half block where the *Commerce Committee* (local businessmen wanted a name too) intended to build their water tower. Day after day under the park's lone tree, a majestic elm, numerous Elmers protested throughout the summer.

By Labor Day, Northern Pacific Junction was a town divided. But miraculously that same afternoon, leaders of both factions announced to a crowd of hundreds that a deal had been reached. The Commerce Committee would be given the park land for the water tower if they agreed to hand over naming rights to the Elmers (no one had ever liked the name *Northern Pacific Junction*).

Gathering in one of the leading Elmer's back yard, ideas were batted around well into the evening. Another fight seemed poised to kick off as names were suggested (*Oldenburg, Paine's Crossing, Carlton*) and rejected in quick succession. Finally, minutes before the Elmers and CC'ers were scheduled to meet in Junction Park for the big announcement, a small boy asked the men a question.

"After you pick a name, what'll happen to that big tree?"

"They'll have to cut it down, son," a man explained. "It's gonna be in the way."

"But I don't wanna lose that tree!" the boy cried.

The man smiled and patted the boy's cheek before turning to the crowd and suggesting, "How about *Lost Elm*?"

*

The re-named town would remain a vital rail center for another four decades, but its glory years were over with the passage of the *Interstate*

15

Highway Act in 1956. Passenger train travel quickly petered out and Lost Elm's depot closed. It was there that Addie often snuck off to, using Billy's forgotten knife to chisel her thoughts deep into the building's aging pine beams:

> *Where can I run to hide from the light?*
> *Steal away from the world like a thief in the night.*
> *Will I be like this forever, alone and apart?*
> *Or do I escape one day and make a new start?*

Beneath the water tower, *First National Bank* and the municipal bar and liquor store anchored an ailing business district throughout the town's steady decline. Aside from these twin pillars, Lost Elm was dotted with a few restaurants, gas stations and auto repair services. Other buildings that didn't house city or county offices never stayed open for long.

Though few people were moving into Lost Elm by the summer of 1977, visitors had been passing through the town for decades. The reason—scenic *Jay Cooke State Park*—lay one mile east of the bank and bar. Jay Cooke, a principal financier of the Northern Pacific Railroad, had donated a tract of land situated on both sides of the fast-flowing St. Louis River, marking it for preservation.

The river rushed under a trestle bridge just a short walk from the park's entrance. Trains had rolled back and forth across it for nearly a century, but those tracks were long gone. Below the bridge and throughout the park, ancient glaciers had left rich deposits of slate. Similar outcroppings were scattered all over town.

West of Lost Elm, miles of marshy wetlands were cut in two by a smaller river, Otter Creek. It flowed parallel to the same railroad tracks Billy and Renny followed in and out of town. Crisscrossing this swampy landscape that locals called *The Bog* was a network of footpaths linking countless shacks and shanties.

These flimsy structures, many still equipped with rusting moonshine gin machines, pointed to Lost Elm's rollicking past. In fact, the Bog had quenched the thirst of an entire region throughout Prohibition, producing a harsh liquor fittingly named *Swamp Rot*. When Prohibition ended in 1933, the Bog emptied of bootleggers and filled with a vast transient population of desperate Americans during the Great Depression. Single drifters and entire families came and went peacefully, but their presence was confirmed by the wisps of heating and cooking smoke that rose above the low treetops for nearly a decade. All gone now, the Bog had been a haven for hundreds until better times returned. But proof of their existence littered every shack Addie explored.

The tangled confusion of the Bog never intimidated her. Even after returning home covered with scratches from her day-long explorations, Addie never cared or complained. The Bog was a world she could escape to over and over again.

Billy didn't love the Bog like Addie did. Though it was just a short walk across the highway from their trailer, he was uneasy whenever he crossed Otter Creek. His home, and the Loop around it, had given Billy all the adventure he needed by the time he turned 13—a fact he reminded Addie of every time he declined another trip with her into the Bog. "That's bullcrap!" she characteristically replied, and then was gone.

The ways Billy and Addie were different mirrored the contradictions of Lost Elm itself. As the summer of 1977 began, he had tumbled face first into the ditch next to Halverson Road while she stood impatiently over him. That scene and their lap around the Loop had defined their relationship—Billy succumbing to familiar doubts, Addie comfortable behind her gruff facade. But events would soon conspire to reveal that a boy's uncertainty can be replaced with confidence while a girl's hardened heart can be pierced by love.

Hi Dad,

It's me, Addie.

I finished 9th grade yesterday. What a long year. Mom kept saying, "You're just changing, Addie. Like all girls do." But I know that's not it. Every day I felt like I didn't belong. The one friend I have left is Renny's sister Sara, but even she seems different now, more like a grown up. I don't know what I'd do if I lost her friendship.

Jake came home yesterday. He's been out of town since Monday, said he was working some road construction job in Hibbing, but I'm sure that's bullcrap. He left town so he could drink in peace, at least that's what he used to call it. Jerk took the car too, so I couldn't practice driving after school. What good is my permit if I never get to drive?

Jake has never liked me, not from day one. Can I help it if he's not you? Besides, he's never really tried to get to know me or Shorty. He's always too busy drinking and disappearing to care about anything or anyone, Mom included. I wish I could remember what she was like when we lived in San Diego. Happier I'm sure, and not so tired all the time.

Something's going to happen soon, Dad. I can feel it. Your friend from Vietnam, Mr. Hopp, passed through town last Christmas and told us about the time you saved his life when you got a feeling something was going to happen to him. Maybe we're alike that way.

There's one thing that's coming for sure, though. Mom wants me and Shorty to work at Carson Farm this summer. She was on the phone with Mr. Carson a few nights ago setting the whole thing up, saying how grateful she was to him and Mrs. Carson and that she thought it would be for the best.

Best? What best? Shorty's fine with it, but for once I have to agree with Jake. He's always saying, "Who does that old man think he is?"

I wish I could talk to you, Dad. More than ever, I feel like I'm going to burst. If it wasn't for Mom and Shorty I don't know what I'd do. At least I can write you. That helps a little.

Love,
Your daughter, Addie

2
CARSON FARM

Virgil Carson was waiting for Billy and Addie by the gate of Carson Farm at 9am on the first Monday after the last day of school. Addie saw him first, standing—arms crossed—in front of the big white farmhouse she used to admire.

"Look at him up there," she muttered as they crossed the Loop and stepped into the lower field. "Does he think we're going to start running or something?" Addie was dressed in a plain white t-shirt and jeans cut off just above the knees. The shirt was one size too big for her, hiding the fact that her mother was right, Addie had changed in the past year. She was becoming a young woman. Otherwise, her straw blonde hair was pulled back in its usual tight ponytail except for a loose strand she blew unsuccessfully away from her face.

Mr. Carson did expect them to run, for he rarely sat still himself. A short, wiry man with thinning gray hair, Mr. Carson walked the length and breadth of his farm daily, tinkering and tending to the property he knew and loved so well. For three decades he had split his time between the farm and a steel mill in Duluth until his retirement there a year ago. He and his wife Helen had raised three daughters and one son. Like Will Travers, Jimmy Carson had been killed in Vietnam.

"What do you think he's like, Ad?" Billy asked. He had sped up, sensing Mr. Carson's impatience. "Kids at school say he butchers his cows with an axe. You don't think we'll have to do any of that, do you?" He looked over at Addie for some sign of reassurance but she wasn't there. Addie lingered twenty feet behind, unwilling to be rushed.

"For once I agree with Jake," she scoffed. "Why did Mom ever agree to this?"

Billy didn't share Addie's opinion. He assumed Mr. Carson was a different kind of man than the one he'd grown up with—smart and hard-working, maybe even honest and kind.

"It is now 9:05," Mr. Carson announced solemnly when Billy reached the top of the hill.

"Sorry, Mr. Carson," Billy replied, slightly out of breath. "We left home a few minutes ago." He glanced down at the trailer a half mile away. It had never looked so small before.

"Yes, I saw you and Miss Pearson here the moment you crossed the road." Addie sauntered up the hill as if she were out for nothing more than a casual morning stroll.

"Hey," Addie nodded with unhidden disdain. "We're here. So what's the plan?"

Virgil Carson studied the tall, freckled girl. *Anna was right about this one,* he thought. *Mad at the world.* "Miss Pearson, my name's not *Hey*, it's Mr. Carson. And 9am means 9am, just like your mom told you."

Addie's hands dug into her hips. She ignored him and looked around the farm, mumbling almost to herself, "What a bunch of bullcrap."

"I'm sorry, Miss Pearson," Mr. Carson asked, understanding Addie perfectly. "What did you say?"

She pretended not hear his question and pointed to a dog of unknown breeding and age advancing cautiously towards them. "Who's that?"

"This is Ranger," he replied, scratching behind the dog's ears. "He's getting up there in years, but he's still a smart dog. Aren'tcha boy?" Addie smiled and patted her legs. Ranger approached her eagerly, nuzzling and licking her hands. Mr. Carson's eyes narrowed as he—ever so slightly— reevaluated the girl.

"We'll be on time tomorrow," Billy promised. "Right, Addie?" Addie shrugged without taking her eyes or hands off of Ranger.

"Good," Mr. Carson nodded. "Then here is *the plan*, Miss Pearson."

"We already know. Our mom told us everything."

"Everything?" Mr. Carson asked with thinly disguised surprise.

"Come here, look around, get a work schedule," she said. "What else is there?"

"Nothing. That's it." His face flickered with relief. "How *is* your mom?"

Addie squinted at Mr. Carson as if he had crossed some invisible line. "Fine. Why do you ask?"

"Helen saw her at the bank last Friday. Said she wasn't feeling well." Mr. Carson tapped his watch impatiently. "Alright, let me show you the barn first. That's where you'll be working this month."

He headed for the big red building at the edge of the upper field, a hundred feet behind the farmhouse. Billy followed a step behind, nervous but excited. Home was just down the hill, but it felt a million miles away. Addie glanced around suspiciously, then down at the Loop. *Looks like the same ol' prison to me,* she thought before catching up to Billy and Mr. Carson. Ranger happily followed.

*

"So that's what I expect," Mr. Carson announced after he had shown Billy and Addie around the farm. They were seated on the screen porch in the front of the house. Mrs. Carson joined them, carrying a pitcher of lemonade and a plate of sugar cookies.

"Two weeks of haying. One next month, the other around Labor Day. In the meantime, bales in the barn need to be moved to the shed next to the cow pen."

"What about the cows?" Billy asked uncertainly. "Do we have to . . .?"

"Those are dairy cows, Billy, not beef cattle. Don't worry," he chuckled. "You won't have to help me axe 'em."

"I just thought . . ." Embarrassed, Billy's voice trailed off.

"Don't believe everything you hear, son. People like to talk."

Despite the unfounded fear that he would have to help Mr. Carson butcher cows, Billy had loved the farm immediately. When Mr. Carson showed them around, he had listened intently. Addie, on the other hand, fired off one question after another. *"How much would they get paid? Why bale the hay at all? Can't the cows just eat it in the field?"* Mr. Carson had patiently ignored her, but Addie never seemed to pay attention anyway. She played with Ranger instead, who had taken an instant liking to her. But now, comfortable on the porch, Mr. Carson asked Addie a few questions of his own.

"Enjoying your lemonade, Miss Pearson?"

"It's pretty good."

"And the cookies? Are those good too?" Addie was reaching for another, but stopped. Her pale cheeks reddened.

"Stop it, Virgil," Mrs. Carson scolded him. "You don't have to be a mule about it. Go on dear, have as many as you like."

The tension was broken by a phone ringing in the kitchen. "I'll get it," Mr. Carson said. "I'm expecting a call." He excused himself but returned a minute later. "That was your mother. I told her I would definitely be able to work with you. So if you agree, we can start tomorrow."

"Hold on a second, Mr. Carson," Addie objected. "You never answered my questions."

"Congratulations, Miss Pearson. That's the first time you've used my name all morning. But I wasn't talking to you. I was talking to your brother. The job is his if he wants it."

Addie's smugness evaporated as she realized what Mr. Carson was saying. "Let's go, Shorty," she muttered. "We've got better things to do this summer than work here."

Billy knew Addie's darkness well, but he had already decided that the farm was where he wanted to be. Even if Mr. Carson was a stern man, Billy thought he might be a fair man too. *How come Addie can't see that?*

Mr. Carson rose from his chair. "Billy you'll be paid $250 at the end of the summer. That's the amount your mother and I agreed on when she asked me if you two could work here. I was willing to go a little higher, but she said no."

"You mean . . . ?" Addie asked him, dumbfounded.

"That's right, Miss Pearson. Working here was your mom's idea, not mine."

Billy approached him and stuck out his hand. "See you tomorrow, Mr. Carson."

"Bright and early, Billy?"

"Yes, sir." Billy walked cautiously past his sister, then leapt off the porch steps and jogged back down the hill.

"When you're willing to work by someone else's rules, Miss Pearson," Mr. Carson said as gently as he could, "Let me know. Not everything has to be so difficult."

"What would you know about difficult?!" Addie snapped. Her face flickered between the only two expressions she ever seemed to show the world—hard and haunted.

"Some advice?" Mr. Carson suggested, his shoulders sagging. "You might want to be a more like Will Travers and less like that man down there." He jerked his thumb toward the Loop.

"How would you know?! You didn't even know my Dad."

Virgil Carson had learned long ago when to stop arguing with a teenager, but he had one more thing to say. "You're wrong, Miss Pearson. I do know a thing or two about difficult."

"Saying so doesn't make it true," Addie replied, the edge in her voice softening.

He joined her in the front yard and pointed across the highway into the Bog. "See that smokestack out there, the one halfway to the horizon?"

"The one with the rusty roof?"

"Well, they all have rusty roofs now," Mr. Carson mused. "When I was Billy's age my brothers and I built that shack, and when I was your age we moved out of it."

"You lived in the Bog?" Addie couldn't hide her astonishment.

"My whole family did."

"I didn't know."

"No one does. Just you and Helen."

"Was it hard?"

"Miserable. Three miserable years."

Humbled, Addie didn't know what else to say.

"Tell your brother 9am sharp," Mr. Carson reminded her. "And Addie, if I didn't cut the hay each summer, what would the cows eat during the winter? Snow?" She smiled sheepishly and gave the Carsons a small wave, then disappeared down the hill.

"Why did you have to go and do that, Virgil?" Helen asked him after he joined her back on the porch. "You know those two are supposed to be a package deal. Besides, you promised me you wouldn't set foot in the barn this summer."

Mr. Carson patted her hand. "It'll be alright, Helen. I won't need Addie until July. Billy will be enough for now."

"I hope so, because I'm not quitting my job just to make sure you follow doctor's orders." Mrs. Carson had worked as a librarian in Lost Elm for the past decade. She wasn't about to give it up for her stubborn husband.

"Everything can still work out like Anna planned," Virgil reassured her. "She's a smart woman."

"But why did you have to shoo the girl away like that?"

"Addie has to want this for herself," he countered. "Don't worry, she'll come around."

25

"I hope you're right, Virgil. For all our sakes."

Me too, Helen," Mr. Carson murmured as they watched Ranger scamper down the hill after his new friend. "Me too."

*

Without any fanfare, Billy went to work the next morning moving hay bales from the barn to the shed. Each bale was a rectangular block four feet long by two feet wide by two feet deep, weighing approximately forty pounds. Mr. Carson showed Billy how to use two hay hooks at once, expertly stabbing both ends of a bale and hoisting it onto the wagon. That demonstration and, "*Stack 'em three bales high, son,*" were his only instructions.

Trying to impress his new boss, Billy loaded the first wagon four bales high from back to front. But when the wagon crossed the threshold of the barn and rolled into a deep rut, half a dozen bales tumbled to the ground, spilling hay everywhere. Eyes wide, Billy looked up at Mr. Carson in embarrassment and dread.

"What happened?" Mr. Carson asked him flatly.

Billy assumed the farmer was angry. Unsure how to respond, he began gathering up the hay.

"Billy?" Mr. Carson asked again. "What happened? What did you do wrong?"

Billy's throat tightened. "I stacked the wagon four high after you told me three," he mumbled hoarsely.

Mr. Carson jumped down from the tractor. Billy dropped the hay and took a step backward. "Son, what's the matter?" Mr. Carson held his hands open. This stuff," he waved at the ground, "It's just hay. I'll bring a few cows by later. They'll take care of it."

"I'm sorry, Mr. Carson. It won't happen again."

Mr. Carson chuckled softly and shook his head. "Trust me, Billy. This wasn't your last mistake—not today and not this summer. But that's okay. What you should have done was ask me why the wagon should be stacked three bales high in the first place."

"How would I know to ask that?"

"Because the only way to figure out what you don't know is to ask questions." Mr. Carson climbed back into the seat and waved Billy up to the narrow running board next to the brake. The tractor jerked once, then chugged on toward the shed.

"Do you have any chores, Billy?" Mr. Carson asked him. "There must be a few things Jake has you doing, isn't there?"

"I'm supposed to mow the lawn but Jake . . . er, my Dad does it. He let me try once but said I was doing it wrong." Billy rolled his eyes. "Straight lines, how hard can that be?"

"Did you ask him what you did wrong?"

"No."

"Why not?"

"I dunno. Didn't seem worth it."

"Same question, son. Why not?"

"It's not as easy as you make it sound, Mr. Carson."

"I understand that, Billy. But not everybody is like Jake Pearson."

They rode on in silence until Mr. Carson maneuvered the tractor next to the shed. He shut the engine off and swung around in his seat. "I'll make you a deal. Promise me you'll ask questions if there's something you don't understand."

"Okay," Billy agreed. "But what's the deal?"

Mr. Carson smiled warmly at the boy. "I won't get mad when you do."

After that, Billy said very little during his first two days on the farm. He couldn't have said much even if he tried. The temperature in the barn was stifling and stacking bale after bale left him continually out of breath. Breaks never came soon enough, but when they did Billy gulped down as much water as he could, pouring the rest over his sweat-soaked head.

"Easy, Billy. Drink slowly," Mr. Carson told him. "You're doing fine, getting better with every wagonload."

"Yes, sir," Billy said. "But is it okay if I keep a water jug on the wagon?"

"See," Mr. Carson smiled. "That was a good question."

＊

"The work's hard, but I like it," Billy explained to his mother and Jake over supper at their small kitchen table the evening after those first two difficult days. He struggled to hold his fork, dropping it twice in a matter of minutes.

27

"All thumbs, Shorty?" Addie teased him. "Show Mom how tough your hands are."

"Let's see, honey."

Billy glared at Addie and reluctantly lifted his hands from his lap. They were raw and blistered.

"Oh, Billy!" Anna exclaimed. "Should I tell Mr. Carson you need a day off?" She reached for the phone but Billy waved her off.

"I'm fine, Mom. Besides, Mr. Carson said they would toughen up in a few days. You should see his hands. They're like leather."

Thus far, Jake had eaten in silence. But after seeing Billy's hands and hearing his words, he banged his silverware on the table and threw his napkin on his plate.

"Fine?! They don't look fine to me! You're done up there, Billy, ya hear me?!" Jake pushed his chair away from the table and stood. "Who does that old man think he is?!"

"I'd say Mr. Carson thinks he's the guy giving out jobs, Jake." Addie hardly ever spoke during meals, but she knew she had to get between Billy and Jake somehow. "Maybe he has something for you to do up there. Or is there more *work* in Hibbing next week?"

"Stop it, Addie," Anna said wearily. The tension between her daughter and her husband was as familiar to her as the rhythm of rain. "You know your father is doing the best he can."

Now it was Addie's turn to push herself away from the table. "Jake!" she hissed, "Is not my father! Never was, never will be!"

"I'm going out," Jake snarled ominously, glaring across the table at Addie. "Don't wait up." A claustrophobic silence fell over the kitchen after he stormed out.

"He's nothing but bullcrap, Mom!" Addie barked. "Why can't you see that?"

Anna exhaled and avoided her children's expectant stares. "I'm going to bed. Can you two do the dishes?" They watched her walk down the cheaply paneled hallway. Billy fought through a wave of pity, but his mind was made up.

"I'm gonna keep working on the farm, Mom. I like the Carsons."

Anna leaned a hand on the wall and straightened her shoulders. "I'm counting on it, honey," she replied with quiet determination. "Good night." Billy and Addie exchanged confused looks, then began clearing the table.

*

"Where ya going, Billy?"

Renny Farelli popped out from behind the trailer just as Billy headed back to Carson Farm on Friday morning, June 10th.

"Same place I've been all week, Ren." Billy pointed up to the now familiar farmhouse.

"What do you do there all day?" Renny asked as the pair made their way across the lower field.

Billy smiled, knowing it wouldn't matter what he told Renny. His friend's question had been the same all week. He turned the conversation to familiar ground.

"How'd Carew do yesterday?"

Renny's tone turned authoritative. "1 for 4, a triple. That makes nine already this year. If he keeps going at this pace, he'll end up with 27." Every Sunday Renny poured over baseball statistics in the sports page, projecting Rod Carew's numbers over the course of a full season.

"What's he hitting now?" Billy asked when they reached the far edge of the field. Renny had followed him this far each of the last three days, but had gone no further. His brow furrowed as he looked back and saw the Loop in the distance. "Just like yesterday, Ren," Billy gently urged his friend. "Keep talking baseball like I'm right there with you." He knew from experience that Renny, for all his genius with numbers, didn't like to go anywhere by himself.

"Okay," Renny mumbled timidly. "See ya later." He turned and began walking back home. Billy watched him for a minute, then leaned into the hill. Mr. Carson was waiting for him when he reached the top.

"Is your friend alright?"

"Renny's fine. I just don't think he likes me working here."

He's probably not the only one, Mr. Carson assumed. "Well, you made it to Friday, Billy," he announced. "Ready to put in some more work?" Like Renny's daily curiosity about the farm, Mr. Carson started each morning with the same question.

"Yes sir," Billy smiled. "I'm ready."

"Hey, Billy!" Renny hollered back up the hill. "I forgot to tell ya! Carew's hitting .379! Just you wait! .400 isn't that far . . ." But the rest of Renny's words went unheard.

As Mr. Carson promised, the rest of the week had been much smoother for Billy. He worked unsupervised in the barn, fetching Mr. Carson from the screen porch only after the wagon was loaded (three bales high) and ready to move. His hands had begun to callous too, though some of the flesh was still tender. But Billy didn't complain when he saw how Mr. Carson's own hands were tough and unforgiving. *I want hands like that*, he decided.

*

Though they talked more and more each day, Billy still wasn't used to Mr. Carson's gentle, disarming manner. Each question he asked was neutral, every comment he made sounded matter-of-fact.

"How does Jake feel about you working here?"

"I dunno. Okay, I guess."

"Really? I thought he might have a stronger opinion than that."

"Well," Billy smiled mischievously, "He does wonder who you think you are."

Mr. Carson laughed out loud. "I bet he does. Seriously though, does Jake mind you working here? I know he's out of town a lot, but he must have said something."

"Yeah, right. Outta town," Billy murmured, his voice faltering. Mr. Carson bent down to inspect the grass for a minute as if he had nowhere else in the world to be.

"I'm glad when Jake's gone!" Billy finally said, much louder than he had meant to. "Mom's happy, Addie's happy—well, not as mad, anyway." Thoughts unspoken for too long spilled out of him. "And even when he is home he doesn't want us around! What did we ever do to him?! It's not our fault he's not . . ."

"Your dad?"

Billy's throat burned as hot tears trickled down his face. "Jake's not the way a dad's supposed to be," he said with unconcealed anguish.

"No, he's not," Mr. Carson agreed, putting a hand on the boy's shoulder. "For as long as I've known Jake, he's been mad at the world.

Pain buried always returns," he sighed. "And that man is carrying a lot of pain."

"Well I wish he'd carry it somewhere else," Billy replied bitterly.

"You know, for a second there you sounded a lot like a certain girl we both know."

"Uh oh." Billy's eyes widened in mock horror.

"Feel better?" Mr. Carson asked. Billy nodded and wiped his cheeks. "You know I'm not just your boss, Billy. I'd like to think we're friends too." He stuck out his hand. "Friends?"

"Yes, sir," Billy answered, shaking Mr. Carson's hand. "I'd like that."

Hi Dad,

It's me, Addie.

Shorty and I met with Mr. Carson last week about working on his farm and he told us it was Mom's idea! At first I thought it would be just one more place where someone would be telling me what to do, but now I'm not so sure.

Mom was pretty angry when I told her that Mr. Carson only hired Shorty. She said, "Why is it so hard for you to keep your mouth shut, Addie? Why?" I said I didn't know.

I'm glad Shorty's working there, though. At first I was mad when he took the job, but I'd rather he be on the farm than around the trailer when Jake's home. I even picked a fight with Jake last Tuesday because he was going to make Shorty quit. I didn't have a choice, Dad. Shorty won't stand up for himself and Mom hardly ever says a word in our defense anymore. And who cares if Jake was gone for a week after our fight? We're better off without him.

A few days ago I searched the Bog for the shack Mr. Carson said he lived in when he was a kid. Geez, and I thought the trailer was small! I used to envy the people who lived in the Bog, but it never crossed my mind that they were just trying to survive and keep their families together. Why can't Mom do that for us, Dad? Why won't she even try?

I do have some good news. Sara called last night and invited me to come over to her house tomorrow. She wants to listen to some new records with me. I don't care what the reason is, I've missed her. We haven't hung out since school ended.

Tomorrow is Shorty's last day on the farm until haying starts next month. I'm going to meet him up there when he's done. He told me to wait until 2 o'clock, but I'm going to get there early. I need to talk to Mr. Carson. If there's even a chance he knew you, Dad, I have to ask. I have so many questions.

I miss you all the time.

Love,
Your daughter, Addie

33

3
CARVINGS

Billy and Addie stepped out of the mud room of their trailer and into a mid-June morning unusually thick with humidity. By the time they reached the Loop their canvas tennis shoes were already wet with dew.

"Another hot one," Addie observed mildly.

"I don't mind," Billy replied. "I like the heat."

Though Billy's admission confirmed a growing confidence Addie had noticed in her brother, he couldn't hide his disappointment at the thought of waiting another month before working with Mr. Carson again.

"I'll see you up there later," she reminded him.

"How come?"

"Maybe I just wanna see Ranger. Didja ever think of that?"

Addie watched him walk across the lower field before scanning the entire Loop, her eyes coming to rest on the Farelli's house. Unlike the Pearson's cramped trailer, Sara and Renny lived in a spacious home built by their father, the president and part-owner of First National Bank, the same bank where Anna worked. Shortly after Will's death, Michael Farelli had offered her an entry-level teller job. Steady promotions had followed over the next decade and she was currently the bank's head bookkeeper.

Addie's gaze—as well as her eagerness to see Sara—was interrupted by the sound of tires skidding on gravel. The Comet's back end fish-tailed onto the Loop from Halverson Road. Addie's hands went instinctively to her hips as the car braked hard next to her.

"Where's your brother, Addie?" Jake asked, his arm dangling carelessly out the window.

Addie sniffed accusingly. "Already, Jake? Isn't nine in the morning a little early to crack open a beer?"

"What about your mom?" Jake said, squirming in his seat. "Where's she?"

"Where do you think? It's Tuesday—Mom's at work. And she had to get a ride from Mr. Farelli again."

"I was at your grandpa's for a few days," Jake said, though Addie hadn't asked or cared.

"You mean your dad—both of my grandpas died before I was born." She understood why he smelled like alcohol. *That's all those two ever do together, drink.*

"Where are you going so early?" Jake asked.

"Sara's," Addie replied without thinking. She hated explaining her whereabouts to Jake, even accidently.

"Oh," he said without interest. "Well, don't do anything I wouldn't." And with that odd warning, Jake sped off. Addie watched the Comet race around the Loop and idle at the stop sign for a long time before turning onto the highway toward Lost Elm.

Addie was about to mumble her usual "*bullcrap*" to Jake's sudden appearance and departure, but the impulse was forgotten when she heard pounding music coming from inside the Farelli's house. An inviting note was taped to the front door. *Come in, Addie. I'm downstairs, Sara.*

She found Sara in her bedroom singing into a hairbrush, swaying back and forth to a rhythmic beat. Mesmerized, Addie watched her from the doorway. Eyes closed and oblivious, Sara sang freely:

> *"Don't stop, thinking about tomorrow,*
> *Don't stop, it'll soon be here,*
> *It'll be better than before,*
> *Yesterday's gone, yesterday's gone..."*

Sixteen year-old Sara Farelli wasn't quite as free as Addie imagined. "*Trapped*," she called it, for two more years until high school graduation. But Sara had already begun planning for a future far from Lost Elm. Her bedroom was filled with books that took her all over the world and walls covered with her own original artwork and photography. Sara was bound for anywhere and everywhere else. The proof was all around her.

Poised and witty, she moved easily between the cliques of Lost Elm High School, connecting with and detaching from classmates at a whim. Sara was just as indifferent to her appearance—tall and statuesque, with long raven hair and penetrating brown eyes—as she was to the effect it had on people. With the exception of Addie, no one ever got too close to her, which was just fine with Sara.

"Hi, Sara!" Addie announced loudly over the music.

Sara opened her eyes and gave Addie a bright smile. "You're here!" she shouted, and lifted the needle off the record. "What a great song, huh?!"

Addie nodded uncertainly. Sara's energy and passion always had a strong effect on her. She blushed as a warm feeling climbed up her neck.

"Fleetwood Mac is amazing!" Sara squealed. "Listen to this one!" She took Addie's hand and was quickly lost in the music again.

Whether it was Sara's contagious enthusiasm or the hostile encounter she'd had with Jake minutes earlier, Addie felt a surge of electricity flow through her body. She was strangely overcome by a deep longing to shed her carefully constructed identity and do what she had demanded of Billy on Halverson Road—*Just Let Go!* Timidly at first, then with a building recklessness, Addie joined in:

> *"Loving you isn't the right thing to do,*
> *How can I ever change the things I feel?*
> *If I could, maybe I'd give you my world,*
> *How can I when you won't take it from me..."*

Her long-simmering bitterness, so swiftly unleashed by the music and Sara's warm hand in hers, boiled over. Aching emotions too long pent up spilled out all at once. Addie danced and sang with a violence she couldn't control even if she had tried.

When the song faded, Addie's eyes were shut and her fist was clenched tight. Sara let go of her hand and turned off the record player. Goaded by the painful silence, Addie tried to catch her breath but let out a wrenching sob instead. The raw, animal sound betrayed an anguish she'd hidden for years. Her eyes widened in horror and her face twisted with pain and humiliation.

"Oh God, oh God! I'm sorry, Sara! I'm sorry!" Addie fled upstairs and out the front door, disappearing into Pete's Woods.

Sara had a pretty good idea where Addie was going, but she skirted around the border of the woods before moving toward its interior. She found Addie there, crouching at the base of a big slate rock outcropping.

"I thought I'd find you..." Sara froze when she saw a knife in Addie's hand. "What are you writing?"

Addie slashed the blade into the rock a few more times, then revealed her work:

I HATE HIM

"What do you think?" she asked Sara sullenly. "Pretty catchy, huh?" Though her face had regained its composure, Addie's eyes flickered with a familiar pain as she folded the blade into its hilt.

"What's it like, Addie?"

Addie winced at the question, careful not to show Sara more tears. "I don't know," she replied, pointing through the woods to the trailer. "But I don't think *that* is normal."

Sara smiled sympathetically. "I'm sure there's all kinds of normal, but no—that's not it." She thought about her own world for a moment—filled with beauty and purpose; books and art and culture with countless tomorrows. *What's Addie's world is like?*

"How do you deal with it all, Addie?"

No one—not her mother, not Billy, certainly not Jake—had asked Addie a question like that in years. She was finding out fast that the brave face she showed the world didn't wear so well around Sara. She paced feverishly and talked about a father she was fast forgetting, a brother she'd spent years protecting, and a mother who was growing more distant every day. And Addie talked about Jake.

"He doesn't like me, Sara! He never has! And he looks at me so strangely sometimes!"

"Is that why you hate him?"

Addie's head fell to her chest. The sun had reddened her freckled forehead, which was mottled with sweat. Struggling to hide more tears, she took out Billy's knife and frantically scratched over the words she'd carved only minutes earlier. At first Sara was confused, then an awful realization struck her.

"Oh Addie, no. Don't hate him," she pleaded. "You can't hate him."

Addie sank to her knees. "Didn't he know what would happen to us if he never came home?!" she cried, grabbing fistfuls of earth to sponge over the words. "I'm sorry, Dad! I'm sorry!" She wiped her cheeks, tears and dirt smearing her face. "I just want this to end, Sara. When is this ever going to end?!"

"I don't know, Addie," Sara murmured, unwilling to patronize her friend, tell her everything was going to be alright. "But I think today was a good start, don't you?"

"I'm sorry," Addie said through her grief. "I feel like a fool."

"You're not a fool. You're amazing."

"If you say so."

"I do say so," Sara insisted. "You go into battle every day for your mom and your brother. That takes courage."

Embarrassed, Addie took a deep breath and exhaled, then squeezed Sara's hands gratefully. "What time is it? I want to be at the Carsons' by 1."

"Come on then," Sara replied, willing to let Addie off the hook for now. "Let's go back to my house and listen to some more music. And don't let me forget, I've got a couple of things for you. I think you're going to like them."

The girls exchanged affectionate smiles. *At least for today I feel normal,* Addie thought as they made their way out of Pete's Woods. *Thanks to Sara.*

*

An hour earlier Jake had left Addie in a cloud of dust on the Loop before braking hard where Halverson Road met the state highway. The blood vessels in his brain were constricted and pinched from the effects of a powerful hangover. He wanted to scream at the unfairness of it all, the unending parade of humiliations conspiring against him, but he wouldn't. *The Loop's not that big,* Jake thought sourly. *Addie will hear me.*

He turned the Comet east towards Lost Elm, straight into a blinding morning sun. Recoiling, Jake squinted thinly until he saw a comforting sign a quarter mile ahead:

AT THIS POINT ON FEBRUARY 15, 1870 . . .

He pulled over onto a dirt patch in front of the historic billboard and staggered from the car. With a fierce urgency, everything Jake had poured into himself the night before rushed out with frightening speed. His eyes were shut tight, shame and relief mingling with bile and alcohol.

The pain was self-inflicted, of course, though Jake was angrier at his father than with himself. Addie was right, drinking was all they ever did together—hard drinking provoked by the absence of Betty Pearson, Jake's mother. She had been gone a long time, but both men still mourned her absence.

Addie's words, *"My grandpas died before I was born,"* pounded in Jake's head as he wiped saliva from his chin. He could hardly argue with her. His dad was definitely no grandfather. Ron Pearson had attended his son's wedding ten years earlier, but Jake was the only Pearson who'd seen him since. He flinched at the memory of his father arriving late and leaving early, missing the ceremony entirely. And rather than congratulate the newlyweds, he pulled Jake aside and issued a stern warning, "Don't ever trust her, ya hear me?"

Vomiting eased Jake's nausea, but his head still thumped furiously. Fortunately, relief was nearby. He thrashed fifty yards through the underbrush and waded across Otter Creek, cursing its early summer chill as he climbed up the steep opposite bank. Thirty feet ahead of him, tied to the base of a poplar tree, was a faded red bandana embroidered with his initials—*JRP*.

After a half dozen hurried steps, Jake pitched forward, falling face first into the wet earth. Groaning, he pulled himself onto all fours and crawled the rest of the way. Like a mindless animal, he clawed at the earth until his hands struck something smooth and cool—a clear glass bottle containing the Bog's legendary Swamp Rot. Jake's hands shook in anticipation as he pried the cork free and raised the bottle to his mouth.

Suddenly, Jake's eyes snapped open. He scrambled to his feet and held the bottle up to the bright sun, studying the clear liquid like a scientist analyzing a drop of blood on a sterile slide. He put his thumb over the mouth of the bottle and drew his arm back, momentum and purpose on his side. *Just throw it, you idiot!* Instead, Jake drank the bottle dry before smashing it on a rock at the edge of the creek.

The pressure in his head subsided as he re-crossed the creek and walked numbly back to the billboard. Buoyed by the Prohibition-era liquor, Jake changed out of his wet jeans and into a dry pair he kept in the trunk for just such an occasion. *Now what?* he wondered as he pulled back onto the highway. *Jay Cooke Park?*

To get to the park, Jake had to drive through Lost Elm's main intersection—Chestnut Avenue & 3rd Street. Ahead of him was First National Bank. To the left was the municipal bar and liquor store, *The Junction*. Without giving Jay Cooke another thought, he pulled into the bar's small parking lot.

The Junction was cool and dark, a soothing balm to Jake's fading hangover. A couple of nods greeted him, mingled with the rattle of billiard balls. Bud, a large, bleary-eyed bartender with a towel perpetually draped over his shoulder, dropped a square napkin onto the bar between them.

"What'll ya have, Jake?"

Jake pointed to a beer tap and threw down two quarters before looking around at the other regulars. No one spoke, though Jake was certain they all knew each other, for he knew them.

"What're ya up to, Jerry?" he asked a forlorn man two stools over. Three or four other men twitched as if they'd been woken from a sound sleep. Jerry shrugged as if to say, "*Not much.*"

A Hamm's Beer sign hung behind the bar in front of Jake's perch. Lights danced behind a plastic waterfall, but his eyes were drawn to the sign's digital calendar. He recalled more of Addie's words after he had asked her where Anna was, "*It's Tuesday—Mom's at work.*" Jake scowled, took a long drink and glanced down the bar again, overcome by a strong urge to leave, get away from these men, as if the problems cursing their lives might be his too.

"What the heck happened to you?" Bud asked as he refilled Jake's glass.

"What?"

"Ya got dirt all over you."

Jake sighed, took another drink and slid off his stool. "I gotta use the can."

Alone in the bathroom, he braced himself on the sink and studied his reflection. Loose skin hung below a grimy, stubbled chin. Vacant, bloodshot eyes stared at a grubby t-shirt that barely covered his flabby belly. *I gotta get the hell outta here*, he decided. After a few furtive looks around the bar, Jake beat a hasty retreat.

41

Two miles later, he drove into Jay Cooke State Park's Visitor Center, but the parking lot was empty. Leaning against the park ranger's booth a sign read: *The Park is closed on June 14th due to repairs on the Swinging Bridge. We apologize for the inconvenience.*

"Now what?" Jake muttered as he turned the Comet around.

Between Jay Cooke and Lost Elm was the little village of Slate Gap. A back door into the park was near the tiny hamlet, a granite-covered rail bed whose tracks had been torn up more than a decade ago.

Jake pulled off the road and eyed the fist-sized rocks uncertainly, knowing a short walk over such wobbly terrain would make even a sober person unsteady—and he was definitely not sober. But two hundred yards down the path a turn-of-the-century trestle bridge spanned the slate-strewn St. Louis River. Jake had to get to that bridge.

A chest-high fence, not there when he was in high school, guarded each side of the bridge from thrill-seeking jumpers. Jake swung his leg over the top of the fence and pitched forward precariously. He nearly plunged fifty feet into the river below, but grabbed an iron beam at the last possible moment, preventing his fall.

When he had steadied himself, Jake jerked his hand off the beam as if it was on fire. For there they were, the three painful words he'd seen scratched into the steel long ago. It was too much for him to take. The alcohol and hot sun yanked Jake irresistibly back to a summer he had tried hard to forget, but would always remember.

*

"What do you think of Anna Olson?" Will Travers asked Jake before jumping off the same trestle bridge and plummeting into the swirling St. Louis River. It was 1959—the summer before their senior year of high school.

Jake looked over the edge as Will's feet slapped the water. Five long seconds passed before his friend broke the surface. "What's that s'posed to mean?!" he yelled down.

Will swam over to the riverbank. "She and I have been hanging out a lot!" he shouted. "I guess we're kind of together now!"

"Together?! I thought you two were just friends!" Jake replied, his voice echoing off the high rock walls on either side of the river. Neighbors since they were kids, Jake had harbored a secret crush on Anna for years.

"We went to prom together," Will grinned after he made his way back onto the bridge. "You knew that." Water sprayed in all directions as he shook his sandy-brown hair. A few weeks shy of his 18th birthday, Will was six feet tall with broad shoulders and a narrow waist and possessing a contagious smile. Jake, however, was unmoved.

"How long has this been going on?"

"Since March," Will said. "Shakespeare class, remember? We were reading *The Taming of the Shrew*. She was Kate, I was Petruchio." Inspired, Will picked up a piece of sharp granite and scratched and slashed out three words onto one of the bridge's steel beams—*WILL AND ANNA*—then recited:

> *"Kate of my consolation,*
> *Hearing thy mildness praised,*
> *Thy virtues spoke of,*
> *Thy beauty sounded,*
> *I am moved to woo thee for my wife."*

Jake watched the performance with a deep, unspoken envy. Will's boldness had probably won Anna over, but Jake had no such talent. His edges were rough and bullying, often angry. What had those qualities ever gotten him? Not much. Certainly not Anna.

"Come on big man, your turn." Will urged him, flicking his towel playfully at Jake's feet. "Over the side."

"I'm done for the day," Jake replied, retrieving a towel and a clear bottle from his gym bag.

"Where'd you get that?"

"Relax, Will," he said and took a quick drink. "I've got a few hidden here and there. No one's gonna find 'em."

"We've got football practice in a few weeks, Jake. And if you show up at Mr. Carson's smelling of booze, I don't know what he'll do. You're still haying with me and Jimmy, aren'tcha?"

Jake said nothing, promised nothing. Instead, he drained the last inch from the bottle and threw it over the top of the bridge. It plopped into the river with a small, distant splash.

When did this start? Will wondered. He didn't know what had brought their afternoon to a sudden end, but something had changed. He was sure of it.

*

That's when everything changed, Jake remembered, staring at the words Will had carved eighteen years earlier. Nothing he had ever done, nothing he could ever do, would erase those three words. WILL AND ANNA was a suffocating reminder of an undying love that had never included Jake.

He raced back into town and pulled into his dad's driveway, located across the street from the high school. From where he parked, Jake had a clear view into Ron Pearson's kitchen. *If I wait a few minutes,* he figured, *I can tell him I stopped by but he wasn't home.* But he knew his lie wouldn't hold water. His father was always home.

Jake slipped through the side door and into the kitchen. It still looked the same as it had the last time he'd seen his mother. Cracked, vinyl-covered chairs surrounded a plastic-veneered table and tarnished chrome canisters were scattered across the countertop. Oblivious of the mess in the sink, Jake walked into the dining room and turned toward the living room. Ron Pearson was there, fast asleep in his recliner.

"Dad, wake up." Jake patted his cheek and eased a beer bottle from his hand.

The man's face told a weary tale. Covering it were thin purplish veins, a grotesque road map of decades of alcohol abuse. At the sound of Jake's voice, Ron Pearson pitched forward, then fell back into a half-conscious stupor.

"Dad!"

"Jake?" he groaned. "Is that you? Tell your mom to fix me something to eat, okay?"

Jake sat on the couch and stared at a picture of himself on the coffee table. He looked to be about Billy's age. Next to him, Ron was holding a drink and sporting a cocky grin, gesturing to something off camera. Father

44

and son—separated by twenty-five years—could have been twins. Now shrunken and gray, Ron Pearson was 58 going on 80. He had retired from the local feed mill three years earlier, drawing a disability pension ever since.

Jake drank the rest of his dad's beer and stood up. The room swam for a moment before he regained his balance. When he did, he noticed his dad's chest began to heave.

"Let's go, Dad! Get up!" Jake yanked him to his feet and, like a well-oiled machine, they rushed into the bathroom. Jake knew he should have pitied his father's violent retching, but he felt nothing. Those days were long gone. Even pity has a shelf life.

"Thank you, Jakey," Ron mumbled. "Your mom'll be home soon. Why don't you go outside and play."

"Sure, Dad," Jake replied as he helped him into his bedroom.

Ron's eyes fluttered as he lay down. He looked at his grown son, then around the room. His world came into harsh focus. "Can you get me some water?"

Jake came back with a full glass and a small plate of crackers. He set each on the nightstand while his father snored quietly. He paused on his way through the dining room and saw a photograph of his mother on the far wall. It had been taken a few months before Will told him he was dating Anna, but the picture was different from any other of Betty Pearson still hanging in the house. Her smile was wide and real. Jake's love and hatred of the photograph had never dimmed.

"Knock it off," he muttered, unable to shake his misery. The scene ended with a sickening familiarity as Jake rifled through the dining room hutch, found another bottle and escaped out the kitchen door. There was someone else he needed to see.

By now Jake was in bad shape. Too much alcohol and too many memories compelled him to drive one mile south of town to Hillside Cemetery, which had been receiving Lost Elm's dead for a century. Jake had been there many times before. But this time, he told himself as he lumbered heavily across the grass, would be his last.

"You shoulda never told me!" he snarled as he sat down on a small bench next to a white marble stone. "But you just couldn't keep your mouth shut, could ya?!" The words tumbled out of him, exactly like the ones he'd screamed the summer before his senior year.

"Let's go, Jake," Will hissed through his friend's open window. "We're gonna be late."

"Go on without me," Jake moaned from beneath his pillow. "Tell Carson I'm sick. It'd be the truth." The bottle he drank on the bridge clearly hadn't been his last.

"No way. You're coming with me." Will circled around to the other side of the house and came in through the Pearson's kitchen door.

"Good morning, William," a soft voice greeted him. Dressed in pink Capri pants and a stylish tapered shirt, Betty Pearson sat in front of a small mirror at her kitchen table.

"Hi, Mrs. Pearson. You're still here? Jake said you were going out of town this weekend."

"Those were Ron's plans," Betty said. "He left last night, which means I get the house all to myself today. Provided you can get Jake up."

"I'll do my best," Will replied vaguely, unable to ignore the red handprint on her cheek that she was frantically applying makeup to. "Is everything okay, ma'am?"

Betty smiled faintly, touched by Will's concern. "It is now, William. Why don't you go see about Jake."

He headed to the back bedroom where Jake was struggling into a white t-shirt. "He lives and breathes!" Will teased. "Mr. Carson told us to wear long sleeves, otherwise the hay will chew us up."

"Are you kidding?! I'm gonna be sweating like a pig as it is. Long sleeves will be torture. Come on, let's get this over with."

Jake's struggles didn't end there. All morning long, he couldn't keep up with the baler or prevent the hay from scratching his arms. Mercifully, Mr. Carson called an early lunch at 11:30. Jake collapsed under the shade of a tall pine, ready to call it quits.

"The worst is over," Will said hopefully. "You'll feel better after we eat."

"Do me a favor? Can you run home and get me a long sleeve shirt?"

"Sure thing, buddy."

Will raced back into Lost Elm. Chestnut Avenue was bustling, preparations already underway for the town's annual summer celebration,

Railway Days, the following weekend. Three blocks away, however, Jake's house appeared quiet.

Will parked on the street and approached the kitchen entrance. He was about to knock but stopped short when he saw two people standing at the threshold between the dining room and kitchen. They were holding each other in a loving, passionate embrace. One person was Betty Pearson, but the other was not her husband. The implications of what Will saw floored him. He silently backed away from the screen door and returned to the farm empty-handed.

The afternoon was a blur. Three questions knocked around Will's brain as he numbly hooked and stacked bale after bale of hay: *Does Mr. Pearson know? Does Jake know? Do I say something?* Luckily, Jake had borrowed a shirt from Mr. Carson so he only asked Will once why he hadn't brought him one from home. Will's rushed reply, "*Your door was locked,*" was accepted without comment. But when Mr. Carson hollered, "Last load boys," Will knew he was out of time.

*

"You okay?" Jake asked Will when they turned onto the highway and sped back into Lost Elm. "The morning was rough, but no harm done, right?"

"You wanna go over to Gap Lake?" Will suggested, barely hearing the question.

"Come on, Will. I'm trying to say I'm sorry."

"What? Oh, nothing to be sorry about," Will replied distractedly. "So, Gap Lake?"

"Stop by my house first, I'll grab a few beers. I'm really thirsty."

Gap Lake was a large reservoir created when the St. Louis River was dammed just above Jay Cooke State Park. With no public beach or boat landing, the lake was usually deserted. *As good a spot as any,* Will figured.

"You're coming back tomorrow, right?"

"Sure," Jake laughed, holding a cold bottle to his forehead. "It can't get any worse."

Will tossed a flat rock into the lake. It skipped half a dozen times before disappearing into the dark water. "How are your mom and dad doing?" he asked cautiously.

"I dunno. Fine, I guess," Jake replied as he combed the shore for a good skipper. "What's going on, Will? You've been acting weird since lunch."

"With me? Nothing." Will didn't know where to steer the conversation, or if he should even try. A tiny kernel of regret began to fester in his mind.

"You said my house was locked earlier, but it wasn't a minute ago. Did you just go into town to see Anna?"

Will hadn't considered that little lie. He fumbled for an answer, knowing that lying again offered him an easy way out.

"No, I went to your house," Will replied, picking at the label on his beer bottle. "The door was open."

"Then why didn't you get me a shirt?!" Jake said, his voice rising.

Will felt disembodied, like he was suspended on the edge of the trestle bridge with the St. Louis River swirling dangerously below. Jumping might be a bad idea, but he couldn't find his footing.

"Your mom was home," he finally answered. "It wasn't a good time to go in."

"So she was there, so what?" Jake cocked his head, Will's reply turning in his brain. "Did you see something? What did you see?"

"I don't . . . I don't know, I just figured I should tell . . ."

"Tell me what?" Jake fumed. "What do you think you saw?!"

"Your mom and . . . and someone else. They were kissing." Will stared out across the lake, mumbling, "I'm really sorry, Jake."

"What?!" Jake threw his beer to the ground. The bottle shattered. "You're lying!" He strode menacingly toward Will and shoved him hard in the chest. Will stood his ground but kept his arms at his sides. If Jake was going to throw a punch, he wouldn't stop him. They stood face to face for what felt like an hour, though it was only a few seconds. But in that time Jake had made up his mind.

"You really think you're something special around here, don'tcha?" he snarled. "But you're not. You're nothing but a liar. And this," his hand motioned back and forth between them. "This is over."

Will had witnessed dozens of Jake's confrontations over the years, but he knew this one was different. Being told the truth of his parents' marriage was too great a burden for Jake to bear. Instead, the casualty would be their friendship.

"What do you mean?"

"Done, finished. You're dead to me, Will. Will Travers is dead."

"What about the farm?"

"I don't give a damn about Mr. Carson or his farm," Jake sneered. "Or you. I quit." He grabbed the unopened bottles of beer and stomped off.

Will didn't stop him. Instead, he skipped rocks for another hour, wondering over and over if he'd done the right thing—a question that would go unanswered for the rest of his life.

Jake's belief that Will had lied only hardened as the summer of 1959 continued. Nothing seemed out of the ordinary between his parents, though nothing was particularly good either. That's when Jake began to notice. His parents never showed each other the simplest affection. Even civility seemed difficult. But Jake had to know for sure.

He followed his mother for days. To the grocery store twice, the bank three times, the post office, other random errands. He was ready to drop the whole thing when Betty Pearson announced at breakfast one morning that she was going shopping in Duluth.

Jake's heart pounded as his mother drove through downtown Duluth. Two miles later, he parked half a block away from an East End home he watched her disappear into. Fifteen minutes passed before he found the nerve to approach the house, then darted behind a hedge as Betty walked past a picture window that looked out onto the street. Scurrying to the side of the house, Jake knelt beneath an open window and—hidden there—began to hear voices.

"When are you going to leave him, Betts? Live here with me?"

"People will talk," Betty countered apprehensively. "Is that what you want—to be the source of constant gossip?"

"But you said we would be together once Jake graduates. That's in less than a year. *Two people who love each other this much should be together.*' That's what you told me."

The conversation buzzed in Jake's ears as he rose from his crouch. The scene was identical to the one Will had described: two people were embracing and one of them was his mother. But she was nearly unrecognizable to Jake—young and vibrant, not at all like the person he saw every day. The difference, as well as the truth, stunned him. *Will was right.* Dazed and disbelieving, Jake continued to stare, determined not to move until his mother saw him.

When she finally did, Betty screamed and raced out the front door. She collided roughly with Jake, who was sprinting for his car. He landed hard on the sidewalk, the back of his head smacking the concrete with a sickening thud. Betty tumbled onto the yard's soft grass, shaken but unhurt.

"Jake honey, are you okay? You're bleeding! Come inside, I'll clean you up."

He looked past her to the front porch where someone was anxiously watching them. "Are you serious?! Get away from me!" Jake put his hands on the back of his head. They were wet with blood.

"I can explain," she said weakly. "It's not what you think."

"Two people who love each other should be together!" he yelled. "You said that, right?!" His face twisted in pain. "If it's not what I think, then what is it?!"

Betty looked away, her face ashen. "Please don't tell your father, Jake," she begged him. "Please!"

"What would I even say?!"

Betty looked from the porch to Jake, then took a deep breath. "This is who I am, Jake. And that's who I love. But you're my son. I love you, too."

"Love me?!" Jake screamed. He held his bloody hands up to her face. "Does this look like love to you?!" Betty Pearson fell to her knees and wept as he turned his back on her forever. For good.

*

Eighteen years later, Jake rose from the graveside bench at Hillside Cemetery. "But you're down there and I'm still up here," he mumbled through tears of grief and alcohol. Pitching forward unsteadily, he grabbed the tombstone to regain his balance. Just like the two names written on the bridge, more words stopped Jake from falling.

"I can't ever get away from you!!" he screamed.

Suddenly, Jake got an idea. For starters, he'd get Billy away from that farm. Today, right now. *This is my family, not Carson's.*

"And it's not yours either. Not anymore."

The body buried beneath him was silent, of course. It said nothing as the Comet squealed onto the highway, bound for Carson Farm. Ghosts alive and dead would be waiting for Jake when he returned. If he never did, then so be it. But the marble marker and its namesake would still haunt him wherever he went.

WILLIAM
HOWARD
TRAVERS
US NAVY
VIETNAM
JUL 1 1942
NOV 25 1965
BRONZE STAR

4
TIRES ON GRAVEL

Addie examined her gifts as she made her way across the lower field to the Carsons' house after her morning with Sara. The first was a book— Jack London's *The Call of the Wild*. Sara had explained that it was the story of Buck, a dog stolen and sold into service in the rugged Yukon Territory of Canada. On Addie's wrist was Sara's other gift, a bracelet of colored string and beads. She had beamed when she saw the letters of her name embedded in the beadwork. "I hope you like it," Sara said with her most endearing smile. Addie loved it.

"Well hello, dear! Are you here to join us?!" Mrs. Carson called out from the porch as Addie cleared the top of the hill. "I'll make up a place for you." Distracted by her morning memories, Addie hadn't noticed Mrs. Carson hurrying back and forth from the kitchen to the porch, getting lunch ready for her husband and Billy.

"That's okay, Mrs. Carson," Addie replied, waving nervously as she approached the house. "I already ate. I was at my friend Sara's house."

"Oh, it's no trouble. I just made a fresh batch of cookies." Mrs. Carson disappeared into the kitchen and returned with a small plate. She pointed to the book in Addie's hand. "What do you have there?"

"*The Call of the Wild*. Sara gave it to me. It's about this dog . . ."

"I read that when I was your age," Mrs. Carson said enthusiastically. "Sara chose well. You'll just love Buck."

"You know Sara?" Addie mumbled between bites of a ginger snap.

"We met at the library a few years ago. She was checking out *Gone With the Wind*. I was so impressed, a book like that at her age. We talked right up until closing time. If it wasn't for Scarlett O'Hara, I doubt we'd be friends today."

"How come?"

"I gave Sara a ride home that day and we decided to read *Gone With the Wind* together. Well, not together exactly. We met here for every Saturday all summer and talked about it. And we've been picking out books ever since. We're reading *To Kill a Mockingbird* right now."

Addie and Mrs. Carson chatted pleasantly for a few more minutes until Ranger appeared around the corner of the house. "This guy sure has been missing you," Mrs. Carson observed. "Every day when he sees your brother he gets excited, starts running in circles. Then when he figures out you're not coming, he lies down by the gate and puts his head on his paws."

Addie snuck half a cookie into Ranger's mouth and scratched behind his ears. "Miss me, boy?"

"Billy and Virgil should be along any second. Ranger always beats them here by a minute or two," Mrs. Carson noted. "Can you help me bring out more food, Addie?"

So sure that morning what she was going to ask Mr. Carson, Addie now felt drained and uncertain. *I suppose I've done enough running for one day*, she decided, recalling her escape from Sara's house into Pete's Woods. But whatever chance Addie might have had to leave with her dignity was gone.

"Hello again, Miss Pearson," Mr. Carson said gently. He climbed the porch steps and settled into a chair as if he'd been expecting Addie for lunch the whole time.

"Hi, Mr. Carson. Hey, Shorty."

"It's Billy," her brother snapped, annoyed by his Addie's presence. "But you already know that."

Ranger's ears perked up, his head darting back and forth between the boy and the girl. Mrs. Carson busied herself in the kitchen, returning each time with more food. Only Mr. Carson seemed unfazed by the brief, uncomfortable silence.

"Geez, take it easy." She was taken aback by Billy's tone but determined not to let it show.

"What are you doing here, Addie?"

"You knew I was coming," she replied warily. "I wanted to talk to the Carsons."

Mr. Carson filled his glass with lemonade and scratched Ranger's belly. Billy and Addie both wished he would say something to end their stalemate. Instead, he disappeared into the kitchen. After a hushed conversation with Helen, he poked his head back out to the screen porch.

"Come on, you two. Let's wash up."

Mrs. Carson had prepared cold turkey sandwiches and fresh fruit for lunch. Mr. Carson and Billy ate heartily while Addie nibbled uneasily on a small dish of blueberries.

"That hit the spot, my dear. Thank you." Mr. Carson patted his stomach and looked up at his wife standing next to him. His arm reached around her waist and rested on her hip. She leaned down and gave him a peck on the cheek.

"You're welcome, Virgil," she cooed. Billy and Addie watched the unexpected moment of tenderness, neither having ever seen anything remotely like it pass between their mother and Jake.

"How 'bout I put you two out of your misery," Mr. Carson chuckled. "What do you think, Helen?"

Mrs. Carson swatted her husband with a cloth napkin. "Kids, ignore him. He shouldn't be enjoying this." But as she cleared the table her eyes locked onto his as if to say, *"Talk to them, Virgil!"*

"I'm glad you're here, Addie," he began. "We were hoping you might've come sooner, but now is better than never."

"Better than never?" Addie repeated. "What does that mean?"

"I'm guessing your bother told you that our son was in Vietnam," Mr. Carson continued.

Addie looked at Billy and nodded.

"And now you're wondering if we might have known Will."

"Did you?" Addie asked with a trace of desperation.

"We did," Mr. Carson replied warmly. "And we knew your mom too. Lost Elm's not a big town. Everybody pretty much knows everybody around here." Addie cringed at the thought of *everybody* knowing her.

"What was he like?" Billy murmured.

"Will Travers was very special, Billy. There weren't many like him, that's for sure. He was such a . . . ." the farmer wavered. Helen stood behind his chair and rested her hands on his shoulders. "Will was a born leader," he said with a catch in his throat. "He had a strength people were drawn to. They went to him for advice, followed him . . . anywhere." Mr. Carson reached into the pocket of his overalls and took out a handkerchief. He wiped away fresh tears and blew his nose.

Billy and Addie didn't take their eyes off Mr. Carson from the moment he began talking. They watched, mesmerized, as his tough exterior cracked the longer he spoke. Neither had ever seen a man come so close to crying before. *And he doesn't seem to care,* Billy realized.

"Our Jimmy joined the Marines a few months after Will volunteered for duty in Vietnam," Mrs. Carson recalled, picking up the story. "He

55

spent a year on the farm after high school and another one in college, but Jimmy didn't know what he wanted to do with his life. Not yet anyway. When he heard that your dad volunteered to go overseas, he wanted to do the same thing. He told us it would be an adventure—a chance to test himself. The war still had a lot of support then."

An unbearable stillness fell over the porch. Crickets chirped in the lower field and cars hummed by on the interstate. Ranger dozed at Addie's feet.

"Will called the day before Jimmy enlisted," Mr. Carson continued. "Begged him to reconsider, but it was too late. He was pretty shook up when Jimmy handed us the phone. Said he was sorry, then asked us to do something for him while he was in Vietnam. *'Look in on Anna for me. She and the kids are coming home right after I ship out.'* And we have ever since."

Mrs. Carson twisted the napkin in her hand. "Jimmy died six weeks after your dad," she murmured.

Addie held her breath. All she could think of was why her Mom had never told her or Billy any of this.

"You can't be too hard on your mother," Mr. Carson said, reading Addie's mind. "Anna had to make some hard choices after Will died and she made them in the midst of the worst kind of loss a person can go through."

"Those two loved each other very much," Mrs. Carson said, shaking her head at the memory.

"So yes, Addie," Mr. Carson concluded sympathetically, "We knew your dad."

Addie smiled gratefully at Mr. and Mrs. Carson, though the smile didn't reach her eyes. She was satisfied, at least for now.

"I'm sorry our dad couldn't talk Jimmy out of joining," Billy said. "But I'm glad he tried."

"Me too, son," Mr. Carson said. "He was a good man and a good worker. He handled hay bales a little better than you, but he was a few years older, as I recall."

"My dad worked on the farm?!"

"Three summers with Jimmy. They were a good team."

"I was wondering, Mr. Carson," Billy asked, now that they were on the subject, "Is there anything more I can do here before haying starts next month?"

"I don't know, Billy. The deal was for the past week and then two rounds of haying."

"I know but . . . I mean I can . . ." he stammered to find the right words. "I don't mind more work. I like it here."

Mr. Carson smiled. "We like you here too, Billy. Don't worry, there's always more work."

"Thank you," Billy replied with tangible relief.

Not content with just Billy, Mr. Carson decided to try his luck with Addie again. "How about it, Miss Pearson? Interested in joining your brother?"

Addie hadn't heard his question. She was looking down the Carson's long driveway. Like a newsflash interrupting a TV program, the sound of tires on gravel filled her with dread. A car had turned off the highway and was racing up the hill toward them.

Mr. Carson's gaze followed hers. "Wait here," he ordered. "Both of you." The screen door creaked open and he marched down the porch steps. The driveway in front of Mr. Carson didn't end—it just sort of petered out, the gravel fading into grass. That's where he met a familiar car and its uninvited driver.

"What can I do for you, Jake?"

"I'mere for the kids." The bottle Jake had taken from his dad's house lay on the seat next to him. He stepped unsteadily from the car.

"Can we get you anything, Jake?" Mr. Carson asked him. "We just finished lunch but it'd be no trouble to fix you a plate."

"I don't want nothin' from you, Carson," Jake spat, stumbling forward. Virgil grabbed his shoulders and held him fast.

"I'm going to say this just once, Jake," he whispered. "You're embarrassing yourself. Those kids didn't sign up for this, but this is what they got. They got you. I am truly sorry for whatever has caused you so much pain, but we all have problems. I suggest you start dealing with yours."

"What would you know 'bout it?!" Jake roared, twisting free from Mr. Carson's grip.

"Probably nothing, Jake," he replied wearily. "But we've tried to help you and you've refused us each time—called it charity. What did you think? That you were going to get something for nothing? I expected you to work hard. That's what I got from your boy."

"He's not my boy."

"No, I suppose he's not," Mr. Carson agreed. "But you're the only father he's ever known and you've wasted the opportunity."

Jake staggered towards the porch. "Billy! Addie! Let's go! Billy, yer done here! Carson'll have to find somebody else to boss around for the rest of the summer!"

Minutes earlier Billy had gotten exactly what he wanted, more time on the farm and more time with Mr. Carson. Now someone masquerading as his father was taking that away from him. Billy didn't say a word, but he didn't move either.

Addie had no trouble finding her voice. "Who's gonna drive us home, Jake?! You?!" She had barely restrained herself from the moment she heard the Comet hit gravel. Whether stirred by her morning with Sara or strengthened by news of her father, Addie let loose again. She kicked the screen door open and stood toe to toe with Jake. "We're not going anywhere, so you can just crawl back to all those places you run off to and leave us alone!"

Enraged, he reached for Addie with both hands. Mr. Carson threw his weight into Jake's chest and knocked him roughly to the ground. Jake's low moans quickly turned to laughter.

"You know that's my house you're livin' in," he muttered.

"What a bunch of bullcrap!" Addie replied with all the contempt she could muster. "You're going to do whatever you want, Jake. You always have. If you hate your life, that's your problem. But I'm tired of hating mine."

"Time to go, Jake," Mr. Carson announced, pointing to the Comet. "You shouldn't drive but Addie's right, once you've made up your mind to hell with the consequences."

Jake slipped grudgingly into the front seat and re-started the car, forgetting that he had left it running. The Comet shrieked in protest. For a heartbeat, his head dropped to the steering wheel before he drove away.

"That was very impressive, Miss Pearson," Mr. Carson told Addie as they watched Jake race out of sight, thankful that he didn't turned onto Halverson Road. "Billy is lucky to have you."

"I don't know about that," Addie shrugged. "I think I just made things a whole lot worse for both of us."

"Maybe, but what's better? More of the same? Jake has to hear the bad news sooner or later. I'm just sorry there's so much of it."

"Me too."

"Thanks, Ad," Billy said as he and Mrs. Carson joined them in the yard.

"No sweat, Shorty," she replied, trying her best to downplay what he'd just witnessed.

"Does this mean I can't work here anymore, Mr. Carson?" Billy asked with obvious concern.

"Let me talk to your mom first, Billy. I don't want to make things worse—for either of you."

"We should get going," Addie said. "Mom will be home soon." She looked at the Carsons with a grateful smile. "Thank you. For everything."

"You're welcome, dear," Mrs. Carson said. "Anytime."

"Are you two going to be okay?" Mr. Carson asked. "You can stay longer if you'd like."

"You saw Jake," Addie replied. "He won't be home for hours, days if we're lucky." After a confirming nod from Billy, they began walking home.

"Is this your book, Addie?!" Mr. Carson called out from the porch, waving her copy of *The Call of the Wild*.

Addie jogged back to the porch steps. "Sara Farelli gave it to me."

Mr. Carson handed her the book but didn't let go of it. "Addie, I was serious. I'm glad your brother has you." He put a hand on her shoulder. "You fight for him."

"Because he won't fight for himself."

"He will one day," Mr. Carson said. "But for now he has you. I didn't know that until today. You know, Will fought for people the same way you just did. That was his gift. He had a very big heart. I'd say you do too."

Roused earlier by the commotion between the humans in the yard, Ranger was comforted by the tender words between his master and the girl. He slipped out the screen door with her as the gentle man disappeared into the farmhouse. His tailed wagged happily at the girl he liked so well.

But when the dog's eyes locked onto hers, his tail froze. The girl's eyes were shiny and wet. Ranger had seen the same thing on his master's face whenever he looked at a piece of paper with the face of a certain boy on it. But this was different. Thin streams of water ran down the girl's face, but her mouth was turned upward. Ranger's tail began to wag again.

Addie knelt down and took the dog's head in her hands. "Maybe everything's going to be okay, boy," she said, wiping her tears on his furry face. "Maybe everything's going to be okay."

Hi Dad,

It's me Addie.

So much has happened this past week I don't even know where to begin. Jake showed up at the Carsons' and left with his tail between his legs, back to his dad's for a while. I thought Shorty would be glad, but he moped around the Loop for days afterward. He even skipped biking into town with Renny last Saturday. I guess I can't blame him, especially after Mom's phone call with Mr. Carson last Wednesday.

She told Shorty he would have to take a break from working on the farm. He never looked at her once when she told him, but right after she finished he said, "We don't need Jake around here, Mom. How come you do?"

Jake finally came home Saturday night. I knew we were in trouble as soon as I saw the way he looked. Whenever Jake showers and shaves, some lame version of "I'm sorry" is never far behind. Sure enough, he told us how he wanted to "be better" and that "it wasn't easy" for him. A pretty lousy apology, but Mom accepted it.

I could sense Shorty watching me the whole time Jake talked, hoping I'd say something, but I kept my mouth shut. When he finished, Shorty just looked at him and said, "Is that all you have to say, Jake?" He's never called him Jake to his face before. I almost felt sorry for the guy, but not after last night.

We were watching TV when Jake announced out of the blue that he wants us to move, have a fresh start together. He said there's a job his dad can get him at a grain elevator in Albert Lea, Minnesota, wherever that is. He asked us to think about it. But when Jake went outside after talking to us, I knew his fresh start was nothing but bullcrap.

I waited a few minutes, then snuck outside and climbed the Pines. From up there I could see Jake looking around Pete's Woods until he found one of his red bandanas. Does he really think I haven't figured out what he uses those things for? The joke's on him, because I've known for years. I have an idea what I want to do with those bandanas, but the plan has to include Shorty. If he's not mad enough to join me now, he never will be.

61

I don't want to move, Dad, but I'm afraid Mom will just give in to Jake like she always does. She hardly says anything these days, except for her secret phone calls with the Carsons. I know they were deciding whether Shorty should keep working on the farm the other night, but what else did they have to talk about for an hour? Then today Mrs. Carson called and asked Mom if we wanted to come over for lunch tomorrow. That only took a minute. Why sixty minutes on the phone one day and sixty seconds the next?

I already have plans with Sara, but I'm glad Shorty is going. Maybe I'll talk to him about the bandanas when he gets home. Mr. Carson was right, "Now is better than never."

I'm starting to get answers, Dad. The Carsons told me things about you that make me proud to be your daughter, but I still want to know more. If only Mom would say something.

I'll write again soon. Something tells me I'm going to have a lot to talk about.

I miss you all the time.

Love,
Your daughter, Addie

5
CHOICES

"Hey there, boy—how ya doing?" Billy asked Ranger as the dog greeted him in the Carson's front yard. He nuzzled Billy's leg then trotted on toward the slope of the lower field.

"Addie's not coming today, Ranger. It's just me." The dog's tail rose and his nose twitched. Confirming Billy's news, he circled a patch of dirt and flopped to the ground.

"Don't feel bad, Billy. There's still two of us who are very happy to see you," Mrs. Carson called out as she and Mr. Carson came down the porch steps.

"I don't know what it is," Billy replied. "But Addie sure has a way with that dog."

"Where *is* your sister?" Mr. Carson asked. "The invitation was for two."

"With Sara," Billy explained. "She wants to spend as much time with her as she can, just in case."

"Just in case what?"

"Didn't my mom tell you?"

"Tell us what, dear?" Mrs. Carson pressed.

"That we're moving." Billy replied, biting his lower lip. "At least that's what Jake wants and it doesn't seem like Mom's gonna stop him. You didn't know?"

Mr. Carson shook his head. "No, we didn't." He looked at Helen and gestured behind them to the upper field. "Come on, Billy," he said, pointing through the bordering pines. "There's something I want to show you."

The morning sun burned bright under the cloudless June sky as Mr. Carson took a Farmall cap from his back pocket and put it on his head. He moved with a restless purpose toward an object in the far corner of his property, near the ditch next to Halverson Road. Billy broke into a slow jog to catch up.

"I love it up here," he murmured. "I'd really miss it if we moved."

"We'd miss you too, son," Mr. Carson replied, putting his arm around the boy's shoulder. "Who knows, maybe you'll stay."

Billy hadn't expected Mr. Carson to be such a gentle man. Every rumor he'd ever heard told of a hard man, uncaring and unkind. But in a just few weeks Billy's trust in Mr. Carson was total. The man's words and wisdom were clear and genuine.

They walked on in silence, Billy's eyes brimming with unshed tears as Mr. Carson hummed softly to himself. A few minutes from the farmhouse, they approached a rust-covered hunk of twisted metal surrounded by a dense patch of thistle. Mr. Carson circled the object slowly, never taking his eyes off it. Billy watched him, expecting some explanation, but was told nothing. Instead, he turned his back to Billy, unzipped his fly and relieved himself on the wreckage, his water spattering against the flaking metal with a continuous, hollow thud. When he finished, Mr. Carson spat into the thistle and returned to Billy's side.

"Why'd you do that?!" Peeing outdoors was one thing, but in broad daylight right next to Halverson Road?

Mr. Carson exhaled, then met Billy's shocked gaze. "Have I told you why I bought the farm?"

"No, sir. You just said it was in 1946."

"Close, 1945. Helen and I moved in the day after Thanksgiving. She gave birth to Jimmy that same weekend, nine months to the day after I got home from the war." He smiled at the memory.

"You were in World War II?" Billy said in astonishment.

"Everybody was, Billy," Mr. Carson nodded. "I joined the army right after Pearl Harbor and landed in France in June of '44. Got my ticket home December 12th that same year."

"Ticket home?"

"My squad was on the German border and their artillery was pounding us pretty good. I took some shrapnel in the back of my leg that nearly cut clean through the artery. I didn't want to worry Helen so I kept my discharge quiet right up 'til the moment I knocked on her parents' front door. That sure was some homecoming."

"What was *this*?" Billy asked, pointing to the twisted wreck.

"This was my dad's car," Mr. Carson sighed. "He crashed it here the night of July 4th, 1945."

"You mean . . ." The truth dawned on Billy. "You didn't own the farm yet?"

"No. I'd just started working at the steel plant and was taking a few agriculture classes in Duluth."

Billy had more questions but he kept them to himself. He sensed Mr. Carson was coming to the point. Besides, he didn't want to interrupt a good story, especially one with so much history.

"I behaved pretty badly those first few months after I got home. I thought I had it coming after the three years I gave the Army." Mr. Carson bent down and plucked a piece of straw from the ground. "War's a hard thing, Billy, but it's hard on the people back home too. Helen showed me a lot more patience than I deserved. After all, I was one of the lucky ones."

Billy wondered what his own father might have gone through in Vietnam, an unlucky young man among tens of thousands of unlucky young men.

"My dad was a lousy father," Mr. Carson admitted. "I never got along with him except for those first few months after I got home. For once, one of my Dad's drinking buddies was me."

Billy looked at Mr. Carson, tried to imagine him as a reckless young man. He couldn't.

"I was hurting pretty bad and not just from my wounds," he said, stuffing his hands in his pockets. "So I buried it all in a bottle. My dad was more than happy to have some company."

Mr. Carson reached across a patch of thistles and twisted off a piece of metal from the wreckage, tapping it idly in the palm of his hand. "That all ended on the 4th of July. We were at the Junction—it was called *The Water Tower* back then. My dad was showing me off to his buddies but pretty soon he got tired of all the attention I was getting. Told everyone how I'd been nothing but a rear echelon flunky during the war. *'If you're so tough,'* he said, *'Prove it. Hit me.'* It was a full house that night, being the 4th near the end of the war."

"What happened?" Billy asked.

"I hit him. Hard. I guess I'd had enough. For the three years in the Bog, for the beatings, for the way he treated my mom. I laid him out on the floor soaking in his own beer. He didn't say a word, just got up and stormed out. That was the last time I ever saw him alive."

Although Mr. Carson spoke with a practiced detachment, Billy felt enormous sympathy for him. He could scarcely believe what he was hearing.

"Doesn't look much like a car, does it?" Mr. Carson asked. "When they pulled my dad from it he didn't look much like a person either."

Billy cringed. "How come you're showing me this, Mr. Carson?"

"Because you need to understand that you always have choices, son," he said wistfully. "My dad wasn't a good person, but not a day goes by that I don't wish I could take back that punch and talk to him instead."

"Are you saying I should talk to Jake?"

"If you're moving I'd say talking to Jake is more important than ever."

"But what if he doesn't listen?" Billy asked with a trace of desperation. "What if he doesn't change?"

Mr. Carson knew sugar-coating the truth would be wrong. "I doubt Jake will do either. So maybe that means you and your sister need to stick up for yourselves from now on. I know that sounds like a pretty tall order, but you can't do it the way Addie has—returning anger for anger. That's never worked."

"What about my Mom?"

Mr. Carson looked away from for a moment. *Not yet,* he reminded himself. "Of course, Billy. She'll always be there to help you."

Billy looked into the wreckage. He knew Mr. Carson was right, but he couldn't imagine what he and Addie could do that would make a difference. *It's not like we can run away,* he thought, his eyes meeting the farmer's penetrating gaze.

"But I still don't understand why you peed on your dad's car."

A wry, sad smile crossed Mr. Carson's face. "For months after the accident I worried that I'd turn out just like him," Mr. Carson replied. "But from the moment I held little Jimmy in my arms I knew I'd never be anything like Roger Carson. So when the farm went up for sale that fall, I knew I had to have it. I've never thought once about removing this—it's a reminder to me that we all have choices."

"But that still doesn't explain the pee."

"I forgave my dad a long time ago, Billy," Mr. Carson said as they walked back to the farmhouse. "But I still get mad at him now and then. The last drink I had was the night he rolled his old Ford into this field. I just figure this is a better way to deal with the hurt than what I did before that night—what Jake's been doing for years."

"Do you come out here a lot?"

"Often enough, son," Mr. Carson said ruefully, glancing back at the thistle and metal and rust. "Often enough."

*

"We're eating inside where it's cool," Mrs. Carson announced when Billy and Mr. Carson returned from the upper field. The dining room table was already set, the overhead fan offering a welcome breeze.

Mr. Carson stared at the food his wife had set before him. His plate was covered with raw carrots, steamed rice and a dish of fresh fruit. He frowned and reached for her hand. She glared right back and pulled him into the kitchen.

"You might not have taken the doctor's orders seriously, mister, but I did," Helen insisted. "High blood pressure, remember?"

"But I've stayed out of the barn," Mr. Carson argued.

"Keep your voice down," she shushed, peeking into the dining room. "Look at him. For heaven's sake, you know what's coming. Don't you think that boy has lost enough already? Haven't I?"

Mr. Carson's resolve vanished. So did his sour expression. He took his wife's face in his hands and kissed her below each eye, where fresh tears had formed.

"Eat your food."

"Yes, ma'am."

When they returned to the dining room, Mr. Carson didn't waste any time before he asked Billy about Jake's intention to move them to Albert Lea. "I understand what Jake wants, Billy," he acknowledged. "But what do you want?"

Billy took a deep breath and let it out slowly. "I don't want Jake for a father anymore," he said, a large tear curling to the bottom of his chin. "Addie's right—he'll never change. Besides, he's not really family so why should we move with him?"

Mr. Carson gave Helen a knowing look. Her eyes widened and she shook her head imperceptibly. *Not yet, Virgil.*

"We don't want you or your mom or Addie to move either," Mr. Carson replied in earnest, conceding to his wife's silent demand.

"Even Addie?" Billy asked.

67

"Yes, even Miss Pearson," he chuckled. "I'll tell you what, Billy. Helen and I are having lunch with your mom at *Paulette's Café* tomorrow. Do you mind if we tell her what you've told us?"

Billy's face paled, but he nodded. "Sure."

"Your mom has a lot on her mind, but she deserves to know how you feel and also what a fine young man you're becoming."

Mrs. Carson rose from the table. "How about a dish of ice cream? I think we have some Neapolitan in the freezer."

"Me too?" Mr. Carson asked hopefully.

"You too, Virgil—but a small bowl. Rome wasn't built in a day."

Billy stayed with the Carsons for the rest of the afternoon, soaking in the loving atmosphere that seeped into every corner of their home. Mr. Carson taught him how to play cribbage and Mrs. Carson showed him some of their old photo albums. Billy looked at one picture for a long time—that of a weary young Lieutenant Virgil Carson in uniform and on crutches. A dog-eared corner of the picture revealed a date written on the back—*March 1, 1945.*

*

As Billy and Mr. Carson crossed the upper field on their way to the rusting wreckage of Roger Carson's car, Addie met Sara in the Farelli's driveway. She was pretty sure she'd never felt more ridiculous in her entire life.

"Wow, Addie! You look so different!" Sara exclaimed.

Addie's face reddened to match the color of her shirt. Instinct screamed at her to run back to the trailer and put on her usual white t-shirt and cut-off jeans.

"What's wrong?" Sara asked, sensing Addie's embarrassment.

"I'm going home to change," she murmured.

"No, you're not." Sara locked eyes with Addie across the low hood of her dark purple El Camino. "I'm not the only one who gets to see how great you look."

She was right. Even Billy said so when Addie emerged from their tiny bathroom earlier that morning. *"Geez, what's with you? You look . . . nice or something."* Gone were her well-worn summer clothes. Instead, Addie wore a pale red top lightly cinched below her ribs. A pair of crisp white shorts had replaced her knee-length cut-offs and a thin layer of makeup masked her freckled cheeks and forehead. The tight ponytail was gone too, replaced by gentle curls that fell below her shoulders.

Sara had phoned the night before with a simple request—more of a command, really. *"You and me tomorrow, okay? No arguments."* Addie was thrilled, but when she saw her usual outfit that morning she was stirred by an unexpected desire to look, as Billy had so clumsily put it, *nice.*

"Where are we going, Sara?" she asked as the El Camino cruised past the Northern Pacific Railroad sign.

Sara hadn't heard her question. The car's AM radio blared over the wind whipping through her open window. Addie, on the other hand, kept hers rolled up. She had labored too long in front of the mirror to give up on her hair already.

As they sped toward Lost Elm, Addie discreetly studied her friend. Sara's dark hair swirled around her face as she sang *Knowing Me, Knowing You* without a hint of self-consciousness.

> *"Breaking up is never easy I know,*
> *But I had to go (I had to go).*
> *Knowing me, knowing you is the best I can do. . ."*

"How do you make it look so easy?" Addie finally blurted out.

Sara, seemingly oblivious of Addie's question, downshifted the El Camino as they cruised into town. She continued to sway to the music until she brought the car to a stop in the gravel lot across the street from First National Bank.

"Don't go anywhere," Sara ordered, a grin spreading across her face. "We need some cash."

Addie watched her disappear into the bank, then adjusted the rearview mirror to assess her wind-damaged hair. That's when she saw Jake.

He was standing outside the post office fifty feet down the street. The stubble had returned to his face and his clothes were wrinkled. Jake looked back and forth, noticeably unsure what his next move might be. Finally, he walked toward Addie and the El Camino, but went right past her.

Without a second thought, Addie got out of the car and followed him. "Where do you think you're going, Jake?"

69

Jake spun around at the familiar voice, but looked blankly at Addie. Only when her hands went to her hips did he recognize her.

"What happened to you?" he asked, slipping his sunglasses down from the top of his head. "You look different."

Addie glared at him contemptuously. "So this is being better, Jake?! Mom's not clueless, you know. None of us are." She braced herself for his usual sarcasm.

"I didn't say you were," Jake replied, forcing a smile. "I told you things were gonna be different and I meant it."

"Did you really think one speech was going to make everything better?!" Addie countered.

"Of course not." Jake wouldn't let himself get drawn into an argument, though he thought his earlier apology and promise should count for something. "But haven't you ever wanted a fresh start, Addie?"

She bristled at his use of her name. The question reminded her how different she must look. Jake sensed her discomfort and pressed on.

"Is that your mom's red shirt?"

Addie's face turned crimson. "Big fan of red, aren'tcha, Jake?" she retorted, hoping he understood her veiled reference to his monogrammed bandanas. "So where are you going? Your usual stops?"

Jake refused to take the bait. "Harold's." He pointed down 3rd Street. *Harold's Service Station*, one of the last filling station and auto repair shops in town, was a few blocks away. "He's patching a tire for me, then I thought I'd run over to Wood City and pick up a pizza for supper. Any requests?"

"Huh?" Addie heard Jake's words, but his pleasant tone disarmed her.

"Requests. You know, toppings."

"I won't be home. I'm hanging out with Sara." Once again, telling Jake her plans bothered Addie more than his oddly normal behavior.

"Alright," he replied. "Have fun."

Addie watched him walk past the Junction. *You don't fool me for a minute, Jerk. No one changes that fast.* She looked down at her outfit. *Not even me.*

"Look who I found, Addie!"

"Let's get out of here, Sara," she said, turning around. But instead of facing Sara, Addie saw the astonished expression of her mother.

"Your mom was on break so I thought I'd show you off," Sara announced, peeking out from behind Anna.

Addie pulled at the curls in her hair. "Sorry, Mom. I should have asked if I could borrow your blouse."

"Never mind that, Addie. Come here." Anna put her hands on Addie's shoulders and brought her over to the full-length glass doors of the bank's entrance. "Honey, you look beautiful."

A faint smile tugged at the corners of Addie's mouth, but then she noticed their reflections. The contrast was unnerved. They were the same height and shape, but her mother looked noticeably pale and tired.

"We should get going," Addie suggested self-consciously.

"Have her home by dark, Sara," Anna said.

"I'll try, Mrs. Pearson."

"Mom, I won't be home for pizza!" Addie shouted after she had crossed the street. "You can break the news to Jake! I'm sure he'll be crushed!"

"Pizza?! We're having leftovers tonight."

Addie shook her head. Jake had lied again.

"You pick, Addie," Sara said. "Where to?"

Addie looked down 3rd Street. The Comet was just pulling out of Harold's and heading north. "Let's go to Wood City."

"Wood City it is. But first to Harold's."

"Why there?" Addie asked as the Comet disappeared from sight a half mile ahead of them.

"Because," Sara said, waving a handful of bills. "The money's not just for fun. We need gas." She drove the El Camino into the service station and rolled to a stop next to a gas pump, triggering a bell inside the building.

"Be right witchya!"

Two legs stuck out from underneath an Oldsmobile in one of Harold's repair bays. Sara put two fingers to her mouth and blew. The piercing whistle startled the person beneath the car. "Come on, Harold!" she hollered playfully. "Shake a leg!"

Harold Hinkum slid out from under the car and shielded his eyes. Closing in fast on 60, he hoisted his stout frame off the ground and shook his head in amusement at the sight of Sara's car.

71

"The Countess Sara!" he boomed. "What has brought you out from the protection of Farelli Manor this fine day? Not mingling with any commoners, I hope."

"Not until now," Sara teased. "Please, Sir Harold. Can you help a damsel in distress?"

The old man smiled warmly. "You can pump the gas all by yourself now, Sara," he pointed out. "Heck, I'm sure some day you won't even have to come inside and pay."

"And deprive myself of your company?" Sara pouted. "Never."

Harold blushed and scratched his graying temple. "Then I shall fill 'er up, Milady," he promised solemnly.

Addie started to speak but Sara put a finger to her lips. Reaching behind her seat, she fished out a book—*The Good Earth*.

"Okay," Harold said after putting the nozzle back in its cradle. "Thirteen gallons at sixty-seven cents a gallon comes to $8.71."

Sara handed him a ten dollar bill and balanced the book on her open window. "Some light reading, my good Sir?"

Harold read the back cover as he brought the money inside. When he returned, he handed Sara her change and a copy of *Watership Down*.

"Who knew a story about rabbits could be so good. I trust this one is too?"

"Have I ever steered you wrong?" Sara asked with mock indignation.

"Harold," Addie began, unsure whether or not to break up the melodrama. "I just saw Jake here. Did he say where he was going?"

"Didn't say," Harold replied, never taking his eyes off the book. "Just in a hurry."

"Okay. Thanks anyway."

"I will now take my leave of this realm," Sara declared. "Take care, Sir Harold, until I return in a fortnight for your literary review."

He bowed stiffly as the El Camino drove off. The filling station shrank from view in the car's back window, but Addie saw Harold perform a little jig by the pumps before he slid back under the Oldsmobile.

"I didn't know you were friends with Harold Hinkum."

Sara set the book down between them and collected her thoughts. "Harold was changing my oil last fall when the sheriff came by and told him his wife died in that bad car accident over on Hay Lake Road. Remember that one? I turned the *Open* sign to *Closed* and we went inside until his son could pick him up and go to the hospital to claim her body. While we waited Harold told me all about her, their kids, how they met—everything." Sara wiped her cheeks. "I think Harold thought if he kept talking, her death wouldn't be real. So he never stopped until his son came."

Addie reached out and held Sara's hand. She wanted to tell her friend how much she admired her. She didn't, but she didn't let go of her hand either.

"Ever since then I come by the gas station a few times a month and bring him books. People like Harold shouldn't have to go through something terrible all by themselves." Sara looked at Addie. "No one should."

A few silent minutes later they cruised into Wood City. Ten times the size of Lost Elm, Wood City boasted a thriving paper industry, evidenced by the sour odor the mill gave off most days of the year. With a fortunate breeze blowing north, the girls didn't smell a thing as they drove by half a dozen businesses before Sara parked across the street from *Jensen & Company*, the only clothing store in town.

"We're going shopping and you're going to have fun, Addie," she proclaimed. "Got that?"

Addie looked in the mirrored visor. A stranger stared back at her desperately trying to unsnarl strands of long, straw-blond hair.

"Your mom's right, you know," Sara said. "You look beautiful. And don't tell me you went to all this trouble just for me."

"I don't know," Addie shrugged, her face reddening.

"When things don't exactly feel right do you ever get that weird feeling right here?" Sara tapped her chest.

"Sometimes."

"Do you have that feeling now?"

"Kind of."

Sara opened the glove compartment and plucked out a rubber band. "Here, maybe this will help."

Addie pulled her hair back into a familiar ponytail and wrapped the rubber band around it.

"Better?"

Addie looked into the mirror again. "Much."

"I heard your question earlier, Addie. When you asked how I make it look easy. If I do, it's only because I'm okay with who I am. We have to be who we are. What other choice is there?"

"But that's just it. Most days I don't know who I'm supposed to be," Addie confessed.

"Well don't you think this is a good start?" Sara replied, gesturing to Addie's changed appearance. "Come on, let's go pick out some new clothes. You might surprise yourself."

The girls dodged a few cars on their way across the street. When they reached the other side, Sara saw a familiar figure disappear into the *Wood City Bar & Lounge* a block and a half away.

"Wasn't that Jake?"

Addie took off running down the sidewalk. She pulled on the bar's thick oak door, ready to do battle with Jake again come what may, but two hands grabbed her firmly by the shoulders.

"Addie, what are you doing?! You can't go in there!"

"Watch me!"

"What's that going to prove?! Jake will just know he got under your skin again. Is that really what you want?"

Addie wanted to tear herself free from Sara's grasp, but she didn't. Instead, she remembered her own words to Jake a week ago. *"If you hate your life, that's your problem. But I'm tired of hating mine."*

"My life is all bullcrap, Sara," Addie winced.

"That's not true and you know it," Sara replied emphatically.

"Maybe," Addie murmured.

"Maybe?!" Sara exclaimed, adopting the same tone she had used with Harold. "Me thinks Lady Adeline has much to look forward to, and I will brook no argument to this keen observation. We will leave the rabble where they sit and proceed forthwith to shop 'til we drop."

"Lead the way," Addie giggled, doing her best to block out the image of Jake in the bar, trying to forget his lies and false promises, but she couldn't—not entirely.

"What are you thinking?" Sara asked, noticing the mixture of emotions playing across Addie's face.

"That it's been a good day. Thanks to you."

*

74

The setting sun disappeared as Addie walked home from Sara's later that evening. Clouds had gathered all afternoon and the sky was now gray and foreboding. When the rain finally came, Addie stood in the middle of the Loop and let the day wash over her. Nearby, their driveway was empty, though a faint light shone through the trailer's living room window where her mom and Billy were watching television.

Addie hurried to the shelter of the Pines and set her packages down on a bed of pine needles. She and Sara had rummaged through Jensen's clothing racks for nearly an hour running back and forth to the changing rooms. Now, beneath the gathering storm, the day's bright memory stood in stark contrast to the perilous plan Addie was determined to set in motion. She looked into the trailer again, then back to Sara's El Camino. Inspired, she pulled out her small notepad and wrote:

> When I've yearned to run wild,
> When I've longed to be free,
> Always two kept me here,
> But now there are three.

Pleased, Addie picked up the packages and ran to the trailer as a driving rain began showering Halverson Road. For now, she was safe.

6
MARKS ON MAPS

Renny wondered if the storm would ever end. He had fallen asleep with rain pounding on his bedroom window and woke up to more ominous clouds overhead. The downpour began anew as he glumly ate a bowl of corn flakes. His sour mood and open-mouthed chewing was interrupted by the ring of a telephone.

"Farelli's."

"Hey, Renny. Good job." Michael Farelli replied. He'd been coaching his son on how to answer the phone because, *"I'm sorry, my dad's at work right now,"* followed by a hang-up had been Renny's response since, well, forever.

"My dad's not home. Can I take a message?" Renny responded mechanically.

"No pal, it's me."

"Hi, Dad," he said. "You're not home right now—can I take a message?" Renny scooped up the last of his cereal and crunched them into the receiver.

Michael laughed despite his impatience. "Having breakfast?"

"Mmm hmm."

"Renny, I've got some good news. I just got off the phone with some men from Minneapolis. Guess what they're mailing me?"

"Twins tickets?!" Renny said, suddenly excited.

"How did you know?!"

"Because I've been asking for tickets since Opening Day!"

"Okay, okay," his father chuckled. "Box seats, Bud. And they're sending me an extra ticket too. I thought you could invite Billy. How does that sound, Renny? Renny?"

Renny hadn't heard the question. His gloomy morning was forgotten and so was the phone. He and Billy were going to the Twin Cities to see Rod Carew and the Minnesota Twins.

*

Addie lay on the couch, hypnotized by the beating rain on the trailer's thin metal roof, when the phone rang. She hurried into the kitchen, but Billy snatched the receiver off the wall first.

"Hey, Ren," he answered. "Pretty lousy outside, huh?"

Addie heard garbled excitement on the other end of the line as she slid a thick piece of bread into the toaster. Billy held the phone away from his ear, urging his friend to slow down.

"Twins tickets, Billy!" Renny screeched. "We're going to Met Stadium on July 10th!"

"I'll have to ask my mom," Billy said, barely listening. Open in front of him was a Rand McNally road atlas displaying a map of Minnesota. On one page Billy had underlined Lost Elm. Far to the south, near the bottom of the opposite page, he traced a continuous circle around Albert Lea.

The toaster dinged. As Addie absently slathered peanut butter on her toast, she studied Billy. His expression betrayed little, but the pencil pressed deeper and deeper into the page with each loop.

"Don'tcha think my dad already asked her?" Renny replied. "They work together."

Billy looked up to see Addie staring at him and the atlas. Neither had talked about Jake's idea for a fresh start, as if the mere mention of moving might make it a reality. But now Billy's marks on the map triggered an immediacy that neither of them could ignore any longer.

"What day is the 10th, Ren?"

"Sunday," Renny replied after a quick calculation. "They play the Mariners. The Twins will win for sure!"

Billy was too busy scanning all the cities and towns along Interstate 35 between Lost Elm and Albert Lea to feel any of Renny's excitement. "Sounds like fun," he said with little enthusiasm. "Who knows, maybe Carew will be hitting .400 by then." Almost as an afterthought Billy added, "Hey, Ren? Do you wanna bike to Ervin's tomorrow?" More whoops and hollers were heard from the receiver before Billy handed it to Addie. He flopped into Jake's chair in the living room and flung the atlas to the floor. It slid across the carpet, coming to rest under their battered couch.

"Hello," Addie answered, unconsciously smoothing her hair. "Hi, Sara. No, Jake didn't show up last night." She untangled the cord and stretched it down the hallway. "Can you help me with something tomorrow?"

"Why not today?"

"I need to go into the Bog, but I don't think the rain's going to let up today."

"What's in the Bog?"

Addie looked into the living room. "I can't talk right now. I don't want Shorty to hear me, not yet anyway."

"Is this about Jake?"

Addie shot to her feet, Sara's question was drowned out by the sound of a car pulling into the driveway. She lowered the phone and stepped further down the hallway to look out the window at the far end of the trailer.

"Meet me in Pete's Woods in fifteen minutes."

"Sure but what's . . ."

"Just meet me by the big rock. And wear some rubber boots. I think we're going to get wet."

Addie hung up the phone as the outer mud room door opened and closed. "I'm going to Sara's, Shorty. Are you going to be okay?"

Billy looked up from the cover of his *Sports Illustrated*. A jockey dressed in black and yellow was astride a horse, holding a riding crop high over his head. He nodded glumly as Addie grabbed the door knob. It wouldn't budge. Guessing that Jake was probably doing the same thing on the other side, she let go. The door swung open.

"Where are you going?"

"Where have you been?"

Recognizing the futility of one more stand-off, Jake slid past Addie and into the kitchen. A red bandana dangling from his back pocket fell to the floor. *That's one*, she thought, picking the bandana up before Jake noticed it was missing. She quickly put on her raincoat and boots and disappeared outside.

"Whatcha reading, Billy?" Jake asked uneasily. Small talk was never his thing.

Billy held up the magazine. "Seattle Slew won the Triple Crown."

"Can you save that for me?" Jake replied. "I wanna read it later."

Say something, Billy urged himself. "Jake, er, Dad. Can I talk to you?"

But Jake had already retreated to the bedroom. When he returned five minutes later he was carrying a duffel bag. "I'm going to Albert Lea 'til next week sometime—maybe work a couple days at their grain elevator, get the lay of the land."

"Does mom know?"

"Yup, I called the bank this morning before I left Grandpa Ron's."

"Oh." Billy didn't hide his disappointment. "Can I talk to you?"

"It'll have to wait 'til I get back," Jake said, looking past Billy to the small bookshelf in the living room. "Have you seen the road atlas? Albert Lea's right off the interstate but I wanna bring a map just in case."

Billy shook his head. "Nope."

"Hey, one more thing, Billy. My dad wasn't feeling too good this morning. Can you tell your mom to check on him after work today?" And with that parting request, Jake was gone.

"Sure thing, *Jake*," Billy muttered. He chucked the Sports Illustrated across the living room. It joined the road atlas underneath the couch.

*

Addie crouched at the base of the slate rock in the center of Pete's Woods, making numerous cuts with Billy's knife, when Sara approached her. She discreetly slipped the knife into the front pocket of her dark green poncho and stood.

"You'd have to look pretty hard to read it now," Addie said. Dozens of slash marks covered *I HATE HIM*, but her own guilty scar remained.

"You know it doesn't mean anything, Addie. Everybody gets mad at their parents."

"I know, but this is different. He's gone."

Sara dropped the subject and addressed Addie's mysterious phone call. "So what's going on? Why are we . . ." Her question was interrupted by a booming crack of thunder overhead. Both girls instinctively ducked. "Why are we out here in the middle of this monsoon?"

Addie unzipped the pocket she'd put the knife in and took out a red bandana. "Because of this. There are at least a dozen more just like it—most of them in the Bog. I need you to help me find them, Sara. Before it's too late."

80

The rain never let up, but neither did Addie. She found one bandana in Pete's Woods, left it fastened to the base of a tree, then crossed the state highway and dove into the Bog. Sara watched intently as Addie hurried to an old birch tree overlooking the rapidly swelling Otter Creek. Addie pulled out an old tobacco pipe from a split in the tree and twisted the stem free from the bowl. Inside it was a rolled up piece of paper. She studied the paper briefly before returning it to the stem.

"Ready, Sara?!" Addie asked over the pelting rain.

"Ready for what?! I get it, we're looking for red bandanas. But every time you find one we just move on to the next." Sara's hands were planted on her hips in a posture Addie knew all too well.

"Come on, I'll show you."

They walked fifty yards down a narrow path next to Otter Creek before stopping at a small landing where the river narrowed. Addie pointed to a small pine tree on the opposite bank. Tied around it was another bandana. She took Sara's hand and led her across the river on three rocks spread conveniently across its width.

"Dig here," Addie pointed, handing Sara the knife. Her foot marked an "X" in the dirt near the base of the tree.

Sara buried the knife into the wet earth and struck something solid. She pulled the blade out and traced a square around the spot. Driving the knife in up to the hilt, the soil gave way easily. Cupping her hands, she shoveled out just enough dirt to expose a small glass bottle filled with a clear liquid.

"You said a dozen of these?"

"Maybe more. The Bog's a big place." Addie pointed to the initials on the bandana—*JRP*. "Jake gets a new pack of these from his dad every Christmas."

"Okay, so we find more bottles. Then what?" Sara said, washing the mud off her hands with the driving rain.

"Yesterday you said a lot of things are starting to change, but they're not changing fast enough." Addie smoothed the dirt back over the bottle and tamped it down with her foot.

"It's only June, Addie! You've got all the time in the world!"

"We're moving, Sara! I've got to do something now—before it's too late!"

"You're what?!" Sara flipped up the brim of Addie's hat and saw the desperate urgency in her friend's eyes. "Moving? Why? When?"

"I don't know. A couple weeks, maybe a month. I don't want to go, Sara." The defeat in Addie's voice was apparent.

"Okay—right now," Sara demanded. "Tell me everything."

*

The girls trudged deeper into the Bog, going from one bandana-clad tree to another for the next hour. After finding each one, Addie took the pipe out of her pocket and studied the slip of paper—a crude map she'd been making marks on for a year—before the girls moved on.

As their search continued, she told Sara of Jake's plans and his promises. Addie's words betrayed her total unwillingness to give Jake even the slightest chance to redeem himself. Instead, Addie told Sara that she had a plan of her own, but said it would only work if Billy joined her. Without him, she insisted, it would be just one more hopeless attempt by an "*angry Addie.*"

"Thanks for coming with, Sara," she said after they re-crossed the highway and reached the edge of the Loop.

"Thanks for what? You didn't need my help, did you?"

"Maybe not," Addie admitted. "But I'm still glad you were with me."

"See? I told you! There's less and less of Buck in you every day." Sara pulled the bandana from Addie's raincoat and waved it between them. "You're doing more than just surviving, Addie."

"I have to be honest with you, Sara. I haven't even started reading *The Call of the Wild.*"

"Doesn't matter," Sara laughed. "The book and the bracelet were just an excuse. I hadn't seen you since school ended—I didn't want to lose your friendship." She wrung the water from the bandana and handed it back to Addie. "Besides, you're Addie Pearson," she proclaimed, as if that was all Addie needed to know.

The girls hiked through Pete's Woods, their steps muted by the unceasing rain. Before they parted, Addie and Sara exchanged looks of determined affection. Back in the Bog, their muddy tracks had already disappeared, washed away by the storm. But the red bandanas were still there, waiting.

Wednesday, June 22ⁿᵈ

Dear Dad,

I'm finally going to do it! I'm going to dig up all those bottles Jake has hidden in the Bog and show them to Mom. That should prove to her once and for all that he's nothing but a liar. She'll see that moving to Albert Lea isn't going to change a thing, not for Jake and definitely not for us. There's no way he'll be able to lie his way out this time.

But if Mom's going to believe me, I can't do it alone. Shorty has to help. I don't see any other way it'll work. When Mom sees that we both found Jake's bottles, our word against his will be a lot more convincing. I didn't want to bring Shorty into this, but the fight he saw between me and Jake at the Carson's last week must have opened his eyes, and probably for good. I guess that means I won't be able to protect him anymore, but he's got just as much to lose as I do if we move, maybe more.

I don't see any other way, Dad, but the truth is I want it this way! I want to see the look on Jake's face when we dump all his bottles on the kitchen floor. It has to happen soon because our time in Lost Elm is running out.

I've got to go. I just heard someone at the door. Hopefully it's Shorty.

I miss you all the time, Dad. Now more than ever.

Love,
Your daughter, Addie

83

7

Soon You Even Stop Trying

Though the sky cleared a few hours after Addie emerged from the Bog with Sara, water still shook off the Pines at dusk with every branch she and Billy climbed. Climbing was her idea. She had wanted to talk to Billy about her plan as soon as she got home, but found a note on the kitchen table—*I'm at Renny's*—instead.

"I thought Mom was having lunch with the Carsons, not supper," she complained.

"She was s'posed to," Billy replied with obvious irritation. "What does it matter?"

"Don't be mad at me, Shorty. I'm not the one who left town," Addie snapped. "Now go over it again, what exactly did Jake tell you?"

Billy repeated everything—how Jake was going to Albert Lea to work a little and get the "lay of the land." Addie knew what that meant. The trip was probably nothing more reconnaissance. Jake wanted to check out the local bars.

"Did he say when he'd be back?"

Billy shrugged. "Next week sometime."

There won't be a better time than now, Addie thought. "Have you ever seen one of these?" She pulled the bandana from her back pocket and tossed it to Billy.

"Sure, that's Jake's. Says so right here." He pointed to the initials, *JRP*.

"Where do you think I got it?"

"How should I know?"

"I found it in the Bog," Addie remarked meaningfully, snatching the bandana from his hand. "And there's a dozen more just like it."

"So?"

"So?! Don't you get it? Jake keeps track of where his bottles are with these." She waved the bandana in his face.

"What bottles?"

"Come on, Shorty. Where do you think that piece of glass in your shoulder came from?"

"So you found some bottles," Billy countered, taking the bandana back from Addie. "So what? Is there one of these tied to the front door of the Junction? Because Jake can walk in there anytime he wants."

"I just thought we could dig them up together," Addie proposed, sensing her idea quickly dying. "Show Mom what Jake's really doing around here."

"You think she doesn't already know?" Billy muttered. "Mr. Carson was right. You get mad, Jake gets mad, but nothing changes." He let go of the bandana and watched it flutter to the ground, then climbed down after it.

Addie briefly watched the cars come and go on the interstate, aware how similar Billy's words were to the ones Sara had spoken earlier that day. Hers Addie could accept. His were harder to swallow.

"What then?!" she shouted down at him. "We just follow Jake and his bullcrap to Albert Lea?! Is that your plan?! Or do you want to talk to him instead?!"

"I dunno, maybe," Billy murmured when she joined him on the ground.

"Seriously?!" Addie asked, wide-eyed. "Who told you to do that? Mr. Carson?"

"He's knows a lot."

"I know he does," she admitted, realizing too late that yelling at her brother was getting her nowhere. "But Mr. Carson's up there. We're stuck down here."

"He hasn't always been up there, ya know." Billy repeated what Mr. Carson had told him the day before. The angry father. The twisted wreckage. The years of regret.

"What else did he say?"

"That we should start sticking up for ourselves."

"See? The time for talk is over."

"I'm not like you, Addie."

"No," she replied, ready to concede defeat. "You're not."

Right on cue, the Carson's truck turned onto the Loop and pulled into the Pearson's driveway. Mr. Carson rolled down his window as Anna got out of the truck and joined her children in the yard.

"Hi, Billy. Hello, Addie," Mr. Carson said warmly. "I'm sorry we stole your mom tonight, but we had a nice visit."

"We certainly did," Mrs. Carson agreed.

"Virgil and Helen reminded me what great kids I have," Anna said. She squeezed in between Billy and Addie and put an arm around each of them. "As if I didn't already know."

"Thanks again, Anna," Mr. Carson said, tipping his cap. "Billy, Addie—I hope we see you again real soon." With a parting wave, the Carsons drove off into the twilight.

"You okay, Mom?" Billy wondered, feeling her weight on his shoulder.

"Of course, honey," she replied dismissively. "Have you two eaten yet? There's some spaghetti in the fridge. Can you heat it up, Addie? I'm going to lay down. It's been a long day."

"Mom?" Addie stopped at the foot of the mud room steps. "When's Jake coming home?"

Anna looked at each of her children in turn. "Early next week sometime. Isn't that what Jake told you, Billy? When he does, we'll have to talk about what happens next."

"You're kidding, right?!" Addie nearly shouted.

"It's just talk, honey." Anna reached out to pat her daughter's cheek but Addie brushed her away.

"Don't you know what's going on around here?!" Addie put her hand on her back pocket, ready to wave Jake's bandana in her face, explain everything it implied.

"I'm not blind, Addie," Anna replied soothingly. "And you're wrong if you think you've got all the answers. You don't know everything."

"How could I?! You never talk to us about . . . about anything anymore." Addie almost said *Dad,* but stopped herself. "Eat without me, Shorty," she said, then stalked off into the night.

"Oh, Addie," Anna sighed, easing herself down onto the porch steps. Billy joined her and they sat quietly for a minute. "Mr. Carson said some nice things about you." She looped her arm through his. "He's very fond of you. Helen is too."

"You said we don't know everything, Mom. What don't we know?"

"Please don't worry, honey," she said, squeezing his hand. "Everything is going to work out for the best. I promise." Billy had no reason to draw comfort from her words, but for some reason he did.

"Should we go in?"

"In a minute. Let's just enjoy this a little longer. It's such a beautiful night."

*

Billy woke early the morning after he rejected Addie's red bandana request. He tiptoed into the living room and found his mother asleep on the couch. Billy looked at her for a moment, struck by how small she appeared. His confusion was interrupted by the ringing telephone.

"Pearson's," he whispered.

"Jakey, is that you?" a man's voice asked. It sounded hoarse and distant.

"He's not here right now. Can I take a message?" Billy searched the kitchen for a pencil and paper.

"Billy?" the voice persisted. "This is your grand . . . This is Ron Pearson, Jake's dad."

"Oh, umm . . . hi, Mr. Pearson." Billy looked into the living room. "Just a second—you probably wanna talk to my mom." He held his hand over the phone and approached his mother. Mercifully, she began to wake.

"Morning, honey," she mumbled. "What time is it?"

"Mom," Billy hissed, holding up the receiver. "It's Jake's dad."

Anna was instantly awake, practically levitating off the couch. She grabbed the phone, cleared her throat and stared out the wide windows at the end of the trailer for five long seconds before speaking.

"Hello, Ron. What can I do for you?"

Billy withdrew to the kitchen but studied his mother's face closely as he retreated. Her mouth didn't move. Her eyes were unblinking.

"I'm sorry you're not feeling well, Ron," Anna finally replied. "No, Jake didn't tell me when he would be home." She followed Billy into the kitchen and put her arm around him. "Ron, my ride to work will be here any minute. If you'd like, I can stop by over my lunch break and check on you."

When Anna offered to look in on her estranged father-in-law, Billy remembered Jake's request the day before. *"Check on him after work" should've been yesterday*, Billy thought, guilt flooding his conscience.

"Jake's dad didn't sound too good," he observed after Anna hung up the phone.

"If you and Renny are going to Ervin's today, can you come with me to Mr. Pearson's house?" Anna did her best to sound nonchalant, but Billy heard the urgency in her voice.

"Sure, Mom. Whatever you need."

*

"Eight points, Billy!" Renny whooped as he threw a rock five feet wide of the Northern Pacific Railroad sign. "Carew went from .382 to .390 in one game!"

"But the Twins lost, Renny. The Rangers got four in the 7th inning and five in the 8th. Our pitching stunk." Billy picked up a rock and called out the *F* in February on the billboard. He struck his target squarely. A splinter of wood popped free and fell at Renny's feet. Billy mounted his bike indifferently and pedaled on toward Lost Elm.

"You okay, Billy?" Renny asked, speeding to catch up.

"I just wish they would have won. The loss drops 'em outta first place." Billy knew his lie was convincing. Jake's dysfunction wouldn't make much sense to Renny so he didn't bother his friend with the ugly truth.

"They'll be back on top today," Renny said assuredly, pulling a small transistor radio from his back pocket.

The radio was a welcome distraction. "I hope you're right, Ren," Billy replied. "Turn the game on. It should be starting any minute."

The red cap of Lost Elm's water tower peeked over the distant trees as the announcer's pleasant drawl mingled with sounds coming from the nearby Bog. *"Good afternoon everybody and welcome to Minnesota Twins baseball! There's a clear blue sky here at Metropolitan Stadium as the Twins try to take two out of three from the Texas Rangers. What a day for a ballgame!"*

*

By the time Billy and Renny arrived at the bank shortly after 1pm, two early hits by Rod Carew had raised his average to .393 and the Twins were in the middle of a rout over the Rangers. Renny was nearly hysterical.

"Hi, boys," Anna grunted, pushing open the bank's heavy glass door. "Have you been waiting long?" Billy was about to answer but was interrupted by Renny, who happily condensed Rod Carew's entire season into a frenzied monologue for her.

"Billy's told me all about it, Renny," she said. "It sounds pretty wonderful."

"Wonderful?! Come on, Mrs. Pearson—this isn't just wonderful!" he cried. "This is .400!"

"We'd better get going," she urged, her enthusiasm quickly dimmed. "I've got to be back to work by 2."

They arrived at Ron Pearson's house minutes later. Anna had largely avoided the house, the school across the street and her childhood home next door (repossessed by the bank shortly after her parents died) whenever she could help it. Head down, she made her way quickly to the side door that led into the kitchen—the same door Will had looked through almost twenty years ago.

"Wait here, okay?" she told the boys. "I won't be long."

Less than a minute later Anna reappeared in the kitchen, a piece of paper crumpled in her fist. She lifted the receiver from the phone and dialed *0*. Billy rose from the porch when he heard the familiar *chu-chu-chu* of the rotary dial and his mom vainly repeating, "Hello, operator?! Hello?!" When she finally hung up in frustration, Billy's eyes followed hers down the wall to where the phone line had been cut.

"What's going on, Mom?"

Anna nearly knocked him over as she burst through the screen door. "I'm going to the Fire Hall, honey! Wait right there!" She ran down the sidewalk toward Lost Elm's volunteer fire department a few blocks away.

Billy sniffed the air and hollered, "I don't smell any smoke!"

Before Anna disappeared around the block, she said something that sent a chill through his body.

"There isn't any! I'm getting an ambulance!"

Billy peered through the screen door. The phone swung like a pendulum, tapping rhythmically on the tile floor. Music drifted into the kitchen from the living room and Billy heard the skipping scratch of a record needle as a man sang a mournful lyric over and over:

> *But you can't forget her, soon you even stop trying,*
> *But you can't forget her, soon you even stop trying. . .*

"He got another one, Billy! Can you believe it?!" Renny squealed. "A single to center. That's .395! Oh man, Carew's gonna do it!!" Renny's volume and excitement had the effect of a gunshot. Billy squeezed the doorknob to keep his balance.

"Shut that off!"

Renny paled and spun the radio dial, staring anxiously across the street into the empty school yard. "I'm sorry, Billy," he whispered. "I didn't mean to make you mad."

"You didn't, Renny—just startled me is all. Go ahead, turn the game back on. But wait here, okay? I gotta check something."

Billy stepped into a small, tidy kitchen. The counters were clear except for an old chrome toaster and a few tarnished canisters. On the table he found a scrap of paper with Jake's handwriting, six terse words: *I'll clean the kitchen when I get back.* Billy frowned. *Clean what?*

He walked into the living room and crept over to a stereo console near the front door. Two older men—one black, one white—smiled warmly at him from an album cover propped up behind the turntable: *Sinatra-Basie: An Historic Musical First.* Billy lifted the needle off the record and examined the rest of the room.

A man was sitting in a chair facing the far wall, his arms hanging limply by his sides, both hands brushing the carpet. Next to one was a beer can. Next to the other was a small bottle, the kind—Billy recognized—that adults got from the pharmacy. The television was on but sat mutely in the corner, Olympian Bruce Jenner silently encouraging viewers to eat their Wheaties. A large mirror hung on the wall above the TV. Staring vacantly into it was the reflection of a pair of lifeless eyes. The man in the chair—Ron Pearson—was dead.

Billy fought down a wave of panic and walked past the chair to shut the TV off. Pity replaced fear when he saw the man's damp trousers. Without thinking, Billy knelt down and grasped the man's hands. But rather than recoil at their cold touch, he place them gently on Ron Pearson's lap.

"Is that your Grandpa?" Renny asked, one hand clutching the dining room table, the other still holding his radio. Its dial had slipped from the ballgame and was emitting only low static.

Billy looked at Ron Pearson's face and couldn't begin to guess his age. But whatever the number and whatever the reason, Billy saw a man who had simply worn himself out.

"No, I never knew my grandparents."

"Then who's that?" Renny asked.

"Jake's dad," Billy replied as a distant siren wailed. "But it's not anymore."

*

Anna, Billy and Addie stuck close to the trailer for the next two days. When she wasn't resting, Anna arranged a funeral for a man she never knew. In between her phone calls to florists and funeral homes, Billy confessed to his mom that Jake had asked him to have her look in on Ron Pearson a full day earlier.

"One more day wouldn't have made a difference, Billy," she said, patting his knee. "Ron would have taken his own life sooner or later. I'm just sorry you had to see it."

Though the air in the trailer was stifling, neither Billy nor Addie left their mom alone for long, in case Jake returned. Consequently, Friday, June 24th, seemed to last forever.

"Has Jake even called?" Addie wondered the next morning over a bowl of Cheerios. "His dad'll be in the ground a week before he finds out."

"That's what I'm afraid of," Anna replied, nearly asleep on her feet in the corner of the kitchen. She held a cup of coffee in both hands, drawing strength from its warmth.

"Do you need anything, Mom?" Billy asked her.

"As a matter of fact, I do. Mrs. Carson made a few hotdishes for us. I told her you'd pick them up around noon."

"Are you gonna be okay while we're gone?" Addie said, echoing Billy's concern.

"What is it with you two?" Anna protested. "I'm not going to shrivel up and blow away. Get dressed, both of you. I'll call Helen and let her know you're coming."

Billy and Addie looked at each other over their breakfast. With Jake's likely return still days away, a visit to Carson Farm would be a welcome distraction. They fled down the hallway, changed clothes and were out the door before Anna could remind them to clear their dishes.

*

"Where ya goin', Addie!" Billy yelled. "The farm's this way!"

After crossing into the lower field, Addie had veered toward Halverson Road. She ignored Billy and followed the narrow footpath behind the Farelli's house that led up Carson Hill.

"Come on, Shorty! We've got plenty of time!"

Though Billy was anxious to see the Carsons, Addie was right. It wasn't even 11 o'clock. He looked toward the farm and saw a small, dark speck racing toward him—Ranger. Together, he and the dog cut across the field and caught up to Addie at the top of Carson Hill.

"What are we doing here, Ad?"

She pointed to Halverson Road. "How 'bout after lunch you give it another try? It's been three weeks."

"Why is it so important for you to watch me crash and burn on Halverson Road again?" Billy replied, looking at the bone-dry gravel. He reached down and rubbed Ranger's belly. "Don'tcha think we have bigger things to worry about right now?"

Addie could hardly argue with him, but she was undeterred. "Come on, Shorty. We do the things we can. Besides, Halverson Road might be the only thing around here that lasts."

"What are you talking about?"

"I'm not going," she murmured.

"Not going where?"

"To Albert Lea. I'm not coming with, I can't. You know everything Jake said last week was bullcrap."

Billy braced himself for another one of Addie's outbursts. But this time he wouldn't get the chance to hear it. Instead, they were both snapped back to reality by the sight of the rust-orange Comet turning onto the Loop. Without another word or question, they raced back down Carson Hill.

Ranger's head tilted in confusion when the girl and boy suddenly left him alone on top of the hill. By the time they had reached the bottom, the pair were in an all-out sprint for the long, skinny shelter Ranger

93

instinctively knew was their home. The dog tensed and barked once before dashing headlong after them.

8
You Wanna Talk to *That*?

The hay crackled beneath Billy and Addie's feet as they tore across the lower field. Neither slowed down until they had slammed into the back of Michael Farelli's large storage shed, across the Loop from their trailer. "Why's Jake home already?!" Billy wondered breathlessly.

"He's not home yet," Addie panted, pointing to the idling Comet parked on the Loop near the Farelli's driveway. The driver's side door was open to a path leading into Pete's Woods.

"Should we tell Mom?!"

Addie turned on Billy. "Do you really want to be around when she tells Jake what his dad did?" she replied uncertainly, blowing away a strand of hair that had come loose from her ponytail. "Come on. I've got a better idea."

"A better idea?!"

"Let's go. There's something you need to see." Addie put her hand out to Ranger, who had just emerged from the tall grass behind them. "Go home, Ranger," she ordered. The dog looked back and forth from the girl to the boy, hoping for an encouraging word. Hearing none, his tail dipped and he wandered away.

After reaching the edge of Pete's Woods, Billy and Addie moved swiftly from one dense patch of cover to another before hunkering down behind a large hazelnut bush. Addie put a finger to her lips and pointed through a narrow opening in the foliage.

Fifty feet away, kneeling at the base of a tree, Jake clutched a red bandana in one hand and a clear glass bottle in the other. When he raised the bottle to his mouth and drank, his entire body seemed to relax. Billy rolled away from the opening in confusion and disgust, realizing that the alcohol had revived Jake somehow.

"You wanna talk to *that*?" Addie muttered in disgust. "Good lu. . ." She clamped her hand over her mouth as Jake moved noisily toward them. Billy held his breath, but Jake was oblivious to everything around him. He stumbled past their hiding spot and wandered out of Pete's Woods.

After a long frozen silence, Billy and Addie crawled out from behind the bush and made their way over to Jake's tree. A dirty cork stuck out of the ground where the bottle had been carelessly re-buried. Billy's face contorted as he pulled the bottle free. Mr. Carson's advice, *"If you're moving, talking to Jake is more important than ever,"* collided with the fact that Addie was right. Jake would never listen.

"Let's go," he replied decisively and flung the bottle high over the trees. "Mom's gonna need us."

They rushed out of the woods and into the yard, stopping by their old sandbox and swing set. Weeds and prairie grass sprouted from the sand. Rust caked the chain links of the swing.

"You're not going into the trailer, are you?" Addie asked, seeing the unwavering look on her brother's face.

The doubt Billy heard in Addie's voice surprised him. He was counting on her to know what to do next. "We can't just do nothing." He rushed to the end of the trailer and crouched under the living room's wide windows. Embarrassed by her own fear and Billy's sudden boldness, Addie strolled towards him, determined to take her sweet time.

"Now what?" she whispered.

Billy pressed himself against the warmth of the trailer. "I dunno. I just wanna be by Mom."

Addie's expression softened as Billy's eyes burned with the same intensity she had seen in pictures of Will Travers.

"What's wrong?"

Addie blinked and looked back into Pete's Woods. "For a second you looked like . . ." Billy was about to ask *who*, but his curiosity was cut short by accusing words coming from inside the trailer.

"Why do you have a note from my dad?!" Jake shouted. He held the piece of paper Anna had held in her hand when she ran past Billy and Renny on her way to the fire station.

"Can I make you something to eat, Jake? Or a cup of coffee?" Anna's voice was drowsy and distant, though she didn't sound surprised to see him. She'd gotten used to his unpredictable comings and goings long ago.

"Didn't Billy give you my message?! Did you check on my dad?!" Jake pressed. "What does this even mean?! *Jake, I cleaned the house so you wouldn't have to.* Did you check on him or not?!"

Billy remembered Jake's note on Ron's kitchen table, *I'll clean the house when I get back.* He and Addie peered into the trailer and saw their mother standing over Jake, who had slumped into his chair.

"I have some terrible news, Jake. Your dad died Thursday. I'm so sorry."

He looked up at Anna as if she were speaking to him in a foreign language. He shook his head in a futile effort to process her words through layers of alcohol and exhaustion.

"What are you talking about?! I've only been gone a few days!" He stood up and reached for the phone.

"It won't ring, Jake. The line was cut," she explained. "Ron cut the line."

Jake dialed his father's number anyway. An awful silence followed, then a shrill voice: *"We're sorry; you have reached a number that has been disconnected or is no longer in service. If you feel you have reached this recording in error or would like to make a call, please hang up and dial again."* He dropped the phone and read his father's note again, straining to understand its meaning. Anna put her hand on his shoulder but he jerked it away.

"You were supposed to check on him! Didn't Billy tell you?!"

"He told me Wednesday as soon as I got home from work." Anna's face was composed and convincing as she lied for Billy.

"Then why didn't you do what I asked?! He'd be alive if you had!"

"How?" Anna's voice was as calm as Jake's was crazed.

"How?! What do you mean, how?!"

"How could I have checked on your father after work? You took the car, Jake."

"You could have figured it out!" he screamed, ignoring her logic and his selfishness.

"Maybe you should have stayed home if you were that worried about him."

Billy and Addie exchanged glances. If they didn't know better, it seemed like their mom was trying to provoke Jake. *But to do what?*

Her tone quickly softened. "He sounded fine on the phone Thursday morning, just tired."

"You talked to him?!"

"Yes. I called right before work. Told him you were gone but that I would stop by on my lunch break."

Billy's fingers sank into Addie's arm. His mother's lies on his behalf sent a surge of adrenaline through his body. Addie winced, but the pain faded when she saw the fear in his eyes.

"Don't you get it?!" Jake said, seizing Anna's shoulders. "He'd be alive if it wasn't for you!" Saliva sprayed from his mouth. Anna tried to twist free, but his grip only tightened.

"That wasn't living," she replied meekly.

"Jake!" Billy shouted, bursting into the trailer. "You need to let Mom go!" He and Addie had raced for the door the instant Jake grabbed their mother. Billy's voice was strong, though his knees were shaking.

Jake blinked and stumbled backward, staring at the crumpled scrap of paper in his fist. Eyes wild with torment, he dimly understood that the only thing Ron had bothered to tell him before taking his own life was that he had spared his son the inconvenience of cleaning up after him. Jake let out an involuntary, feral cry, then charged past Billy and Addie out the door.

Like a balloon slowly leaking air, the pressure inside the trailer subsided. To her children's demands of, "*Now what, Mom*?!" Anna could only answer, "I'll figure everything out later. I just need to rest for a bit." When she disappeared into her bedroom, Billy looked hard at Addie. She watched his expression pass from sorrow and acceptance to resolve. He tugged on the red cloth sticking out of her pants pocket.

"You win, Addie," he sighed, holding the bandana between them. "Whatever it takes to get rid of Jake, I'm with you."

*

The air grew thick as Saturday dragged on. Everything around the Loop seemed to wilt and hold its collective breath. Even the typical sounds of summer fell silent. After waking from her nap, Anna spent the rest of that steamy day at the kitchen table finalizing Ron's funeral plans. Slips of paper headed with single words—*Visitation, Program, Burial, Reception, Food*—were spread out before her as she made call after call for her dead father-in-law.

Sunday morning, June 26th, dawned dry and clear. Whatever dew had formed on the ground overnight evaporated with the rising sun. The blue sky seemed to herald another sweltering day, but scattered clouds were gathering beyond the interstate, a growing mob on the western horizon.

Addie called Sara after breakfast and spoke with an edge in her voice that troubled her friend. Billy huddled with Renny under the Pines but said little, content to let Renny chatter on about Carew's chances of climbing over .400 that day. The Carsons dropped off the food Billy and Addie hadn't picked up the day before, promising to bring Anna and the kids to the funeral home if Jake didn't appear.

Anna called the Junction. "Jake was here last night," Bud told her. "But only for a couple beers." She tried the Wood City Bar & Lounge. "*You just missed him.*" Her last call was to the Carsons. She and the kids needed that ride.

Everything—from the visitation to the service to the reception afterward—was an ordeal. Ron Pearson's daughter Jeannie, unseen for years, arrived late and left early. She had fled Lost Elm for the Twin Cities long ago, and it was clear to everyone in attendance that even this brief return was more than she cared to endure.

Jake was a no-show. Anna did her best to make excuses for him, but eventually an unwitting shrug was all she could muster. The only thing that roused the mourners was a graveside appearance by Betty Pearson, vanished from Lost Elm nearly twenty years ago. Fortunately for the gossips, Ron's Hillside Cemetery plot was 150 feet from the road. Betty's long walk gave them plenty of time to heap their silent judgments on her, as well as speculate about the identity of the person waiting for her back in the car. But as soon as the casket was lowered into the ground, the former Mrs. Ronald Pearson took a few furtive glances around the cemetery—presumably looking for Jake—before making a swift departure.

*

It was nearly 6 o'clock when the Carsons dropped Anna, Billy and Addie off at the trailer. The promising morning sun was long gone, replaced by an eerie sky that gave the colors all around Halverson Road a strange glow. Billy and Addie looked up at the clouds but kept their curiosity to themselves. Anna, weighed down by all her efforts, didn't have the energy to notice.

They changed clothes and went out to the back yard, underneath the Pines. Addie had a red bandana wrapped tightly around her hand. Billy clutched a vinyl orange duffel bag with the logo, *Wheaties-Breakfast of Champions*, emblazoned across it. Two black plastic handles were fastened on both sides of a long, zippered opening.

The bag was empty except for a flashlight and a small garden shovel. Soon it would be filled with other items which, until the day before, Billy had been only dimly aware. But no more. From the cover of the hazelnut bush he had discovered that Jake was, for reasons he couldn't fathom, chained to alcohol.

"Let's get this over with," he muttered.

Addie understood Billy's anger well. *How did I think I could protect him from Jake?* She saw again in her brother's face the memory she had tried so hard to safeguard.

"Have you ever noticed how much you look like Dad?" she said unexpectedly. Billy dropped the bag and thrust his hands into his pockets. "Well, you do, Shorty. So much sometimes that I've wanted you to be just like him someday." She fished Billy's knife out of her pocket and fumbled with the blade. "That sounds kind of crazy, huh?"

"How did you think that was that ever going to happen, Ad?" he replied, gesturing to the trailer. "I mean, look around here."

"I just thought I could . . ." Her voice trailed off.

"Keep all the *bullcrap* away from me?" Billy responded, trying Addie's word on for size. "If it makes you feel any better, you kinda did."

On some gut level, they both understood that turning points were real and they were facing one now. Billy picked up his bag and Addie pocketed the knife. Together, in the dream-like early evening light, they moved rapidly through Pete's Woods toward the state highway and the Bog beyond it.

*

"Where do ya think they're going, Sara?" Renny asked from his perch on the Farelli's front steps. "I need to tell Billy about the Twins' game today."

"Now's not a good time, Renny," she replied as they watched Billy and Addie disappear into Pete's Woods. "I'm guessing there's something they've got to do."

Sara had been watching the trailer even before Billy and Addie appeared in the back yard. Though she hadn't heard what they were talking about, she had no doubt where they were going.

"But I gotta tell Billy about Rod Carew!" Renny groaned. "He had the game of a lifetime!"

"It'll have to wait 'til tomorrow," Sara said, unmoved by his excitement. "Let's go inside. It's time to eat."

Renny's enthusiasm was barely dampened. He recapped the slugger's day, at-bat by at-bat, to anyone who would listen. But Sara wouldn't be there to hear it. She tied her long dark hair into a tight ponytail, grabbed her car keys from the kitchen counter and sped off into the twilight.

9
WHEN THE WOLF IS GONE

"Twelve more of these?" Billy asked Addie as they came out of Pete's Woods and ran across the state highway. A single bottle clanged against the flashlight in his Wheaties bag.

"Twelve that I know of."

She jogged along a foot path through a sentry of tall pines that led into the Bog. Billy tripped over the uneven surface, pitching forward into the hard earth. As he fell the bottle slipped out of the open duffel bag and shattered on a rock at the trail's edge, scattering its shards in front of him.

"You okay, Shorty?!" Addie hollered, reversing course when she heard the breaking glass.

Billy waved her off, remembering her reaction when he slid into the ditch next to Halverson Road. But this time she waited patiently by his side.

"Is this plan even gonna work?"

She shrugged. "Maybe biking no-handed down Halverson Road doesn't matter," Addie confessed, picked up a piece of glass and waving it in his face. "But don'tcha think this does?"

"You're not really leaving are you, Ad?"

Addie hated to admit that she had no plan and nowhere to go, but she couldn't bear the thought of living one more day feeling so helpless. "No, but if there's even a chance this could make a difference . . ."

"How come Jake thinks moving will help?" Billy wondered.

"Who knows? Maybe he's been banned from the Junction and needs some new bars to get kicked out of."

"I'm serious."

"So am I." She saw from the look on Billy's face that he wanted real answers, even wrong ones. "Whatever his reasons are, they don't have anything to do with us," she assured him. "So, are we doing this or not?"

Billy nodded. "Should we pick this up?" he said, pointing to the broken bottle.

Addie swept the glass off the trail with her foot. "Leave it. There's plenty more where that came from."

*

After crossing Otter Creek over a fallen tree, they made short work of Jake's first seven hiding spots. In silent tandem, Addie untied each bandana as Billy worked the shovel into the ground. Every bottle he dug up was identical, though each contained varying amounts of alcohol.

"I'm gonna have to empty some of these bottles," Billy noticed as they moved further into the Bog. "The bag's getting heavy. These handles might break."

"But I want Mom to see what's in them," Addie replied, tying the bandanas together end to end and looping it around her neck like a scarf. "Alright, five to go."

"You're sure you know where the rest are? It's getting kinda dark."

"The next four should bring us to the depot and the last one isn't too far from the billboard."

As Addie led Billy down a trail that curved toward Lost Elm, lightning danced convulsively overhead, chaotic strands of electricity momentarily suspended between hostile clouds. Fortunately, the next three bandanas were just a short jog off the path, each fifty yards apart.

"Good thing the depot's next," Billy commented. "We'll be stuck there awhile if it starts raining." He reorganized the bottles in the bag to make room for the last two, then slipped the shovel handle through his belt loop and stuck the flashlight in his back pocket. "Alright, Ad. Which way? Addie?" Billy peered up and down the trail. *She was just here,* he thought, taking a deep breath to fight down a rising panic.

"I'm right here!" she shouted.

Billy looked all around him, trying to locate her voice. He followed the trail a few more steps before Addie repeated herself.

"Where?!"

"Follow my voice!"

To Billy's surprise Addie began to sing. Her words mingled with a low, thundering rumble:

> *"Loving you isn't the right thing to do.*
> *How can I ever change the things I feel?*
> *If I could, maybe I'd give you my world."*

Billy peeked through an unnaturally dense patch of dry, dead brush that Addie had fallen into, apparently constructed to hide something from prying eyes.

"I can't believe I haven't seen this before," she said in disgust. Behind her stood a low shack not much bigger than their living room and no higher than Billy's shoulder. The entire structure was leaning dangerously to one side. Topping it all were four sheets of aged, curling plywood.

"Were you just singing?" he asked in astonishment.

"It worked, didn't it? You found me." Addie's face reddened, though Billy pretended not to notice.

"What is it?"

"It's just a song, Shorty," she snapped.

"No, I mean *what is it?*" Billy pointed to the shack behind her.

"It was for making this," Addie said, holding up an empty bottle. "They're all over the Bog, or at least they used to be." She lifted a corner of the shack's warped roof. A dirt floor lay below ground level, far enough down for a man to stand up in. Billy waved his flashlight around the shack. Each corner housed an aging, rust-brown barrel. Sprouting from every top was tarnished copper tubing linked to a cast-iron contraption sitting, Buddha-like, in the center.

"Swamp Rot?" he guessed.

"You know about that?"

Billy did, though that era of Lost Elm's history never seemed real to him—at least not until he met Virgil Carson. "Do you think Mr. Carson's dad made this stuff?"

"I doubt it. You said he was thirteen years-old when they moved into the Bog. Prohibition was over by then."

"Do ya think Jake knows about this place?"

Addie opened her mouth to answer, but was interrupted by a tremendous explosion overhead. Billy dropped to the ground as a shockwave cascaded through his body like a rolling pin. He tensed for another volley, but none came. Lightning flared within the clouds, popping and fizzing, its energy temporarily spent.

"Come on, Ad. Don'tcha think we've dug up enough of these?! Let's skip the rest." Billy didn't want to be in the Bog when the sky recharged. He wanted to go home.

A low moan was Addie's only response. Startled by the thunder, she had fallen backwards into a patch of broken glass.

"You okay?"

She wasn't. A red stain quickly expanded out from her right shoulder blade where a jagged piece of glass protruded. Reacting automatically, Billy placed his hand on her back and swiftly pulled it free, but Addie felt no relief.

"Give me the knife," he said coolly. She fought down more pain and handed it to him. "Hold still—this is gonna hurt." He pulled down the collar of her shirt and examined the wound with his flashlight. A thin sliver of glass was buried in the raw flesh. Widening the cut slightly with his thumb and forefinger, Billy pried the piece out with the tip of the knife. Addie's breathing immediately slowed and deepened.

"Hand me the bandanas."

Addie obediently unwound them from around her neck with her uninjured arm. Billy looped the chain under her arms and over her shoulders a few times, then tied each end together in the middle of her back.

"Feels better," she remarked, studying Billy with an intense curiosity.

"That should help with the bleeding," he said hopefully. "But don't raise your arm if you don't have to."

"Where'd you learn to do that?"

Billy's face went blank. "I dunno. I guess I just . . . did it." He retrieved the battered orange bag and followed her back to the trail.

They had to cross back over Otter Creek, but this time it wouldn't be so easy. A dozen stones, five to ten feet apart, zig-zagged across a wide and deep part of the river near the abandoned depot. The passage was a challenge under the best of circumstances. An attempt now, with darkness upon them, seemed sure to fail.

"Why don't we just wade across?" Billy suggested.

"Current's too strong with all the rain we've gotten lately," Addie replied, wincing in pain. "You go first. I'll light the way."

Addie knew the location of each rock well enough to talk Billy across. Still, he nearly fell in after catching the flashlight at the river's edge when she tossed it to him.

"Your turn!"

Addie grunted in pain as she leapt from rock to rock, her right arm useless as she struggled to maintain her balance. To make matters worse, another barrage of lightning and thunder lit up the sky when she reached the middle of the creek. Billy stood his ground this time, but the flashlight slipped from his hand and rolled into the underbrush. Trapped in the dark, Addie could only look to the sky and wait. Right on cue, bolts of lightning dove at each other, locking together in a brilliant embrace. The remaining boulders were laid out before her. She saw Billy too, scrambling in the bushes for the lost flashlight, the depot outlined behind him.

Addie practically ran the rest of the way, expecting darkness to envelop her with every step. When it finally did, she was standing triumphantly on solid ground.

"You made it?!" Billy exclaimed, appearing from a tangle of undergrowth, flashlight in hand.

"Of course," Addie replied, adjusting Billy's makeshift harness to ease a fresh wave of burning pain. "Let's get in the depot. It's going to pour any minute."

Billy aimed the flashlight around the building. The Northern Pacific Railroad had built it from the abundance of pine in the area shortly after the first tracks were laid in 1870. The same length as their trailer but twice as wide, the depot had been stripped of everything not bolted down after passenger train travel in and out of Lost Elm ended a generation ago. All that was left were a few rows of pew-like benches lining its perimeter.

"I haven't been here since last summer," Billy remarked. "Looks like there's a new poem on the wall." The author of the depot's poetry was a local mystery. Addie preferred to keep it that way.

"Bring the light back here," she said. "I think I'm still bleeding."

Billy ignored her and worked his way to the far end of the building, reading aloud:

I can't go until he's free from this,
Unmarked and unbroken, nothing amiss.
For now I'll keep the darkness at bay,
Then leave when the wolf is gone,
Fly far, far away.

107

Billy trained the light back on Addie. "When did you write this?" he asked her quietly. She didn't answer, her silence telling him everything he needed to know.

The depot's gloom hid their mutual embarrassment—Addie for being found out and Billy for discovering a layer of tenderness in his sister he would have thought impossible a month ago. Not knowing what else to say, he focused the flashlight on her wound. "Bleeding's stopped. How does it feel?"

"Like it's on fire," she said, winding the bandanas around her forearm. "But we're almost done. One more bottle to go."

Billy didn't try to convince Addie that they'd already done enough. He knew she wanted to see her plan through to the end. And despite the darkness, so did he.

A warm wind swirled around them when they stepped outside. Addie took the flashlight and searched for the trail that would lead them to the billboard.

"Let's just follow the tracks," Billy suggested.

"Oh, right. I almost for. . ." Addie's words were cut short by a dim glow behind them. A car's headlights cut through the void. She switched off the flashlight and they crouched low, though the night already rendered them invisible.

The car coasted another quarter mile past them, wavering between firm pavement and the gravel shoulder, then crawled to a stop. It made a creeping left turn, twin beams of light slapping against the white plywood of the Northern Pacific sign:

AT THIS POINT ON FEBRUARY 15, 1870 . . .

"Can you get us to the billboard without the flashlight?!" Addie asked with an unmistakable urgency.

"Yeah, but isn't that . . . ?" Billy's voice tightened.

"If it is, we don't have much time." She looked at Billy for some sign of resolve, but couldn't see his face. "You're gonna have to do the rest, Shorty."

"Come on, Addie. Let's skip the last bottle."

"I've got a better idea," she replied. "You're going to break the ones we've got."

"You mean . . ." Addie's change of plan became instantly clear to him. Billy weighed the odds of her new, braver rebellion and judged it worth the risk. "Okay," he nodded invisibly. "Follow me."

Unnoticed across the highway from the billboard, on a dead-end gravel road, a second car was parked. It had been sitting there, like a cat in tall grass, for hours. The eyes within it were fixed straight ahead, ignoring the roiling storm overhead that would soon be unleashed.

10

RESIDUE OF INNOCENCE

They fell only once. Unwilling to use his flashlight, Billy stumbled blindly onto the tracks as they neared the Northern Pacific Railroad sign. He absorbed the fall without a sound, but Addie cried out in pain as she toppled onto the unforgiving wooden ties.

"Are you sure you got all the glass out?" she whimpered.

Billy was about to admit that he might not have when a car door slammed ahead of them. Next to it a hulking figure attempted to light a match, cursing each failure. One finally sparked and a kerosene lantern was lit. The area around the car glowed faintly, but the lamp and its owner moved quickly past the billboard into the tangled scrub of the Bog.

"Hand me the flashlight, Shorty."

"Do you want me to wrap your shoulder again?" Fresh blood had seeped into Billy's makeshift bandage.

"Later."

"Are you sure? It looks pretty bad."

Addie ignored Billy's concern as they covered the remaining distance and came to a stop in front of the Comet. She grabbed the Wheaties bag and walked toward the billboard.

"Since I'm not a lefty you win by forfeit. But I'm still going to make you throw." Addie pulled the bag's handles apart and the cheap fabric finally tore free. None of the bottles broke, but the sound of glass colliding and crashing to the ground echoed far into the night. Nevertheless, Jake's lamp light continued to shrink until it disappeared from sight.

"What do I win?"

Addie smiled grimly at the question. "You get to keep Lost Elm. We both do."

"My kind of bet."

"Okay," she replied. "But the words are your target, not letters. It's dark, after all."

Billy considered his sister as she handed him the first bottle. He understood what Addie had done for him for so long and why, but the events of June had finally stripped her of that responsibility. From now on he would protect himself. And with that realization, Billy's last residue of

111

innocence melted away. Jake had utterly failed them, and for reasons still unclear, something was very wrong with their mother. But in spite of everything that was now undeniable, a shining smile lit Billy's face. *You never failed me, Addie.*

"Call 'em out," he told her.

They worked fast. Over and over, Addie chose a word and Billy hit it. His eyes never left the billboard. Her eyes never left him.

"THIS!" Smash.

"POINT!" Smash.

"FEBRUARY!" Smash.

"15!" Smash.

"1870!" Smash.

Billy paused and parted his lips to catch a few raindrops that had begun to fall. They were almost out of time. The storm was nearly upon them.

"CONSTRUCTION!" Smash.

"NORTHERN!" Smash.

"PACIFIC!" Smash.

Glass littered the ground beneath the sign. Swamp Rot streamed down the billboard. The duffel bag was almost empty.

"RAILROAD!" Smash.

"WAS!" Smash.

She handed him the last bottle.

"COMMENCED!"

"What are you waiting for, Shorty? COMMENCED!"

The answer was written all over Billy's face. His eyes were wide as the bottle dangled from his fingertips. On the other side of the billboard—with a bottle of his own in one hand and the lantern in the other—stood Jake.

"Whu ya doin' 'ere?" he mumbled. His clothes were wet and torn. The river crossing to get Billy and Addie's last bottle had gone badly. "I ast you a qweshun!" Jake lurched forward, his feet crunching the glass beneath the sign. He blinked hard, staring at the ground around him.

"You want answers, Jake?!" Addie snarled. "Maybe this'll help!" She thrust her clenched fist in the air. From wrist to elbow, the bandanas were illuminated by the Comet's headlights. Her arm cast a defiant shadow on the sign above him.

"I said it before!" she yelled, the burning in her shoulder bleeding into her heart. "You hate your life, that's your problem." Jake's wild eyes narrowed as he hung on Addie's next words. "Your mom was at the cemetery today! Did you know that?! But you couldn't pull yourself together long enough to make it to your own father's funeral!"

Billy was horrified. Addie had gone too far. Sympathy tugged at him even as Jake's rage boiled over. He dropped the lantern and threw his only bottle at Addie's head.

Billy pulled her to the ground as the bottle whistled over her shoulder and buried itself in the Comet's right headlight, plunging the area into semi-darkness. Billy motioned for Addie to stay down, then he stood, whirled and fired *his* last bottle.

It hit COMMENCED dead-center. The impact rang out as glass and liquid showered down on Jake, who cowered under the onslaught. When the sharp echo of Billy's throw melted into the night, Jake's wrath returned.

"Ya gonna be jus' like yer tomboy sister?!" he slurred. "Some kinda tough guy?!"

"He's just trying to get under your skin, Addie!" Billy yelled over the muffled drumbeats high above them. "This time we win!"

"Win?!" Jake cackled. "Whaddya think you won?!"

"Why do you have to hurt us, Jake?!" Billy hollered, approaching the billboard. "'Specially, Mom. You always do whatever you want, but you never include us. If that was your plan all along, why'd you marry her in the first place?"

If Jake could have been honest with himself, he would have told Billy and Addie that marrying Anna Travers was a childish dream to soothe his grown-up nightmare—a seething contempt for his father, the irreplaceable loss of his mother and the death of his estranged best friend in Vietnam.

"We're going home!" Billy shouted as he picked up Jake's lantern. "Stay at your dad's house and leave us alone!"

The blunt words snapped Jake out of his stupor. Later he would tell himself that Billy had been in the wrong place at the wrong time. He liked the kid—he always had. He just never knew how to show it.

Whatever remorse Jake might feel the next day didn't matter to Addie. It couldn't erase what she witnessed in front of the billboard. Frozen in place, Addie watched Jake try to wrench the lantern from her brother's grip, pulling back and forth on the handle until a final ferocious tug sent Billy and the lantern sailing through the air. Both landed hard on the broken glass. The lamp tipped over on its side, igniting the grain alcohol that had soaked into the ground. The flames advanced menacingly on Billy.

Addie had seen enough. She charged into Jake as he bent down to retrieve the lantern, driving her undamaged shoulder into his midsection. He fell in a heap, dazed and groaning. Billy's face and hands were red and orange. The red was his blood, the orange were flames reflected in the shards of glass buried in his skin.

Addie yanked him to his feet and grabbed the lantern before the fire could reach them. Most of the glass fell harmlessly from Billy as he was jostled upward, but his blue and gold number *12* t-shirt was ruined and shallow cuts peppered his arms. Addie breathed a sigh of relief when she realized he wasn't badly hurt.

The same couldn't be said for Jake. He howled like an animal caught in a trap as the fire ignited his clothing. Frantic, he rolled on the grass behind the billboard. The flames were quickly squelched, but not before ugly red blotches appeared on his arms.

"Are you okay, Shorty?!" Addie yelled over another peal of thunder. Billy nodded. "Good! Let's get outta here!"

"Go on, go home!" Jake croaked behind them. "I'll be there soon 'nough!" Smoke drifted off his body as a light rain hissed against his burnt flesh and clothing.

Addie's shoulders sagged at the familiar threat, but she was too tired to argue. Pulling Billy along with her, Addie strode over to the Comet's one working headlight and smashed it with the butt of the flashlight.

"Fine!" she yelled, training her light on Jake's dumbfounded expression. "But if you plan on making it home tonight you're gonna need this!" Addie flung the lantern high in the air. As she let go, its handle caught her bracelet, snapping the twine from her wrist. Beads scattered on the ground as the lantern burst open against the billboard's peeling plywood. Flames chased kerosene and Swamp Rot across its entire length and breadth. Billy and Addie shrank back from the heat that surged off the sign.

"My bracelet!" Addie shrieked, clutching her wrist.

"What?!"

114

"The bracelet Sara made for me!"

"She can make another one! We gotta go!"

Billy commandeered the flashlight and led her across the highway and into the ditch. Jake lurched towards the Comet. Headlights or not, he was going to make a run for the trailer.

"Shorty, shut the light off!" Addie hissed.

"Please stop calling me Shorty! You've been calling me that all night!"

"Do you really think now's a good time?!" Addie couldn't believe her ears. "Fine, just kill the light!"

Billy fumbled for the switch but fell forward as the ditch rose sharply onto a dirt road. The flashlight bounced to the ground, its light extinguished. He rose to his feet but Addie pushed him back down.

"What're you doing?!"

Addie mutely squatted on top of Billy as the blind Comet drove cautiously past them. Overhead, the clouds finally burst open. Thick sheets of water fell as Addie helped Billy to his feet.

"Where'd this road come from?!" he asked, feeling the gravel for the lost light.

"It's always been here, hasn't it?"

Billy abandoned his search as another pair of headlights shot out of the darkness. A car eased slowly toward them.

"Get in!" Sara yelled from her open window. "We can still beat Jake to the Loop!"

Stunned, Billy jumped into the back bed of the El Camino and huddled by the small window behind the front seat. Beaming, Addie climbed in next to Sara. She'd never been rescued before, in any sense of the word.

"It's you?!"

"Of course it's me, silly," Sara said. "You didn't think I was going to let you have all the fun tonight."

"I can't believe you're here," Addie replied, thoroughly astonished. "No one's ever . . . How did you . . . ?"

"I saw you and Billy in your yard. I figured tonight was the night." Sara pointed to the bandanas up and down Addie's arm. "I sure didn't think it was going to turn out like that though!" Across the road, the billboard's flames were being rapidly extinguished. Sara pulled onto the highway, her windshield wipers nearly overwhelmed by the driving rain.

Jake had it far worse. Driving blind, he slowed to a crawl. Addie gripped the dashboard as they sped by, but Jake zeroed in on the El Camino's tail lights as Sara accelerated further. The sudden surge threw Billy backwards into the car's tailgate. He managed to roll onto his stomach and peer into the darkness. Jake, outlined against the Comet's faint dashboard lights, was gaining on them.

"You okay, Shorty?!" Addie asked through the rear window. Billy held to his lookout but gave her a quick thumbs-up over his shoulder.

"Hang on back there!" Sara shouted. "It's gonna get a little bumpy!" She pumped the brakes and turned onto Halverson Road. When the tires struck gravel, the car's rear end swung sharply to the left. Billy rolled from his perch and slammed against the wheel well. Heedless, the El Camino shot up the short incline before skidding to a stop next to Pete's Woods.

Sara jumped out and ran halfway down the hill. Addie sprinted to catch up while Billy, dazed from their wild ride, pulled himself to his feet. Between the jostling, his torn clothes and blood-stained cuts, Billy looked like he'd just been through a war.

"I'm fine, in case you're wondering!" he shouted dismally.

"Sara, where are you going?!" Addie hollered.

"I saw something in the rear-view mirror when we made the turn!" She pointed to the ditch where Halverson Road met the highway. There, flipped over like a turtle, lay the Comet.

"Should we do something?!" Addie wondered. Helping Jake would have been out of the question mere minutes ago, but she knew leaving the wreck for someone else to find was wrong.

"What are you waiting for?" Billy yelled, running past them. He circled the car cautiously. As much as he'd seen and done that night, he wasn't sure he wanted to see more.

"Where's the driver-side door?" Sara wondered.

"Where's Jake, you mean," Addie said.

"That's not very funny," Billy replied.

"I'm not kidding. Look for yourself." Billy and Sara knelt down. The front seat was bent and full of debris, but there was no sign of Jake.

They walked down the highway and stumbled into the unhinged door a hundred feet behind the wreckage. The rain lessened and a sliver of moonlight snuck through a gap in the clouds to reveal Jake, immobile and face down on the asphalt.

"Is he dead?" Addie asked. Billy and Sara were thinking the same thing.

Moments earlier, he had foolishly believed he could chase down the El Camino. But when Sara turned onto Halverson Road, Jake lost control of the Comet and swerved violently toward the ditch. The car flipped over, but not before he managed to jump clear.

"Gemme off the road," Jake moaned, answering their question.

Billy automatically took one step forward, then froze. Addie and Sara held their ground. Jake staggered over to the side of the road before promptly falling to his knees.

"Should I run home and call an ambulance?" Billy asked him.

"I don' need one," Jake muttered stubbornly, his bruised face framed in the moonlight.

"Are you sure, Jake? You don't look so good."

"I'm used to yer sisser callin' me that, but you never use' to. Wha' changed? Wassit Carson?"

"I changed," Billy replied, suddenly defiant. "How come you never did?" He took a step backward and brushed next to Addie. She reached out and took his hand in hers.

"Let's go home," she said.

Jake's expression had wavered when Billy spoke, but at Addie's suggestion his mask returned. "Ya know who else never changed?" he barked. "The great Will Travers. Whatever you heard 'bout him is bullcrap! Zat how you say it, Addie? *Bullcrap?* You din' know we were friends, didja? An' if he loved your mom so much, why'd he abannon her?"

Even in the pale light, Jake saw Addie's mouth drop open and tears roll down her cheeks.

"He wrecked my family! Said he saw my mom . . ." Anguished at the memory, his voice broke. "He was my friend an' he betrayed me!" Jake spat. "Will Travers was no one worth 'memberin'! You should be glad he's dead. I am!"

Unwilling to let Addie hear another word, Sara moved on Jake and swung viciously with balled-up fists. After two blows to the chin, he toppled over into the ditch.

"Some people just can't shut up," she said, shaking her hands painfully. "I think we should run, don't you?!" They did, charging back up

117

Halverson Road as more rain pelted them. Sara opened her car door to get in, but Addie stopped her.

"We're going to cut through the woods!"

"Don't you think you two should stay at my house tonight?!"

Addie smiled but shook her head. She knew Jake was probably getting to his feet and coming after them, but she didn't care. "No one's ever done for me what you did tonight! Ever!" Addie threw her arms around Sara and held on tight.

"You are the bravest person I know, Adeline Pearson," Sara whispered in her ear.

"I hate to break this up, but we're outta time!" Billy shouted over the rain pounding on the El Camino's hood.

"This might sound kind of strange," Sara said before they parted. "But I had fun tonight!"

Billy and Addie picked their way across Pete's Woods with Jake only minutes behind them. When they reached the old sandbox Addie unwound the bandanas from her arm. Ahead of them, the trailer's small porch was dimly lit.

"Here, Shorty—take this!" She handed him one end of the bandana chain and tied the other end around the knob of the mudroom's screen door. "Lay it out down the steps. There's no way Jake will miss it!" While Billy did as instructed, they heard shouting from the far side of Pete's Woods.

"Inside, quick!"

Rushing into the mudroom, Billy grabbed a spare key hidden beneath a heavy antique iron they used as a doorstop on hot days. After locking the inner door behind them, Addie used the iron to break the key off in the knob. Jake would have to knock the door down if he wanted to get in.

"What in the world are you two doing?!" Anna asked them as she came out of her bedroom. "And why are you both soaking wet and bleeding?!"

"Mom, what's the number for the sheriff?!"

Why do you need the . . .?"

Billy handed her the phone. Anna studied their faces as she dialed the Sheriff's Department. "Where's Jake? Is Jake home?"

"Any minute now," Addie said impatiently. She grabbed the phone and explained to the county dispatcher what had happened, leaving out a few incriminating details.

118

Moments after she hung up, Jake yanked on the length of bandanas until the screen door came off of its hinges. He twisted and turned the inner door handle, but the broken key held fast. He was about to throw his full weight into the door when a siren wailed in the distance. Jake pounded half-heartedly a few more times, but the fight had gone out of him. Bloody and defeated, he slumped to the mudroom floor. Out of options and out of alcohol, Jake began to sob like a child.

"What did you two do?" Anna whispered accusingly.

"What did we do?!" Addie hissed, nearly leaping out of her skin. "We did what you should've done a long time ago!"

"Addie, sit down—let me look at your shoulder. That must really hurt."

"This?! This is nothing compared to that!" Addie seethed, pointing to the trailer door. She stalked off to her room where she would soon collapse into a fitful sleep.

On the other side of the trailer door, two deputies mounted the porch steps and helped Jake to his feet. He was quickly handcuffed and escorted to a waiting squad car. After Billy used a pair of plyers to remove the broken key from the lock, he repeated the same story to the deputy in charge that Addie had told the dispatcher.

"Do you want to press charges, ma'am?" he asked Anna. Billy looked at her expectantly, but she shook her head.

"That's your choice, but we're going to put him in a 72-hour hold and recommend a referral to *Miller-Dwan* in Duluth."

"Alcohol treatment?"

"Yes, ma'am. And if you're lucky, Mr. Pearson will take it."

"What about the car, Mom? We can't just leave it there."

"A tow truck's already been called, son."

"Thank you," Anna replied gratefully. The deputy jotted down a few more notes then left.

"What happened, Mom?" The plea in Billy's voice was unmistakable.

"I fell asleep, honey."

"No, I mean what happened to you? You know what's going on around here. How come you don't do anything?!"

Not a word, she reminded herself. *Not yet.* "Billy, I love you and your sister more than you can possibly know. I know nothing seems like it makes any sense right now, but it will soon, I promise. We just have to get through all this first—sort everything out with Jake." Then, for what seemed like the millionth time to Billy, he watched his mother retreat down the hallway.

"Before I forget, honey. Renny came by earlier, seemed pretty excited. He left a note for you on the table."

Billy unfolded the piece of paper and read it. He knew he should care what it said, but he didn't. Instead, he couldn't shake the notion that nothing would ever be the same again. The person he was, the one who had followed Addie into the Bog—that Billy was gone for good. He tried to comprehend more—grasp the enormity of it all—but he was too exhausted.

Billy read the note again and tried to laugh, but what came out were silent, wrenching sobs. He stumbled over to the couch and was asleep in minutes, his mind overwhelmed by the pain Addie had protected him from for so long, but no longer. Renny's message slipped from his hand and fell, forgotten, to the floor.

Carew did it today, Billy! He did it! Look at his box score!

AB	*R*	*H*	*RBI*
5	*5*	*4*	*6*

He's hitting .403!!

Is this a GREAT SUMMER or what?!

Wednesday, June 29ᵗʰ

Hi Dad,

Sorry I haven't written sooner. So much has happened in the past week I could fill a whole notebook getting you caught up.

I should be happy, I know that much. Mom just told us that Jake will be a "guest" of the Miller-Dwan Treatment Center in Duluth for the next month. She said it was his choice, but I doubt it. Whatever the reason, Mom said that moving is "off the table." But if that's true, if we really are staying in Lost Elm, why am I still worried? I guess there's a lot I should tell you.

Ron Pearson killed himself last week. Jake lost his mind when he found out. It didn't help that Shorty and I broke his bottles the same day as the funeral, but I don't feel bad about that. Jake hid them, we didn't.

You should have seen Shorty, Dad! You would've been so proud of him. He got cut up pretty bad at the billboard, but when Mom asked him the next day if he was hurt, Shorty just shrugged and said, "I'm fine, Mom. We're both fine." She tried to get me to go to the emergency room to have a doctor look at my shoulder but I refused. And when she said I would have a scar I told her I hoped I would.

Did we do the right thing, Dad? Or did we just make things worse? I keep thinking about what Sara told me. She said, "There are always going to be more bottles." Will Jake pick up right where he left off when he gets out of Miller-Dwan? Will Mom let him? Maybe that's why I feel worse when I should feel better.

Sara was amazing. She was there for us when we needed her most. She even said Mom could borrow her car while she and her family are in Minneapolis. They left this morning and won't be back until Saturday. That's the kind of friend Sara is, Dad. A true one.

She wasn't the only one who saved us though. Shorty finally stood up to Jake. I guess I should have seen it coming. After all, how did I think I could protect him and get him to stand up for himself at the same time? Either way, Shorty was right. For one night, we won.

But if we really did, Dad, how come I still feel so lost?

Love,
Your daughter, Addie

11
YEARS OF YESTERDAYS

"Yer car's totaled, Mrs. Pearson," Harold Hinkum explained over the phone on Friday morning, July 1st. "But I'll give ya two hundred bucks for it." The Comet had been towed to his garage five days earlier, the same night Jake rolled it into the ditch.

"Please, Mr. Hinkum, call me Anna," she insisted. "Two hundred dollars? Isn't it worthless?"

"Harold, ma'am. Two hundred for the parts. One of my guys will have it stripped by the end of the day if you just give me the word."

Anna mulled his offer and looked at the clock—7:30am. With the Farellis still in Minneapolis and the Carsons visiting their new grand-daughter in Fargo, walking to work again didn't sound like much fun.

"Okay, but on one condition."

"Name it."

"Can you give me a ride into town?"

"I'll do ya one better, ma'am. I have a friend in Wood City who's got a nice little Volkswagen in his lot. If you're available, we can drive over there at lunch. I'm sure I can talk his asking price down a bit."

"Do those cars have stick shifts?"

"Yup, the Beetles are 4-speeds. Thatta problem, ma'am?"

"Not at all," Anna lied. "Alright, keep the two hundred dollars. I'll put it towards the car and get the rest from the bank. But I can't go over a thousand, Mr. Hinkum."

"You won't pay that much," Harold boasted. "Besides, I've got a bargaining chip my friend won't see coming."

Anna took a deep breath and exhaled. "Mr. Hinkum, you are a lifesaver."

"That's what they tell me, ma'am," he chuckled. "Anything else you need?"

"Yes, one more thing. There's an El Camino in my driveway. Can you move it when you get here?"

"Sure, but can I ask you a question?"

"I know what you're going to say, Mr. Hinkum. And the answer is no—I have no idea how to drive a stick shift."

"Then this is your lucky day, ma'am. The first lesson's on me."

Anna Pearson was having a good week, though there was no reason she should have been. Her father-in-law was dead and her husband, pushed beyond his limits, was a broken man. Gone for thirty days, Jake would bide his time in confessional circles at an alcohol treatment center.

The suspicion Addie had mentioned in her diary was correct. Jake's placement at Miller Dwan in nearby Duluth had been anything but voluntary. Anna met him the day before his 72-hour hold in county lockup expired to spell out his "options." She had every right to reel off his past misdeeds and shortcomings, but she doggedly stuck to her script instead. *"Be better, Jake. But don't do it for me. Do it for yourself."* Beyond that, Anna made no bargains or promises. Jake meekly mumbled his agreement as the security door buzzed open, then closed behind her.

*

Anna beamed with pride at the memory as she stuck her head out the tow truck window. The sick feeling that always accompanied Jake's binges was absent. He wouldn't be around for her to sober up or rescue for an entire month. Anna didn't consciously comprehend any of this—she only knew she could breathe again.

"Everything okay, ma'am?" Harold asked as they coasted into Lost Elm.

Anna studied his big belly. *I was actually hungry this morning*, she thought. *Feels like it's been months.*

"Everything's perfect, Mr. Hink . . . Harold. Say, can you drop me off at Woodland Insurance up ahead? They need a few more details about Jake's accident."

"Bean counters," Harold snorted. "Always figuring out ways to keep more of our money."

Anna nodded and smiled. "Thank you for the ride. I'll be by later with my driving gloves on."

"Looking forward to it, Anna."

"Me too, Harold."

*

124

Friday was a payday for most of Lost Elm, so First National Bank was buzzing with activity. Anna rarely worked the lobby anymore, but she didn't want to spend the hours before lunch chained to a desk with only her thoughts to keep her company. If she did, Anna feared the resolve she'd shown Jake might weaken.

But like hay in a field, her doubts grew. As noon approached she was frantic, certain that Jake would burst in any second, if only to show her that he could do whatever he damn well pleased. So, whether to escape her panic or his unlikely appearance, Anna grabbed her purse and her lunch and rushed for the exit.

The bright sun revealed crowded sidewalks all around her. This wasn't unusual for a Friday in July, but no one seemed to be moving with any sense of purpose. Instead, knots of people lingered on street corners discussing the recently burned and blackened Northern Pacific Railroad billboard.

Across the street in front of Paulette's Café, two old men in overalls listened to a third suggest that arson was the cause. "Kids!" he complained loudly. "They got no respect for history." A man in the Junction parking lot scoffed at his girlfriend's notion that it was caused by lightning. "What about all that broken glass?" he countered. Crowds outside the courthouse and post office were out of earshot, but Anna assumed they were talking about the old billboard too.

Harold's Service Station was two blocks north of the bank, across 3rd Street from the side entrance to the county courthouse. Anna, buoyed by the dazzling midday sunlight, practically skipped down the sidewalk. Ahead of her, alone at a picnic table on the courthouse lawn, sat Harold Hinkum.

"May I join you, Harold?"

"Sure thing, Anna. I just got here myself." The old mechanic was actually much closer to finishing his lunch than starting it. Scattered on the table in front of him was a hodgepodge of half eaten food Anna guessed were all the leftovers from his fridge. Tucked under the collar of his oil-stained blue jumpsuit was a broad white napkin.

She smoothed her pale pink dress and sat down, removing an apple, a turkey sandwich and a small bag of carrots from a plain paper bag. Her mouth twitched upward with the realization that she was hungry again.

"Meed a mapkin?" Harold mumbled, his mouth full of cold chicken. "Uh always 'arry ooh."

"Thank you, Harold. What would I do without you?"

Harold frowned and pulled his napkin from his shirt, twisting it anxiously and staring down at his food.

"Did I say something wrong?"

"No, ma'am. That was just something Sharon used to say. I haven't heard that since . . . well, since."

Anna brushed away a strand of long brown hair that framed her pale, narrow face. "I hardly left the house the first six months after Will died," she recalled. "I was afraid I might fall apart if anyone so much as said hello to me." An ancient pain flashed across her face. "I wish I hadn't done that. I could have used a friend."

"I know what you mean," Harold said with a catch in his throat. "Most of my customers still come and go pretty quick."

Anna squeezed his hand. "I'm sorry, Harold. I guess I've been one of those people."

"That's okay, I know your plate's been pretty full. My kids check on me now and then, and a few other people stop by to make sure I'm doin' okay." He smiled at Sara's copy of *The Good Earth* next to his lunch pail. "They don't think I know what they're up to, but I do."

"I'm glad," she said. "Talking helps."

"It does," he nodded, his reply cut short by a loud belch. Embarrassed, he laughed until Anna giggled along with him.

"Sharon always clucked at me whenever I did that, but I think she was pleased. She knew I loved her cooking."

Anna smiled at the sweetness of the man. He had obviously adored his wife.

"So did you just stop by to eat lunch with a fat old man or are you ready to buy that car?" They laughed again until they were both in tears.

"Both. But it's such a nice day, Harold. The car can wait a little longer."

*

Harold drove Anna to *Pete's 66 Service Station* in Wood City, a few blocks up the street from Jensen & Company. He eased into the lot and parked next to their prize—a metallic-green, 1972 Volkswagen Beetle.

"Don't let Pete Younger scare ya, ma'am," Harold advised her. "He's more bark than bite. But let me do the talking just in case."

Anna watched the two men greet each other with a flurry of insults. When it was over, their bellies shook with laughter. A lively discussion of their business woes followed before negotiations could begin. Only then did Pete take notice of Anna.

"Ya got a girlfriend, Harold?!" he boomed. "She blind or something?" He walked over to Anna and winked. "If this old fart gives you any trouble ma'am, you let me know."

"Leave comedy to the comedians, Pete. You remember Anna Olson— Byron and Darlene's girl? She married Will Travers years ago, back when you still had hair."

Pete's expression softened. "Sorry Mrs. Travers, I didn't mean any offense," he said, taking off his cap. "Will was a good boy."

"Thank you, Mr. Younger," Anna replied sweetly. "I haven't been called Mrs. Travers in a long time."

"Call me Pete, ma'am," he said. "So you're here for the Beetle, huh? Harold gonna do your horse trading for you?"

"I'm not very hopeful," Anna shrugged. "He said you're a tough negotiator." Harold smiled over Pete's shoulder. *Good girl. Soften him up.*

"He's right," Pete agreed, stroking his chin thoughtfully. "Whaddya think, Harold? Would Mrs. Travers be robbing me if I asked for $750?"

Harold's brow arched slightly, but he shook his head. "Who's the bigger fool, Pete? Me or Anna?"

"You gotta give me a tougher question than that," Pete snickered. He scratched the gray stubble above his ear. "How about $600? That way I still make a profit."

"Deal!" Anna said before Pete could change his mind. "Can the car be ready by tomorrow morning?"

"She's ready right now, ma'am. You won't need this amateur giving it a tune-up. I'll grab the keys and the title for ya." Pete gave Harold a knowing look and moseyed over to his office.

"That went pretty well," Anna said as she circled the car.

"Better than you think," Harold replied. "Once Pete knew who you were, the best he could do on the sale was break even."

"But he said . . ."

"Pete Younger's ex-Marine. There was no way he was going to make any money off a Navy Corpsman's widow."

"Why not?"

"Because a Corpsman just like Will saved his life on Okinawa in '45," Harold explained. "Don't feel bad, ma'am. Pete doesn't. He'll be smiling about this for weeks."

Pete emerged from his office and smiled warmly at Anna. "I s'pose this dogface said he'd teach you how to drive a stick."

"Hey, I drove a tank across Europe, ya old grunt," Harold sputtered.

"Ma'am, when you need proper instruction, *and you will*," Pete teased, "Come and see me. I'll get ya squared away."

"Thank you, Mr. Younger," Anna replied, kissing him lightly on the cheek. "You're a true gentleman."

"Please, ma'am—call me Pete."

*

Anna's workday slowed to a crawl. Never a clock-watcher, she looked up from her desk constantly. The instant 4:30 arrived, she was out the door and on her way back to Harold's.

Harold had chosen the barest road he could think of for Anna's driving lesson—a straight shot four miles south of Hillside Cemetery. Along the way he went over everything with her—where the gears were, when to push in the clutch, how to find reverse, down-shifting, coasting to a stop, everything. During the tutorial, Harold slowed down and sped up in a series of demonstrations.

Anna watched his hands and feet work seamlessly together from one gear to another. She listened for the changing pitch of the engine, immediately fond of the Beetle's distinctive *putt-putt* sound. *The little engine that could,* she thought as Harold steered the car to the side of the road near a lonely intersection.

"Your turn."

Anna ran around to the driver's side door before Harold could even step out of the car. Her eagerness was only slightly dimmed by her failure

128

to find first gear on her first five tries. She squealed with excitement each time the car jerked and stalled, followed by the same six words, "What did I do wrong, Harold?" When the Beetle finally lurched successfully into first gear, Anna practically levitated off her seat.

"Second gear, second gear!" Harold howled over the rising whine of the engine. Anna pressed in the clutch and pulled back on the stick shift. The car shuddered and stalled.

"What happened this time?"

"That was fourth gear," Harold said, looking over his shoulder to see if any cars were coming. "Okay, let's go over 'em again." Anna kept the clutch in and maneuvered the stick from first through fourth gear, then back down again. "Thatta, girl. See? You can do this." She smiled and for a fleeting moment felt young again. Life's unfairness and cruelties hadn't visited her yet. The future was still in the distance, far away down a clear, straight road.

Buoyed by Harold's confidence in her, Anna found first gear and the car moved smoothly forward. When he urged her to shift into second, the little car leapt ahead further still. "Listen for it, Anna. Listen," he whispered. She slammed the stick into third gear before the engine could protest. Squirming in her seat, Anna bit her lower lip while Harold nodded and grinned. "You're doing great, Anna—now give it some gas!" With a triumphant smile, she maneuvered the car easily into fourth gear and raced down the highway.

Anna shifted up and down through all four gears on the drive back to Lost Elm, doing everything Harold asked of her with a deftness that surprised him. Her last task was to coast down the length of the long slope next to Hillside Cemetery, but halfway down Anna braked onto the shoulder and made a U-turn back to the cemetery.

"Do you mind, Harold?"

"Not at all. There's someone I should visit too."

The car jerked and stalled exactly where Jake had parked the Comet a few weeks earlier. "What just happened?" Anna asked, irritation frowning her face.

"Hmm?" Harold was looking at a modest headstone nestled into the hill. "Oh, when you shut the car off in gear you have to push in the clutch first, otherwise it'll stall."

"Good to know," Anna replied, sensing they were both doing some stalling of their own. She looked at Will's grave. A crow was guarding it, perched motionless on a nearby bench.

"Tell you what," Harold suggested. "You come with me to mine. I'll go with you to yours." He stepped out of the car and trudged up the short slope. Anna set the emergency brake and followed him.

"We bought these plots a few years ago," Harold said. "Didn't think we'd need 'em for a while though." He shook his head. "That's all Sharon wanted on her headstone—*Beloved Wife and Mother*. Both are true but neither did her justice. She was a wonderful woman."

They lingered a little longer then walked down to Will's grave. Anna had always gone to the cemetery alone before, but she was glad for the company this time. *And today of all days,* she mused.

"*July 1, 1942*. Hey, isn't that . . ."

"Happy birthday, Will," Anna whispered.

"Oh gosh, I'm sorry, Anna. I can wait in the car."

"It's okay, Harold. Come sit with me." She patted the bench. The crow was long gone.

"If you don't mind me asking, ma'am, Jake never really had a chance, did he? I'm sorry, I had no right to ask that."

"I was so angry when Will joined the Navy," Anna said with quiet intensity. "And then going to Vietnam—I hated him almost as much as I loved him. I guess that's what saved us—the *almost*." She knelt over his grave and ran her fingers through the grass. "So I come here on his birthday and miss him and love him and hate him all over again." She stood, tears streaming down her cheeks. "No, Jake never had a chance."

Will Travers' widow wasn't what Harold had expected. There was more to this shy, reserved woman than he would have guessed twelve hours earlier. Her usual fraught bearing was gone. Standing before him was a woman whose eyes blazed with a renewed sense of urgency—the belief that tomorrow was too late because she had let years of yesterdays torment her. But now Anna couldn't wait—not one more day.

She dropped Harold off at his service station and drove out of town, merging west onto the state highway. As she found fourth gear, her past and her choices seemed easier to live with than they had that morning, though she still feared that a familiar guilt might lure her back to Jake.

Whether it did or not, Anna was consoled by the fact that every choice she made in the next thirty days would be entirely her own.

A mile out of town, she coasted to a stop next to the fresh ruins of the Northern Pacific Railroad sign. There was more broken glass than she had expected, but whatever other evidence Billy and Addie had left appeared to be gone, washed away by the same rain that had smothered the fire. Anna tried to imagine the stand her children made that night—Addie's armful of red bandanas, Billy smashing one bottle after another against the billboard—but her shame wouldn't allow it.

"Why didn't you just stay with us?!" Anna screamed, her hands shaking the steering wheel in futility. "Weren't we enough?!" Convulsions racked her body as she sobbed hard, harder than she had in a long time. Every feeling she'd buried in the last ten years was overwhelmed by the fact that Billy and Addie's secret journey into the Bog had been fueled by their loss of faith in her to protect them.

"I don't hate you, Will," she wept quietly. "But you'd hate yourself if you knew how great our kids are. You would have never left." Her anguish spent, Anna took a long, deep breath and let it out slowly. *Time's running out*, she knew, taking one last look at the scene of Billy and Addie's triumph. *But it's not too late.*

12
PETRUCHIO AND KATE

Crickets chirped lazily around the Loop as Anna parked her Volkswagen Beetle and burst into the trailer. Billy and Addie, sprawled on the living room rug watching a re-run of *The Rockford Files*, immediately noticed their mother's breathless smile. Without a word, she pulled them off the floor and out the door.

"What do you think?!" Anna shrieked, showing off the car like a game show host. Behind her the sun still hung a few hours above horizon. "Who wants to go for a ride?!"

Billy and Addie looked at each other. Babbling non-stop before them was their mother, though she bore no resemblance to the weary person they were used to.

"What are you waiting for, an engraved invitation? Get in our new car!" she teased.

"What's going on, Mom?" Addie asked suspiciously.

Anna sighed, deflated by her daughter's guarded response. But then she remembered her own shame at the billboard. *It's not Addie's fault. She's just doing what she's always had to do.*

"What's going on is we're taking this little beauty out for a quick spin. Now hop in."

*

The next morning Anna woke early, packed a picnic lunch and instructed Billy and Addie to throw their beach towels in the car as soon as they finished their breakfast. By 10am they were on the road again, heading twenty miles south to the small town of Moose Lake. Up front with her mother, Addie searched the glove compartment and fiddled with the radio. In the cramped back seat, Billy studied the Bug's tan interior while the rear engine vibrated behind him.

Anna outlined the day's schedule over the dull roar of the car's open windows. First, to Moose Lake's public beach for a swim and lunch. After that, to nearby City Park where the town's Fourth of July carnival was in full swing. Lastly, to Wood City for fireworks at Pineview Park.

133

No lie detector test could prove that the woman chattering behind the wheel wasn't their mother, but Billy had never seen her smile so easily before. By the time they cruised into Moose Lake he had shaken the image—at least for the day—of the same perpetually tired woman shuffling down their trailer's narrow hallway.

Addie had the opposite reaction. She leaned away from her mother, anxious to escape the claustrophobic confines of the car as soon as she could. Dormant memories had awakened within her, recollections too distant to see clearly, but evoking feelings in Addie that were real nonetheless.

"What a beautiful day!" Anna remarked optimistically. "Won't a swim feel good?"

She turned cautiously into the parking lot. Nearby, the beach was already filling up with families who'd woken up that morning with the same idea.

"Why didn't we just go to Pineview in the first place?" Addie complained. "Wood City's carnival is better and I don't wanna swim here anyway. Do you, Shorty?"

Anna was mum as Billy and Addie bickered for the umpteenth time over her use of his nickname. Instead, she found reverse and eased the car into an empty space—a smooth finish to her first long drive. The same could not be said for her children. Their argument spilled into the parking lot as Anna opened the trunk and handed Billy the picnic basket.

"Can you find us a spot, honey? Somewhere with shade."

"A table or on the ground?"

"Doesn't matter to me. What do you think, Addie?"

Addie rolled her eyes. "No one asked us if we wanted to move halfway across the state, but now you want my opinion about where we should eat lunch?" She spun on her heels but Anna grabbed her arm before she could walk away.

"Find the best spot you can, Billy," she said, never taking her eyes off Addie. "I need to talk to your sister for a minute."

"What is *wrong* with you today?!" Anna asked once Billy was out of earshot.

"I was going ask you the same thing," Addie replied with her usual snark. "Where's my Mom and what have you done with her?"

"That's not very nice, Addie. It's one thing to talk to Jake like that, but I deserve better."

"Do you?!" The instant the words left Addie's mouth, she regretted saying them. The pain on her mother's face only made it worse.

"Mom I'm . . ."

Anna waved her off. "I'm the one who should apologize, Addie."

"For what? Being in a good mood?"

"Because I haven't given you or Billy much to be happy about in a very long time." Anna took Addie's face in her hands. "Are you thinking about your Dad today?"

Addie's face creased and reddened. As her mom's question sank in she dove back into the car, horrified that she might fall apart the way she did in front of Sara. Anna followed her into the front seat.

"Do you still remember your Dad, honey?"

Addie squeezed her eyes shut. She had waited so long to talk to her mother about Will Travers, but she knew if she uttered a single word it drown in fresh tears.

"Do you know what I think?" Anna murmured. "I think the idea of spending a day with me like this—having fun—feels like a betrayal."

"A betrayal?"

"Of your dad. If it were me, I'd be sad too."

Addie wanted to rebel against her mother's intuition, but she couldn't. "How come you're not?"

"I still am, honey. Every day. You know, If I died tomorrow I'd hate knowing I could have made our lives better, but didn't. So better starts today, okay?"

"Does better include Jake?" Addie braced herself for the usual excuses.

"No."

Addie searched her mother's face for any sign of doubt, but saw only a loving smile. "What does *no* mean?"

"It means you and Billy won't have to worry about Jake anymore," Anna promised. "He's my problem, not yours. He'll never be your problem again."

"Do you mean it, Mom?"

"I do." Anna brushed her daughter's cheek. "I'll make you a deal. Let's just enjoy the day. Tomorrow you can ask me anything you want."

135

Addie's face brightened as Billy pounded his fist on the back window. "Come on you two! I found a spot five minutes ago. Last one in is a rotten egg!"

*

By the time Billy and Addie wandered into the kitchen the next morning, Anna had already made pancakes and eggs. She smiled contentedly as they loaded their plates.

"What's the occasion, Mom?" Billy mumbled between bites. "We haven't had pancakes in forever."

Anna tousled his brown hair. The same cowlick Will had had on the back of his head was plain to see on Billy's too. "We used to every Sunday, remember?"

Addie ate in silence. If Jake was there she would have been hunched over, eyes downcast. Not today. Instead of eating quickly and leaving the table, she sat up straight and took her time.

"You look nice, honey. Did you get that outfit at Jensen's?"

"Sara helped me pick it out." Addie was pleased that her mom noticed. She hadn't completely remade herself, but gone were her daily t-shirts and cut-off jeans.

"You look beautiful. Don't you think so, Billy?"

Billy considered his sister between mouthfuls of scrambled eggs. "Looks the same to me," he lied. To show her brother that some things hadn't changed, Addie gave him a well-aimed punch on his shoulder. Anna only laughed.

"Are you two ready for another drive after breakfast?" she asked, slowly sipping her coffee.

"Are we going to be gone all day, Mom? Sara comes home today. We were going to listen to her new records later."

"Did she say why they were in Minneapolis? Michael mentioned the trip at work, but nothing more. Odd," Anna mused. "He never takes a day off."

"Renny didn't say anything to me. Just thought he might run into Rod Carew somehow," Billy grinned. "I don't think he knows how big Minneapolis is. Besides, the Twins are in Chicago this weekend."

"We won't be gone long," Anna assured Addie. "There are just a couple things I want to show you."

"Like what?" Billy frowned.

"You'll see," Anna said as she tried to smooth down his cowlick. "Now clear your dishes or we'll never get out of here."

"Where are we going?" Addie asked, a faint wrinkle appearing between her eyebrows.

"First stop, Duluth."

*

Once known as *"The San Francisco of the Midwest"* for its hillsides and streetcar service, Duluth, Minnesota rose steeply from its Lake Superior shoreline. Ethnic, blue-collar neighborhoods stretched west and south of the harbor, while blue-blood, old-money mansions lay north of downtown and the iconic lift bridge.

Addie ignored this scenery as the Volkswagen began its long descent into the port city. Unlike the drive to Moose Lake, she knew exactly what was bothering her. Jake was close, and getting closer.

"How are you doing back there?" Anna asked her. "Do you want me to wind up my window?"

"I'm fine," Addie replied, forcing a smile. "So what's the big mystery, Mom? Why can't you tell us where we're going?" Her agitation was palpable as the Beetle zoomed past huge iron ore carrier ships moored at loading docks near the shore of the big lake.

Anna looked at her daughter through the rear-view mirror and understood what was on her mind. "We're going to Brighton Beach," she announced, hoping that would lighten Addie's mood.

"Where's Brighton Beach?"

"On the far side of town, past all the big homes."

Addie tensed as they cruised through one green light after another, but Anna didn't flinch as they passed the medical building that housed Miller-Dwan Treatment Center. Instead, she accelerated through the intersection leaving Jake—and their marriage—behind her. Five miles later, neither Billy nor Addie noticed Anna squeeze the steering wheel convulsively as she turned the car onto a pebbled path marked by a wood-carved sign: *Brighton Beach, Lake Superior*.

After cutting the engine and telling Billy and Addie where to set up for lunch, Anna made a beeline toward the shore a hundred feet away. Her children looked on as she removed her shoes and waded into the freezing lake. Recognizing something at her feet, Anna dropped into the ankle deep water and pressed her hands on a large rock just below the surface. Addie set the picnic basket down and raced over to her. Billy followed close behind.

"Mom, what's wrong?! Are you okay?!"

"It's still here!" Anna gasped. "I can't believe it's still here." Up and down the shore, other beachcombers had stopped to gawk at them. Billy leaned down and put his hand under her arm.

"Mom, maybe you should . . ."

"No, no, no!" she insisted, lifting her hands. "Look!" Billy and Addie saw three words carved into the rock—*PETRUCHIO AND KATE*—but their meaning was a mystery.

"Pet-rock-i-o?" Billy recited, mangling the pronunciation.

"Pu-troo-kee-o," Anna corrected him. Her shining smile penetrated their confusion.

"Is this you and Dad?!" they asked in unison.

Like waking from a dream, Anna passed her hand over the rock again, then retreated to the picnic table while Billy and Addie quietly unpacked their lunch. The hypnotic breakers of Lake Superior were almost an abstraction to them, blending with the people on the beach and the scavenging gulls overhead, creating a gentle chorus—filling the time and space until their mother was ready to talk.

Billy had no idea what secrets *PETRUCHIO AND KATE* might reveal. Will Travers had never been more than an elusive figure to him, someone always just out of his reach. Maybe his mother's words would change all that, but Billy wasn't sure it mattered as long as she was happy.

Addie barely tasted her food. Between meager bites, she snuck glances at her mother. Anna stared past them both, her gaze ricocheting between joy and pain until it coalesced into an expression Addie couldn't name or understand. But she knew her answers lay there, behind her mother's weary, watery eyes. The details weren't important to her anymore. Addie simply wanted to confirm what she had always believed—that her father had been a good and true man and he had loved her.

Anna didn't mean for Billy and Addie to wait, but she was glad they didn't barrage her with questions from the moment she sat down. The truth was, for all her newfound energy and inspiration, Anna didn't know where to start. She tapped her chin repeatedly, the tips of her fingers still cold from the frigid lake. The lake. The rock. *The Beginning.*

*

Anna Olson thought it was all a joke, and a cruel one at that. Will Travers had never noticed her before, so why now? Besides, she was nobody. Well, not nobody—just not like him. Even as the attention Anna received from Will continued throughout the spring of 1959, she never let herself believe it meant anything. But all that changed when Will asked her to the junior prom.

"What do you think you're doing, Will?" Anna asked him accusingly.

He thought his question had been obvious. In fact, he'd rehearsed it for nearly an hour, not including another thirty minutes working up the courage to dial the phone.

"What do you mean?" he replied in bewilderment. "Didn't you hear me?"

"I heard you just fine."

Will put the phone to his chest and replayed his speech in his head. *"Hi Anna, this is Will. Listen, I was wondering, um . . . If you don't have a date yet or anything . . . I don't know, would you like to go to prom with me?"* Hardly perfect, he thought, but perfectly clear.

"Anna, I'm just trying to . . ."

"Be funny? Come on, Will. We both know what day it is tomorrow." Will looked at a calendar taped to the fridge. *X*'s covered all of March's thirty-one days.

"This isn't an April Fool's joke, Anna. This is real." There was silence on the other end of the line for five full seconds as his hopes rapidly faded.

"Are you asking me to prom, Will?" Anna whispered.

"Of course I'm asking you to prom!" he shouted in joyful exasperation. "What did you think I've been doing for the last three weeks?"

"I thought you were just being nice."

"I was!" Will exhaled. "To you. I like you, Anna."

For all the hero worship Will received, he'd always been a little bashful around girls. So no one was more surprised than he when he shook off his fear and pursued Anna Olson that spring. And he had one person to thank for it. Well, maybe two.

*

"Brian Lawrence?"

"Here."

"Susan Nystrom?"

"Present."

"Anna Olson?"

"Here."

"Jacob Pearson?"

"Yo."

"Jacob Pearson?"

"Here."

"William Travers."

"It's Will, sir."

Bill Meisner scanned his class roster and compared it to the sixteen students seated before him. He highly doubted *Intro to Shakespeare* had been anyone's first choice at last fall's class registration. But that didn't matter to Mr. Meisner. He loved William Shakespeare. When he was offered the English job at Lost Elm High School three years earlier, he'd asked for only thing—a chance to teach The Bard's plays. The principal had been in no position to bargain with the passionate young teacher. Mr. Meisner was his only applicant.

"For the next twelve weeks," he announced to the class, pausing for effect, "William Shakespeare is going to seep into the very marrow of your bones. At first his plays will sound like gibberish in your ears, but then there will come a moment . . ." Mr. Meisner paused again, his rich baritone punctuating each word. "Then there will come a moment when his genius will fall so neatly into place that you will wonder how you didn't understand him from the start. Mark my words," he concluded, jabbing a finger repeatedly at four rows of desks. "It has happened before. It will happen again."

Most of the class stared at their desks as his words sank in, but three students didn't. Anna and Will looked right at him. She seemed a little terrified, but Mr. Meisner knew he could work on that. The Travers kid was a bit of a surprise, though he was encouraged by the thinly veiled intensity in the boy's eyes. The same couldn't be said for the third student, Jacob Pearson.

"Marrow of your bones?" Jake sneered. "Bill, is that your bone or mine?"

There's always one, Mr. Meisner reminded himself. He came out from behind his desk, sensing none of the tension the students were feeling after Jake's blatant disrespect. With his Roman nose and jutting chin, Mr. Meisner looked like a patrician about to address the Imperial Senate. He anchored his wide frame to the ground and clasped his hands behind his back.

"Who here has heard of a man named *Shylock*?"

Will's hand rose uncertainly. "Isn't he in *The Merchant of Venice*?"

Mr. Meisner hadn't expected anyone to answer the question, much less correctly. "Very good, Mr. Travers," he nodded. "Shylock is a man surrounded by hypocrites. In the play, they justify their prejudice against him because of how badly they expect he will treat them in return."

"What's your point?" Jake said with naked petulance. He searched the room for allies, but found none.

"The point," Mr. Meisner said with relish. "Is this. From Act III, Scene 1 of *The Merchant of Venice*: *If you prick us, do we not bleed? If you poison us, do we not die? And if you wrong us, shall we not revenge?* Well, Mr. Pearson, shall I?"

A mischievous smile crept up around the corners of Will's mouth. Whatever doubts he had about William Shakespeare or William Meisner were gone. *Wrong us, shall we not revenge? How cool is that?!* He looked at Jake, who vaguely understood that the unflappable man standing before them had made his point.

"You obviously signed up for this class for a reason," Mr. Meisner said. "Though I can't imagine what that reason was. Regardless, it is now irrelevant."

Jake had been outsmarted and he knew it. He did his best to recover a measure of indifference, but failed. When he turned to his friend for support, Will never looked his way.

141

"That is your cue to leave, Mr. Pearson," Mr. Meisner said, gesturing toward the door. "I'll let the office know you're on your way to sign up for a class better suited to your level of interest."

Jake abruptly stood, his desk scraping across the floor. He looked at Anna two rows over. He hadn't wanted to be there in the first place, but figured having a class with her might help him break through the simple friendship they'd had since junior high. *And now this*, Jake thought, unwilling to shoulder any of the blame for his sudden ejection.

"Fine," he surrendered. "You coming, Will?"

Catch you later, Jake, Will thought, though he said nothing. Instead, he looked at Mr. Meisner and got the distinct feeling he was being sized up somehow. Never taking his eyes off the man, Will shook his head.

"Suit yourself," Jake said and skulked from the room.

"Now that we've gotten the pleasantries out of the way," Mr. Meisner announced, sensing the students' collective relief, "Let's talk about William Shakespeare."

*

He was right. For the first few weeks of class, Shakespeare's plays might as well have been written in a foreign language. On another planet. In a distant galaxy. Old English words like *anon* and *bequeath* floated just beyond the students' reach. Plots and plot twists were lost in *betwixt* and *besmirch*. They slogged through the intrigue of *Julius Caesar* and the comic deception of *Much Ado About Nothing*. "It will come," Mr. Meisner insisted. "Understanding will come." Eventually, in fits and starts, it did. By the time the class turned to Act I, Scene 1 of *The Taming of the Shrew*, he knew they were on the verge of a breakthrough.

Will and Anna's march from strangers to friends followed much the same path as their grasp of Shakespeare. His growing awareness of the quiet, fair-skinned Anna proved to be a daily distraction. More than once Will lost his place reading lines, only to receive amused reminders from Mr. Meisner. "Sorry, sir—*Friends, Romans, countrymen, lend me your ears; I come to bury Caesar, not to praise him*."

Though they had been classmates since first grade, Will couldn't recall ever having anything but a casual conversation with Anna. But when the characters in *Much Ado About Nothing* donned their disguises for the scene at the masquerade ball, Will shed his mask and began a quiet courtship. Slowly, Anna reciprocated his attention. Day after day, he approached her locker and they talked about the latest play they were reading or whatever other excuse Will could think of. Soon, short conversations lengthened beyond their lockers and continued down the hall. By the time Mr. Meisner assigned parts for *The Taming of The Shrew*, Will had made up his mind. He would ask Anna to prom.

"Mr. Travers, I would like you to read the part of Petruchio," Mr. Meisner chuckled. "It shouldn't be much of a stretch." He peered over his glasses and scanned the room until he zeroed in on Anna. "Miss Olson, forgive me. What I am about to say may be a false assumption, but here goes. You are most definitely not a Kate, but I still want you to read her part."

"Why am I not a Kate?" Anna asked, skimming through the cast of characters.

"For starters, do you like being taken for granted?" Mr. Meisner asked off-handedly.

"No," she said, shifting uncomfortably in her seat.

"Neither does Kate. And she is an outspoken woman who wants nothing to do with our friend Petruchio here." He gestured to a red-faced Will.

Mr. Meisner walked back and forth as he spoke, the wood floors creaking under his feet. Though he was addressing Anna, he made eye contact with every other girl in the classroom, searching for some flicker of recognition that they understood what he was discreetly telling them. *Speak up, ladies! Dream for yourselves. Find your own futures.*

"Under all those manners of yours, Miss Olson, may lie the same strength and spirit as our fiery Kate. Find that fire within yourself and read it like the woman I just described," he urged, waving his well-worn copy in the air. "Tell our scheming Petruchio how you really feel."

*

"And so I did," Anna told Billy and Addie. "I was no Kate, that's for sure. But I found something true in her words. So when Will asked me to prom I eventually believed him and said yes. We drove here the day after and had a picnic right over there." She pointed to a patch of grass at the

143

edge of the rocky shore where a young couple and their baby were playing on a blanket. "Before we left, Will took out his knife and carved PETRUCHIO AND KATE on that rock and put it in the water."

Billy and Addie hadn't moved a muscle since their mother began talking. The breeze off the lake, the waves against the shore, the people coming and going, none of it registered to their senses. The only thing they heard was the story of a boy and a girl and how they had met many years ago.

Anna's tale had mesmerized Billy. He felt like he'd been in Mr. Meisner's class with his parents, wandered the halls next to them. Now his mother was sitting across from him and saying that there once was a boy she had loved.

"Do you still have your dad's knife, Billy? The one Jake gave you." Anna reached for Billy's hand and tapped the faded scar on his palm. "You still have it, don't you?"

Addie put her hand over her front pocket and felt the outline of the knife. What she had always assumed was nothing more than a clumsy token from Jake was now something else entirely. *I carved all those poems with Dad's knife!*

Billy glanced at Addie and nodded. "I keep it in my dresser."

"Can you believe that same knife carved those three words?" Anna reminisced.

"Is that when you knew, Mom?" Addie asked.

"I remember exactly when I knew, honey. It was the fall of our senior year. But for that story we have to drive to Jay Cooke Park. There's something else I want to show you."

Billy and Addie waited for her to say more, but Anna put her uneaten food back in the basket instead. Rather than press her for more information, they bit their tongues and did the same. Answers to long unspoken questions weren't far away—just a few more miles down the road.

144

13
THE SAME REASON

When Will dropped back to pass late in the 4th quarter of Lost Elm's final game of his high school career, he thought his troubles with Jake were over. Their friendship had ended at Gap Lake three months earlier, but that hadn't affected their teamwork on the football field throughout 1959 season. When a handoff was called for Jake, Will gave him the ball. If Will needed protection from his fullback, Jake supplied it. He did, that is, until the last Friday night in late October against the Sandstone Panthers.

Coach Jim Erickson's Lakers had been perfect all season, beating each of their first eight opponents handily. Sandstone too, entered the game undefeated. The conference championship was on the line.

No one who watched Will play that fall would have guessed his heart wasn't in any of it. Play after play on offense, tackle after tackle on defense, he fooled them all, save one—Anna Olson. She saw it in his face at the end of every game. More relieved than happy, Will declined questions from local sportswriters with the same excuse every week, "Coach is the one you wanna talk to. He's the reason we won."

Not surprisingly, the end of the season was very much on Will's mind as he led his team out of the huddle for the final play of the championship game. It had been a seesaw contest all night, from Lost Elm's first possession to its last—which was now deep in Panthers territory. Neither team had moved the ball with much authority, but Sandstone had scored in the 3rd quarter when Jake bobbled a screen pass from Will long enough for an opponent to pluck the ball out of the air and return it sixty-four yards for the game's only score.

With seven seconds left and the ball on the Panthers 16 yard line, Will took his place under center. *This is it,* he thought as he scanned the defense. *Last play.* But he wouldn't remember what everyone else saw in those next few seconds, or for fifteen minutes afterward. The missed blocking assignment, the crushing tackle on his blindside or the hushed crowd as he was loaded, unconscious, into an ambulance and transported to Memorial Hospital in Wood City. For Will, everything just went black.

"Did we win, Coach?"

Jim Erickson was tired. Between the vending machine coffee and the cramped waiting room chairs, he hadn't slept a wink. But he heard Will's faint plea as he stared across the parking lot from the boy's second floor hospital room window.

"Hey, Will," he murmured. "How are you feeling?"

Will let out a long groan. "Like I'm not really here, you know?"

Mr. Erickson nodded. "The first game of my sophomore year in college I got my bell rung so hard that I went to the wrong huddle after the whistle. The other team tried to tell me, but I ignored them. Eventually, one of the refs walked me to the sideline. I didn't play another snap for two weeks."

Will looked around the darkened room. "Mr. E.—where's my mom?"

"I sent her home to get some sleep. Told her I'd call first thing in the morning."

"What time is it?"

"Just after 3am. The doctor said you can go home around noon if everything checks out okay."

"Have you been here the whole time?"

Mr. Erickson took off his cap and fiddled with the brim. "Where else would I be, Will? I'm not a father yet, but if my boy got hurt the way you did tonight no one could drag me out of here."

Will had taken for granted just how much he counted on this quiet, steady man to simply "be there," and how much he admired him. *I wanna be like that*, Will thought. But before he could thank him, Mr. Erickson changed the subject to something that had been on his mind since the game ended.

"Will, I know you're tired, but tell me about the last play. We ran that thing a million times in practice. Everyone knew their assignments. What happened?"

Despite a splitting headache, Will knew what his coach was talking about. A hurried drop back, a look left downfield, a check right for his missing protection, then a doctor pointing a light in his eye. "I dunno, Coach," he answered evasively. "There was a lot of crowd noise. Maybe some of the guys didn't hear the play call."

"Some of the guys?" Mr. Erickson pressed him. "Or just one?"

"Doesn't matter, Coach. Season's over."

Mr. Erickson practically tore his cap in two. *The boy is covering for Jake Pearson even though he nearly got his head knocked off!* He took a deep breath and let it out slowly. "I admire your loyalty, Will. You've shown it to me and you've shown it to the team all season. But misplaced loyalty can get a person hurt."

Will knew Mr. Erickson was right. Jake had blown his blocking assignment on purpose and only he knew why—payback for telling Jake about his mother. Now, three months later and still not sure he'd done the right thing, Will's choice weighed on him all over again.

"I know. I just thought . . . hoped, I guess . . ."

"Whatever it is, Will, it can wait," Mr. Erickson said, letting him off the hook. "I'll be right outside if you need anything."

"Mr. Erickson? Thanks for everything—for the last three years. Ever since my dad died you've always been there."

Mr. Erickson smiled at the boy he knew was quickly passing into adulthood. "It's been my great pleasure, Will. You're one of the good ones." He hadn't gotten two steps out the door before he turned around. "Say, we've been getting so sappy in here, I almost forgot. You've got a visitor." He opened the door to reveal a very worried Anna Olson. "I'll leave you two alone. She looks like better company than me anyway."

*

A week later Will was sitting at a table in the high school library staring at a photograph on the front page of *The Wood City Journal*. There he was, hurrying to throw the football while a Sandstone defender was suspended in mid-air, bracing for the tackle. The caption beneath the picture told only the facts: *"COLLISION COURSE! Sandstone's Adam Saarela ended Lost Elm's undefeated season with a hit on local star Will Travers. The Lakers' quarterback spent the night in the hospital under observation, but was released in good health the next morning."*

The image of Saarela about to send Will to the hospital made no impression on him, but what he saw just past the Panther defender did. Obscured in the background—and definitely not where he was supposed to be on that final play—was a Laker teammate. Now that same person strode into the library.

147

"Hi, Jake," Will said, pushing the newspaper aside. "How ya been? Haven't seen you around lately."

Jake wasn't having a very good week. No one had said anything to him about his on-field "mistake," but there was a definite chill in the halls of Lost Elm High School. And when *The Journal* arrived, the silence only deepened.

"Been busy," Jake replied brusquely. "I started working at Reed's Diner in Wood City after school." He spied the paper on the table and stiffened.

"Good season, huh?" Will said, gesturing to the front page.

"Good things end," Jake replied dismissively. He stepped past the table but Will grabbed his arm.

"I'm sorry about this summer, Jake," Will whispered. "That was none of my business. It's your family, not mine. I just thought . . ."

"You just thought what?!" Jake seethed, yanking his arm free. "That you were doing the right thing?!" He snatched *The Journal* from the table and waved it in Will's face. "This could've happened anytime, Will! You're just lucky I waited 'til the end of the season!" He threw the paper in the trash and stormed out of the library. Anna walked in moments later.

"What's wrong with Jake? He practically knocked me over a second ago. It's like he didn't even see me."

"I doubt he did."

"Are you okay, Will? You look tired." Anna sat down and put her hand on his cheek. "Come on, let's get out of here. I've got study hall last period and you're Will Travers," she teased. "You can do anything you want around here."

He took her hand and interlocked his fingers with hers. "You're just what the doctor ordered, Anna," he said wearily.

Her pulse quickened. She squeezed his hand and felt her neck redden. With supreme effort, she looked into his eyes. "Am I, Will?"

He absorbed the passion in Anna's words. He looked down at her hand intertwined in his but couldn't feel his fingers. His head began to ring, but not from the concussion.

"Did you drive to school?" he asked her, rising from his chair. "The doctor said I shouldn't for another week."

Anna said that she had.

"Good, there's something I want to show you."

148

Will sat quietly next to Anna as she steered her family's gray-green '51 Nash toward Slate Gap and Jay Cooke State Park. His conversation with Mr. Erickson, followed by nearly a week in bed, had given him a lot to think about. Telling Jake he was sorry, regardless of how futile the gesture was, had been an easy decision for Will to make. He was only sorry it had taken so long. And while he recovered at home, Will realized something even more important—he didn't want to leave other things unsaid either. *I've done that since Dad died,* he thought. *I can't, I won't—not one more day.* As Anna pulled off the road next to the Jay Cooke State Park sign, Will knew that now was a good time and place to start.

With November only days away, a bleak chill had settled over Lost Elm. Will offered Anna his letter jacket and led her toward the same railroad bridge he and Jake had jumped off of the previous summer. They followed a straight line between the tracks, which were scheduled for removal the following spring. *"To be torn up for lack of use,"* The Journal had reported a few weeks earlier. *"The interstate freeway linking Duluth to the Twin Cities isn't slated for completion until 1964, but its effects are already being felt in the Northland."*

Those effects weren't on Will or Anna's minds as they made their way to the bridge. She knew what she wanted to say and he knew what he wanted to do. Nonetheless, they made nervous chitchat, their quiet banter mingling with the rushing St. Louis River nearby. Both content and enthralled in Will's company, Anna swung their joined hands and said more than she planned to, but everything she meant.

"Oh, Will—I love you."

She let go of his hand as both of hers flew up to her face. "No, no, no!" she cried. "I didn't mean to say that! I mean, I meant to say it, but . . . !"

Will's first reaction was to laugh, but he wasn't laughing at Anna. He was laughing because of how happy she made him feel. *We came here for the same reason,* he thought, smiling at her endearing exasperation.

"Say something, Will!"

He reached out and took her face in his hands. His mouth pressed on hers until the biting cold faded away. Then he kissed her forehead and led her to the side of the bridge.

"This is what I wanted to show you." He pointed to the names he had carved on the iron beam months earlier. "I love you too, Anna."

Anna ran her hand over the rusted steel, tracing a finger over each letter. First *WILL* then *ANNA*. She looked down into the dark brown water below, then to the slate peaks and neighboring forest where the leaves were fighting a losing battle against a cold wind that Anna wouldn't feel for most of the next six years.

"Now what, Will?" Her question wasn't demanding or impatient. She had simply made her choice.

"I need to tell you something," he began with an unexpected sadness that caught Anna off guard. She braced for some bombshell, but Will had none to lob. Instead, he told her about the day his friendship with Jake ended on the banks of Gap Lake. She saw the anguish in his face as he repeated Jake's parting words. *"You're dead to me. Will Travers is dead."*

"I've lived next to the Pearsons my whole life, Will," Anna said, pulling him close. "I've seen things too."

"But I had no right to tell him what I saw," Will replied with unmistakable torment.

"Maybe, maybe not. But I know no one in that house was ever happy."

Will looked at her. His anxiety, if not his doubt, subsided. "You asked, *now what,*" he said, spinning his class ring free from his finger and giving it to her. "Anna, I don't know where I'm going to be in a year—I just know that wherever I am, I want you with me."

She stared at the ring and turned it over, her finger outlining a small *19* and *60* on each side of a pale blue stone. The unknown future he spoke of suddenly became a little clearer to her, to both of them. "I want me with you too, Will. Always."

*

Anna took her hand off the beam's engraving and closed her eyes. The mid-summer sun warmed her face just like Will's kiss had many years earlier. Billy and Addie stood uncertainly a few feet away, neither of them willing to disturb their mother or her memories.

"That's when I knew, Addie." Anna reached into her pocket and fished out Will's ring. "I should have showed this to you a long time ago," she said, gesturing not so much to the ring as to her entire life with Will Travers. "I'm so sorry I didn't."

That's okay, Mom," Billy said. "I think we understand better now."

Addie studied the ring, now tarnished and faded. "Did it happen right here?"

Anna looked all around the bridge. The railroad tracks were gone and a bordering fence discouraged jumpers, but the changes hardly mattered. She smiled and nodded. "Right here."

"Then why did you ever marry Jake?"

"I don't know, honey," Anna replied evasively. "I wasn't thinking very clearly after Will died." That was a lie, of course. She knew exactly why she had married Jake Pearson.

Maybe Addie didn't want to consider the possibility that her mother might have loved Jake once. Or maybe she just didn't want to dampen an otherwise perfect weekend. Whichever, Addie dropped the subject.

"Should we go home?" Billy suggested. "I'm kinda hungry again."

"Actually, I have one more surprise," Anna remembered. "Mrs. Carson invited us over for supper tonight. She said Mr. Carson wanted to talk to you about haying next week. How does that sound?"

"You mean I still can?!"

"We're not moving, so I don't see why not. How about it, Addie? Interested in joining your brother?"

"Maybe," Addie shrugged.

I'll take a maybe, Anna decided as her children jogged ahead of her back to the Volkswagen. *Even if Jake finishes treatment, everything can still work out. And we might just have more time than I thought.*

Hi Dad,

Mom did it, she talked about you! I can still hardly believe it! She told us how nervous you were when you asked her to prom, how upset you were when your friendship with Jake ended, and how unsure you were about your future after high school. For the first time you seemed like you were a real person. And Mom sounded so happy when she talked about you!

She's been happy with her new car too, I just wish it wasn't a stick shift. What good is my permit without a car I actually know how to drive? Every night this week she made up some excuse to take us for a ride. Last night would have been four in a row, but Jake called right when we were walking out the door. Mom hardly said a word, but went for a walk around the Loop by herself after she got off the phone. She seemed fine when she got home, a little tired maybe.

You're not going to believe it, but I'm working with Shorty on the farm next week. We had supper with the Carsons last Sunday and I said yes when Mr. Carson asked me. I teased Mom later, told her that she set me up to say yes with all her stories about you. She laughed and said, "You're right, Addie. That was my plan all along." I did like being at the Carson's though. They didn't make me feel like a guest. It was more like being with family.

I forgot to tell you, we're going to the Twin Cities in a couple days with Sara and Renny! Mr. Farelli got Twins tickets for Shorty and Renny a few weeks ago. He was going to go with them, but he has a meeting with some bankers in Minneapolis that he said he can't miss. The best part is Sara and I get to explore all on our own. I can't wait!

I still miss you all the time, Dad.

Love,
Your daughter, Addie

14

IF THE LADY ADELINE IS PLEASED

The two and a half hour drive to Metropolitan Stadium Sunday morning hadn't sapped any of Renny's excitement. Fully aware of this, Mr. Farelli spoke to Billy rather than his own son when they pulled into the ballpark's expansive parking lot.

"We should be back by four, Billy. Meet us right here—Lot C. Sound good?"

"Yes, sir. We'll be fine."

"C'mon, Billy!" Renny urged him. "We can watch batting practice!" They quickly waved goodbye, then melted into the crowd heading for their seats on a perfect, blue sky afternoon.

"Are they going to be okay, Dad?" Sara asked.

"I can't think of a better place for two boys to be than at a ballgame. Renny won't miss a single pitch."

"That kid is obsessed with Rod Carew," Addie mumbled from the back seat.

"Tell me about it," Mr. Farelli said as he steered his burgundy Chevy Caprice back onto the freeway. Within minutes they arrived at their second destination.

"Where are you two headed?" Mr. Farelli inquired after waving to three men waiting for him by the front doors of a branch of *Marquette Bank*, one of the Twin Cities' leading financial institutions. Addie studied them and noticed Mr. Farelli's demeanor change to match theirs. He wasn't dressed in a suit like they were, but his pressed slacks and collared shirt weren't too far off.

"It's a secret," Sara grinned, sliding over to the driver's seat while Addie climbed up front to join her. "Dad, what time should we be back?"

Mr. Farelli nodded to the men, then glanced at his watch. "How about 3:30? Addie, there's a map in the glove compartment. Little Miss Sara here thinks she knows where she's going, but better have the map handy, just in case."

Sara made a face. "Better not leave those suits waiting, *Mister* Farelli," she said with a mocking tone.

Michael made a face of his own, though his expression quickly brightened. "A little louder and you might blow this for all of us, Sara," he teased. "Drive safe, honey. Have fun."

"So do you know how to get where we're going?" Addie asked as Sara turned onto a wide street.

"Kind of," Sara replied, stretching out the words. "We're going to *Lake Harriet*. From there we can bike to all sorts of cool places."

Addie found Lake Harriet on the map, along with two other lakes connected by a thin ribbon of green she guessed was some sort of path. "It looks like the street we're on will take us right to the lake."

"How far?"

"Maybe a mile," Addie said, preoccupied by something Mr. Farelli had mentioned minutes earlier. "What did your dad mean—*you might blow this for all of us*?"

"Who knows? Bank stuff probably."

"Seemed important."

"Everything my dad does is *so* important," Sara remarked with an eye roll. "It's all he ever talks about—bank this and bank that." Her nonchalance was vintage Sara, but Addie wasn't convinced.

"There's Harriet!" Sara exclaimed. "Isn't she beautiful?!"

The only other lake of its size Addie had ever spent any time at was Fern Lake, a few miles south of Lost Elm. Fern Lake had a beach, picnic areas and ballparks, but most of its lakefront was privately owned. Not Harriet or any of Minneapolis' other dozen lakes. No home could lay claim to any of their shoreline. They were public lakes for the public's welfare.

Addie didn't know any of this as she lifted a bike off the back rack, anxious to join the hordes of people circling the lake's paved path. Her excitement felt a little out of place as she began peddling, but not unwelcome. *I always feel this way when I'm with Sara.* Soon she spotted small sailboats skimming along the water, runners jogging on one of the lake's two paths and stately homes just outside the parkway. Addie was in a strange land, but she didn't feel like a stranger as they headed north and linked up with another lake, this one named *Calhoun*. Instead, she wondered if other people had once felt like she did before escaping to the city and finding acceptance waiting for them.

"Hungry, Addie?!" Sara hollered. "There's a food stand up ahead!" A quarter mile further, on the north side of Calhoun, the girls dismounted. The area was humming with activity. The food stand sold typical summer fare, while nearby canoes and small dinghies were available to rent by the hour.

"Why don't they rent those somewhere else?" Addie remarked after they had each bought an ice cream cone. She gestured to dozens of watercraft anchored to shore. "It's really crowded here."

"Two lakes for the price of one," Sara explained. "Calhoun hooks up with *Lake of the Isles* right over there." She pointed to a narrow channel of water beneath a busy road.

"Can you hold this for a sec?" Addie held out her cone to Sara. "I need to use the restroom." She walked around the side of the building, but not before Sara saw her retrieve a small notepad from her back pocket. Addie returned a minute later with the notepad safely tucked away again. Sara was about to ask what was in it but had a better idea.

"Should we rent a canoe?"

"We didn't bring our swimsuits," Addie protested, gesturing to her outfit. She was wearing the same white shorts she had on the first day they went shopping together in Wood City, but this time the pair was accompanied by a pale green sleeveless top that she didn't want to get wet.

"You're in good hands," Sara laughed. "Besides," she added, spinning around to show off her golden yellow sundress, "I don't want to get wet either."

Five minutes and five dollars later, they paddled into the tunnel bound for Lake of the Isles. Just as quickly, the humanity that surrounded them melted away. Addie raised her head to the sky and felt the sun's warm rays. Sara let the canoe drift on its own as the lake spread out before them.

"You like it here, don't you, Addie?"

"I know we just got here, but I feel more like myself. Does that sound crazy?"

"Not at all. Maybe you're just answering your own little *Call of the Wild.*"

"Very funny," Addie smirked. "I'm not even close to finishing that book."

"Doesn't matter. The comparison fits."

"Okay, *Little Miss Sara*. What in the world you're talking about?"

"I'm talking about you, Addie! You've been fighting someone or something ever since your dad got on that plane years ago, the same way Buck did when he was stolen from Judge Miller."

"Hey, I remember Judge Miller!"

"I should hope so. He shows up on page one." Sara paddled the canoe away from shore toward a nearby island. "Difference is, you have a chance to do what Buck never could."

"What's that?"

"Let go—not just be the girl who says *bullcrap* to everything."

"Well, that is kind of my motto," Addie joked.

"It doesn't have to be," Sara insisted. "Think about it—that day we listened to music in my room, when we went to Jensen's instead of following Jake into the bar, even the search for those bandanas in the Bog. We did all that together."

"I can't get my hopes up, Sara."

"Why not?! What makes you think you don't deserve to?"

Sara's words tugged at Addie, but so did Mr. Carson's. "*Lost Elm's not a big town. Everybody knows everybody around here.*" The anonymity of Minneapolis had already charmed her—a city where Addie could be herself without small-town minds making their small-town judgments.

"How'd you get so smart?"

"I read a lot," Sara laughed, splashing Addie with her oar. "Now come on, start paddling. We're going around that big island up ahead, then back to the bikes. There's something else I want to show you."

Thirty minutes later the girls had paddled back to Lake Calhoun and mounted their bikes. Sara led Addie toward a road teeming with cars. Despite the congestion, the cars gave them a wide berth. Seven blocks later they locked their bikes to a slender tree and walked another block to a busy intersection—Hennepin Avenue and Lake Street.

"I know it's the farthest thing from the Bog you could ever imagine, but what do you think?!" Sara asked, sweeping her arm around to every corner of the crossing.

"Where are we?"

"The coolest place in Minnesota—this is *Uptown*!"

Addie understood immediately why Sara liked it so much. It had everything her friend loved. People sold artwork on the sidewalks, competing bookstores crawled with customers and music pulsed all around them. Despite all the commerce, Uptown was really a vestige of the Counterculture Movement of the late 1960's. Rents were cheap, the music raw and real, the stores local and everyone free to be themselves.

"Come on, Addie! Let's explore!"

Sara skipped across the intersection as the light turned red. Traffic momentarily separated the girls as a cluster of teenage boys swarmed around Sara. She ignored them and made a face instead, sticking her tongue out and rolling her eyes. Addie laughed but felt something else too—jealousy. *But jealous of who?* By the time she re-joined Sara, the boys had moved on.

She led Addie up the sidewalk and talked about her future—art school in Minneapolis, living her own life. "You should move here after high school, Addie! You know you'd love it."

Addie listened, but noticed something else too. Every male who passed them gave Sara a quick but obvious glance. *I can't blame them*, she thought. *Sara's beautiful.*

"Did I say something wrong, Addie?"

"Hmm?"

"Did I say something wrong? You had the strangest look on your face a second ago."

"I was just thinking about the rest of the summer," Addie fibbed. "It's nice to have something to look forward to for a change."

"I told you! You deserve it!" Sara said, squeezing Addie's hands. She looked around to get her bearings. "Let's bike a little more then head back to the car. That should give us plenty of time before we have to pick up my dad."

Addie's feelings about Minneapolis burned brightly as they made their way back to the car, but didn't compare with her affection for Sara. She had gotten exactly what she'd been promised—a great day.

*

The last hour home from Minneapolis was a quiet one. Only a hushed conversation in the front seat between Sara and her father broke the silence. Jammed in the backseat with Billy and Renny, Addie sorted through her unexpected feelings about the day. Not all of it seemed real,

159

nor was she sure her feelings would last, but that hardly mattered. Addie only knew that her time with Sara had been special. Other truths that might have been flushed free from her heart would have to wait. They were almost home.

Renny stirred as the car braked at the bottom of the freeway exit to Lost Elm, a scorecard from the game still clutched in his hand. Inning after inning, he and Billy had charted the Twins 15-0 drubbing of the Mariners in case anyone wanted a summary on the way home. No one did, though that hadn't discouraged Renny.

"Sorry ya missed the game, Sara?" he asked as they turned onto Halverson Road.

"A little. How'd your man do today?"

"1 for 3. Walked twice, scored twice."

"Is he still over .400, Bud?" his father asked as he pulled the car into the driveway.

"401!" Renny exclaimed, looking around for anything close to his level of enthusiasm. Instead, all four doors opened simultaneously.

"Thanks for the tickets, Mr. Farelli," Billy yawned. "I had a lot of fun."

"You're welcome, Billy," he replied, removing the two bikes mounted on a rack attached to the car's trunk. "But I should be thanking you. Renny would have never forgiven me if he missed the game."

See you tomorrow, Ren?"

"Sure thing, Billy. I told you, didn't I? He's gonna do it!" And with that unwavering certainty, Renny and his father turned in. Billy headed home too, leaving Addie and Sara alone together in the driveway.

"I had the best day, Sara," Addie remarked shyly. "It was exactly what I was hoping for."

"Then if the Lady Adeline is pleased," Sara said with a low bow, "I have fulfilled my duties for the day."

"You have, milady," Addie nodded playfully.

Before Sara turned to go, Addie pressed a scrap of paper in her hand. "I wrote this today, kind of a thank you for everything. I hope you like it."

They quickly parted but remained linked by the sweet, unfathomable connection of their mutual friendship. Sara lingered in the driveway after Addie walked home, unfolding the piece of paper and reading it by the waning crescent moon. A faint smile, visible to no one but real nonetheless, tugged at the corners of her mouth as she read:

160

"Lies and bottles and slashes in slate,
Fade fast like some bygone era,
Swapped for lakes of lively blue,
Though none can rival you, Sara. "

Addie had never written anyone a poem before. *But if I can't write one for Sara, who could I write one for?* She shook her head at the idea of sharing her private thoughts with anyone a month ago. *Then again, I used to walk into the trailer ready to fight Jake every single day.*

"Not anymore." Addie announced as she opened the trailer's inner door. Billy and Anna were seated at the kitchen table, their expressions shrouded. "What's wrong with you two? You look like you've seen . . ."

"Jake, honey," Anna murmured.

"I was going to say a ghost," Addie snickered. "But Jake works too."

They didn't laugh at Addie's joke. Instead, Anna looked past her into the living room.

"Hello, Addie," a voice behind her rumbled. "Did you have a nice day?" She spun around as a hulking shape stepped into the light. Jake was home.

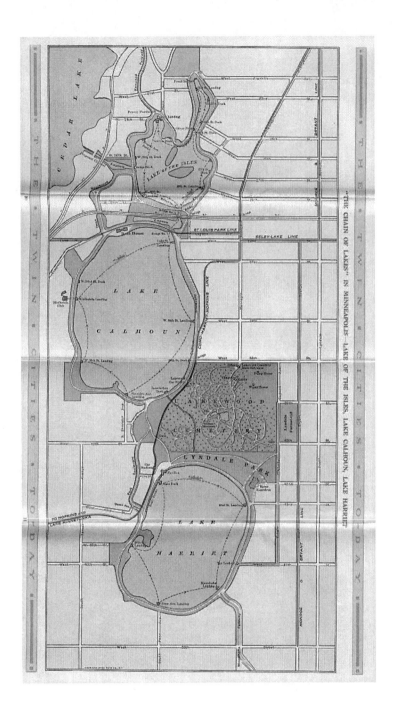

"THE CHAIN OF LAKES" IN MINNEAPOLIS: LAKE OF THE ISLES, LAKE CALHOUN, LAKE HARRIET

162

15
Some Sort of Salvation

The same day Billy and Addie journeyed to Minneapolis, Jake abruptly left treatment. He had been searching for some kind of relief from the moment he entered Miller-Dwan, but after eleven agitated days Jake knew he wouldn't find any there. Instead, his thirst only grew.

The drive back to Lost Elm was a sweaty blur. He fumbled with his dad's house keys before opening the side door, his eyes immediately locking onto the telephone. *"We're sorry; you have reached a number that has been disconnected. . ."*

"Don't try to be strong," the doctors counseled him before he left. *"Throw away every temptation."* Racing from room to room, Jake gathered a dizzying array of alcohol in the kitchen sink, uncorking and emptying every bottle, afraid if he paused for even a second one might find its way to his mouth.

He didn't stop there. As Addie and Sara began their looping ride around Lake Harriet, he emerged from a small shed in the back yard carrying an armful of burlap bags Ron Pearson had collected from his years working at the feed mill. Gutting every closet and bedroom, Jake wasted little time on sentiment. Sacks of clothing, bedding, old magazines and just plain junk bulged from the back of his dad's truck. It took three hours and three trips to the Salvation Army in Wood City before the living room and bedrooms were mostly bare.

Now what? Jake wondered as he drove past the ruins of the Northern Pacific Railroad sign. He gave the blackened billboard only a quick glance, but the sting of his scarred, healing forearms confirmed the truth of that painful night. With no more trips to make, Jake turned automatically into the Junction's parking lot, shut off the engine and stepped out of the truck.

"What the heck ya doing, Jake?" a voice behind him asked. "You know we're closed Sunday."

Jake spun around to find Bud tossing bags of Saturday night's empties into the Junction's dumpster. The two men stared at one another for a moment, each waiting for some sort of explanation. Jake blinked, suddenly comprehending where he was. The counselors at Miller-Dwan had warned him this might happen.

"Hi, Bud. I, ah . . . thought I mighta left my wallet here a few weeks ago."

"A few weeks? Gonna be hard to backtrack that far, ain't it?" Bud remarked, pitching the last bag over the side. "Say, I was sorry to hear about yer dad. He was a good guy."

Not if you knew him, Jake thought.

"Let me buy you a beer. In honor of Ron."

Jake's mouth watered. "I gotta mow the lawn, Bud. Maybe some other time." He rushed back to his truck and sped away.

The old bartender took Jake's snub in stride. He had seen every kind of drunk come and go over the years, witnessed all their private battles. If they asked him for a drink, he mixed them a drink. If they wanted a beer, he poured them a beer. It was all the same to Bud. If they never returned, he wished them well. *But that's just it,* he accepted with a shrug. *They always come back.*

*

Jake hadn't planned on mowing his father's lawn. Whether it was dumb luck or inspired desperation, the idea simply popped into his head as he was being pulled like a magnet back into the Junction. That the grass didn't need cutting hardly mattered. Jake had found a reason to leave. He wheeled the mower out of the shed and gassed it up, but it wasn't until he had circled the yard a few times that his world came back into focus. *"When you're struggling, find something to do,"* a Miller-Dwan counselor had suggested. *"And keep doing it until you feel better."*

As two laps became three, then four, the anxious perspiration dotting Jake's face was replaced by the sweat of real exertion. Doing something as simple as cutting the grass, then seeing the job to completion, instilled something in Jake that he hadn't felt in years—real hope. Why now, he didn't know. *And why hope?* He had mowed the unkempt lawn inside the Loop hundreds of times but always with the incentive of a beer afterward. Hell, even during. This time, inexplicably, finishing the job seemed to be its own reward.

Jake decided to clean and organize the small shed next, but seeing more of his father's junk only depressed him. Still, the job had to be done. Soon the fresh cut grass was covered with tarps, tools and other odds and ends Ron Pearson had accumulated over the years. It wasn't until Jake reached a shelf of paint cans that he stopped to catch his breath. That's when an idea struck him.

He stumbled out of the shed and raced into the house, his feet literally skidding down the basement steps. Stacks of more useless items were piled on the concrete floor as Jake rooted around the shelves lining the basement's dank walls. *My brushes have to be around here somewhere! The last time I saw them I . . .* Then he remembered. They were in the trailer. Jake grabbed the keys from the kitchen table and headed for Halverson Road before he could talk himself out of going.

At the same time Addie was lost in thought on her way home from the Twin Cities, Jake parked his dad's truck in front of the billboard. He sifted through the broken glass, gently kicking here and there until he uncovered a small white cube. It was a single bead with the letter *A* inscribed on it. Searching further, four other beads revealed themselves. Jake rolled them around his hand, then set out for the trailer on foot. He had no idea what kind of greeting he might receive or who would be there when he arrived, but he braced himself for the worst.

*

"What the hell, Mom!" Addie snarled as Jake emerged from the shadows of the living room.

Anna motioned for Addie to calm down but it wasn't her usual appeal for the sake of one more truce between her husband and her daughter. Instead, she wore an expression of detached pity for Jake. Even so, Addie couldn't hold her tongue.

"Well, are you gonna say something?!"

Jake hadn't thought of what he might say if someone answered the door. Instead, he had hoped no one would be home so he could slip in, find his brushes and leave unnoticed. But Addie was right—he had to say something.

"Can I get you anything, Jake?" Anna asked. He waved her off with a measure of courtesy she'd never seen from him before.

"Have you ever tried to run from something," he began, his face growing taut as he tried to explain himself. "But you just couldn't quite get away?"

Anna and her children exchanged confused looks as Jake gazed out the living room window.

"I'm allergic to bees, did you know that? I got stung once when I was little, almost died. I had nightmares all the time after that. In every one I could never outrun those bees."

"Why did you leave Miller-Dwan, Jake?" Anna probed gently.

"I've been a lousy husband, a lousy father," he replied, seemingly not hearing her question. No one spoke a word in his defense, though Addie stiffened at his use of the word *father*. He smiled meekly at their silence. "I've been running for a long time—into the Bog, the Junction, Wood City. As long as I had somewhere to run, no bees ever caught up with me."

"Bees, Jake? What do you mean?"

"People," Jake whispered. "Whenever I think about my mom leaving it still seems like it was just yesterday. My dad was mad all the time after that. And then Will died before I had a chance to . . ." He was going to say, *make things right*, but the words caught in his throat.

"I understand that," Anna acknowledged. "But why did you leave treatment?" Billy and Addie braced themselves waiting for his response, but Jake withdrew to the couch instead.

"I know what you're all thinking. I didn't even make it two weeks. But have you ever had a moment when things finally made sense and you couldn't wait one more day to start your life again?"

Anna knew exactly what Jake was talking about. Whatever the reason—his absence, her new car or something else—she had begun to reclaim her lost life. But now Jake was back, telling her he had experienced the same thing.

"Can you really do this on your own, Jake? Because it won't be with my help, and I think you're going to need all the help you can get."

Jake absorbed the meaning in her words, then remembered the Miller-Dwan staff's final bit of advice: *"Don't beg your way back home. They probably won't want you there."*

"I spent a week listening to people just like me—complainers. Then when it was my turn, they practically cheered me on." He looked at Anna and shrugged. "I don't know if I can do it on my own, but I sure couldn't

166

do it there. No one really wanted to get better. They just wanted someone to blame. I've done that long enough."

While Jake spoke, Billy and Addie unconsciously leaned forward in a protective posture. But his words sank in.

"It's late, Jake," Anna said, glancing at the kitchen clock. "We have to be up early tomorrow." She handed him the duffel bag he had filled before Billy and Addie got home. "Do you need a ride somewhere?"

"No, I've got my dad's truck."

"Where?" Addie asked suspiciously. "I didn't see it parked on the Loop."

"I'm, uh . . . it's down the road . . . by the . . ."

"By the billboard?!"

"It's not what you think, Addie." He reached into his pocket and pulled out five small beads. They were smeared with ash and mud, but each letter of her name was still visible. "Here," he said, holding them out to her. "I found these, figured you'd want them back."

Addie stared at Sara's broken gift, turning each bead over in the palm of her hand. A confused, "thanks," was all she could muster.

Jake accepted her appreciation with a small nod. "I'll be at my dad's, Anna. There's plenty to do there. The people at Miller-Dwan told me to keep busy."

"Sure," she nodded, doubtful that the scene of so much of Jake's pain would be good for him. "Do what you have to do."

"Before I go, there's something I forgot in the hallway closet," he said, suddenly self-conscious. "Do you mind?"

Anna stepped aside and gestured down the hall. Three pair of eyes watched Jake reach into the far corner of the hallway closet and discreetly pull out a small clutch of old paintbrushes and stuff them in his bag.

"If you need anything just give me a . . ." Then he remembered Anna's words two weeks ago, *"It won't ring, Jake. Ron cut the line."* He took a deep breath. "Well, just let me know."

"We'll be fine," she replied, resisting the urge to make him the same offer.

Hearing her simple declaration and nothing more, Jake left. Whether he meant every word or intended to disappear into a bottle again, no one knew. But his confession had smacked of an honesty they couldn't easily dismiss. Addie tried, though she was distracted by what he had put in his bag. *Since when does Jake paint?*

*

He hadn't in nearly twenty years. A talent cultivated as a teenager, painting had been Jake's refuge until the fateful summer of 1959. Too embarrassed to submit himself to his father's criticism, he toiled in secret in the high school's vast art room. A few times a week he snuck across the street to paint, his eyes darting back and forth from the canvas to his subjects—usually pictures from one of the library's stacks of *Look* or *Life* magazine. The world melted away when Jake held a brush in his hand. His anger, the hostility, even the memory of Ron Pearson's hand across his mother's face—all gone.

He eventually shared some of his artwork, but like Addie's depot poems, the paintings' artist remained a local mystery. By the end of Jake's junior year, numerous businesses in Lost Elm had anonymous gifts hanging in their lobbies or behind their cash registers. No two were alike, but each complimented the establishments they hung in. The bank sported a likeness of an antique counting scale. The courthouse received a portrait of blind justice. Even Harold Hinkum found a painting of colorful oil cans waiting for him at his service station one morning.

Sadly, Jake's clandestine hobby ended the same day he collided with his mother on the sidewalk in front of the house in Duluth, the one belonging to the stranger who had asked her, *"When are you going to leave him, Betts? Live here with me?"* With blood from the back of his head drying on his hands and steering wheel, Jake had raced back to Lost Elm. The blood was the same shade he'd used for the water tower and its crimson-coned cap—a painting, when finished, he had planned to sneak into Lost Elm's municipal building.

But when school began a month later, the unfinished work still sat on an easel in the middle of the art room, discovered by a confused first-year teacher who couldn't understand why anyone would slash the canvas of such a fine painting. Regardless, Jake's unclaimed *Water Tower* was tossed into the school's dumpster. His desire to paint was, like Betty Pearson, apparently gone for good.

In the split-second after Jake's hand grasped his brushes in the trailer's hallway closet, a long lost desire seized him. All he could do was utter a hasty goodbye before running the entire way back to his dad's truck parked next to the billboard.

Back in town, Jake found his way into the school through an unlocked window and rummaged around the art room until he had gathered an oval palette and enough half-used tubes of paint to make a go of it. Squeezing himself out the same window, Jake noticed that the alley light behind his dad's house was casting a glow on an old door he'd taken out of the shed a few hours earlier. With pounding heart, Jake lugged it into the basement and laid it across two old sawhorses. After cleaning his brushes in the laundry basin and squirting a sample of colors on his palette, he was ready to begin.

Whatever saliva was left in his mouth evaporated. Jake's hands trembled as he dipped the brush into a blot of paint. Whether it was nerves or the pangs of withdrawal, Jake didn't know. But neither mattered, for he was about to paint for the first time in what felt like forever, hoping he might have found some sort of salvation.

16
WHEN YOU'RE DEAD

Helen Carson called down to the Pearsons' trailer Sunday evening, a few hours before Billy and Addie returned from Minneapolis. After several rings, Anna answered.

"What do you think about having breakfast together tomorrow?" Helen suggested. "A big meal to kick off the first week of haying. It might be a nice way to, I don't know, start the transition?"

The transition. Anna had thought of little else all day. "Breakfast sounds wonderful, Helen."

Billy and Addie grumbled loudly when she woke them at 6:30 the next morning. But soon Monday became Tuesday, then Wednesday. By Friday, July 15th—after five straight mornings eating breakfast with the Carsons—invited guests felt more like family. Billy would set the table and Addie would clear it. Every day they washed and dried the dishes while the adults drank coffee on the screen porch.

Whether it was the routine of haying with Mr. Carson or the prospect of another one of Mrs. Carson's hearty breakfasts, Billy and Addie both woke early Saturday. They were dressed and ready to go when Anna emerged from her bedroom. Despite the heavy morning air, she was wrapped in a thick bathrobe.

"Do you think you'll have to work today?" she wondered sleepily. "It rained most of the night."

Right on cue, the phone rang. Billy grabbed it, his expression changing quickly from optimism to disappointment. He nodded, his face brightening again. "Okay, Mr. Carson, see ya soon!"

"Tell me the hay's too wet to bale today, Shorty?" Addie said in a vain attempt to loosen her aching shoulders.

Billy hung up the phone and headed for the door. "Yup."

"Then where are you going?"

Billy's face spread into a wide grin. "To breakfast."

"You two go on without me."

Addie frowned. "You okay, Mom?"

"I'm perfect, honey," she replied, patting Addie's cheek. "Tell Virgil and Helen you're all theirs today."

"Are you sure?" Billy asked her.

Anna nodded as they slipped on their shoes and hustled out the door. *It's working,* she told herself. *Just the way I planned.*

*

Mr. Carson sifted through a damp patch of cut hay and mulled over the past few days. The protests he had expected from Addie never materialized. She wasn't enthusiastic about the work, but Mr. Carson had labored on a farm too long not to recognize the satisfied expression of a job well done. By the end of the week it was written all over the girl's face.

Addie was certain she had betrayed nothing. But something akin to the same calm Jake found when he circled his father's yard with a lawnmower came over her too. The repetitious loading and unloading of the wagon quieted her troubled mind. The past and present—as well as their uncertain future—ceased to be the constant distraction it had become.

Naturally, Addie was determined not only to keep up with her brother, but outdo him as well. She did, though they both wilted under the withering July sun in their jeans and long-sleeved shirts. Billy didn't care. He was just happy to be back on the farm.

Virgil and Helen were happy too. It had been only the two of them on the farm for almost a decade. In all that time, they'd forgotten how much they enjoyed having a full house. So despite Saturday's wet hay, another breakfast invitation seemed fitting. But Billy and Addie weren't the only ones who needed the farm. Jake did too.

*

He had done nothing but paint all week. One old door quickly turned into two more. His first try, a rugged mountain scene, was followed by Duluth's aerial lift bridge, then a rough likeness of a Great Lakes ore carrier. By Thursday, when Anna, Billy and Addie were sitting down to another breakfast with the Carsons, Jake had painted over each door twice.

He stuck with it, growing more pleased with each attempt. But the old spark was absent—the intensity Jake used to have for painting that he didn't feel seventeen long years later. Without it he grew frantic and, eventually, thirsty.

Between the blistering heat and his increasing agitation, Jake soaked through the thin sheets in his dad's guest room night after night. Restless sleep ended when his cravings returned—a feverish nausea that sent him hurtling to the toilet. Each time he was reminded of his father and their pathetic waltz to the bathroom. But unlike Ron Pearson, what came up for Jake was mostly water and bile. He'd hardly eaten since leaving Miller-Dwan.

As Billy and Addie mounted the hay wagon Friday morning, Jake risked a trip to Paulette's Café. The restaurant was dangerously close to the Junction, but what else could he do? He needed food.

He may as well have walked into the Junction, for there at the café counter was Bud and three of the bar's regulars. Jake's eyes fell to the floor when they paused between mouthfuls of food to offer their garbled greetings. He declined the stool next to Bud, slipping instead into a narrow booth in the back of the restaurant.

His scrambled eggs, toast and hash browns went untouched as he waited for Bud to leave, knowing the others would follow him across the street to the Junction. When they finally did, Jake took a few halfhearted bites before dropping his fork onto the plate. His food had gone cold.

He sifted through his wallet and paid with the last few dollars he had left. Ron Pearson's estate, such as it was, was tied up in court pending the discovery of a will. Jake assumed he and his sister would split whatever their father might have, but until a will materialized he had nothing to live on.

Leaving Paulette's with a doggie bag in hand, Jake decided to go to the bank and see if he had any money left in his savings account, though he knew that his balance was likely near zero. When he reached the far curb he saw Anna inside, approaching the exit. After dashing half a block down the sidewalk, Jake turned and saw her get into an unfamiliar green Volkswagen. The car puttered to life and eased onto 3rd Street, apparently heading for Wood City. Jake looked at the bank clock—10:45 am—and thought about following her, but a counselor's words rang in his ears, *"She probably won't want to see you."* Nevertheless, he struggled mightily against the impulse. But after a few hurried steps across the street, he slowed to a walk. *Now what?*

Cars sped to and fro through the intersection, all going somewhere. Not Jake. One hundred feet from the Junction, he was literally standing at a crossroads. As if snapping out of trance, Jake blinked and looked up at the water tower. *For chrissakes, how did I miss that?!* He hurried off for his dad's house at a jog, turning around every few seconds to make sure it was still there. *Where else would it be?*

After devouring his cold breakfast at the kitchen table, Jake plunged into the basement. He grabbed a whitewashed door, leaned it vertically against the wall and squirted blobs of red and gray paint on his palette. Soon the red-coned top of the water tower began to take shape. With silent tears streaming down his face, he remembered the last painting that had mattered to him. But this time Jake knew he would finish it.

*

Anna scarcely slept after Billy and Addie left for the farm Saturday morning. A dull ache right below her ribs kept her awake. "You won't find the pain, Mrs. Pearson," she'd been told the day before at a morning appointment at Wood City Memorial Hospital. "It's too deep." Still, her renewed energy and appetite had been cause for hope. "I'm sorry, ma'am. We knew that would be temporary. I hope you were able to take advantage of it while it's lasted."

Anna put her robe back on and shuffled into the bathroom. Above the sink an image that had become more unrecognizable every new day stared back at her through the mirror. The whites of her eyes were covered by a filmy, yellow hue. A once smooth, soft face was creased with lines that deepened daily. *Maybe a shower will help.*

Warm water gushed into the tub as Anna closed the shower curtain. Simultaneously, a sharp pain stabbed at her abdomen. She clutched the curtain for support and pulled herself over to the toilet seat. As the pain ebbed, Anna was seized by a crushing fear that threatened to squeeze the air from her lungs all over again. *What happens next? To me? To the kids?!* Two questions, though Anna had ignored the one she couldn't control. Until now.

She undid the sash of her bathrobe and stepped in front of the mirror again to examine herself. Her collar bones protruded alarmingly. Fragile skin strained against protruding ribs. And across Anna's face new strands of gray hair stood in stark contrast against a full head of once lustrous brown, now faded and dry. Mercifully, the shower's steam fogged over her reflection which, like the woman herself, seemed to disappear.

Anna buried her head under the shower and let the hot water flow down her face and neck. She bent gingerly at the waist, allowing a steady stream to target her lower back, momentarily easing an ache that never quite left her. After lathering her head with shampoo, Anna let the water wash over her again, watching the soapy bubbles meander between her toes before vanishing down the drain.

I'm only 35! she thought frantically. *When I'm gone, who will know I was ever here?!* But then she looked up from her feet and placed a hand over her flat belly. Fingers gently traced over the faint lines where her skin had been stretched by two pregnancies—by Addie and Billy.

"Enough!"

Anna shut off the water and flung open the shower curtain. She returned to the sink and wiped her hand across the steamy mirror. A brush was savagely pulled through wet hair until the snarls were freed. Tears were dried from eyes that blazed with fear. The hairbrush fell to the floor and she braced herself against the sink.

"You're done crying, do you hear me?! You can cry when you're dead!"

She was wrong. One final tear would come, though when it did Anna's work would be done.

*

Despite their mother's desperation, Billy and Addie didn't consciously suspect anything was wrong inside the Loop. Instead, they grew more and more accustomed to life and work on the farm. Addie had farther to go than Billy to find comfort there, but the pleasant weather and Mr. Carson helped her every step of the way. He knew she wouldn't get there immediately, however.

"She can spot a phony a mile away," he had told Anna over the phone. "If she thinks I'm pushing the farm on her, she might leave. And like you said, it's not time yet." But when Mr. Carson saw Addie join her brother for Saturday morning breakfast, he decided the time was right—and he would use the wet hay to his advantage.

"Like I told Billy on the phone, we can't hay today. But that doesn't mean there's not work to do." Billy and Addie looked at each other and nodded, thinking his words were their cue to clear the table and wash the dishes. They reached for their plates and utensils, but the farmer waved them off. "I've got something else in mind. I want to show you how to rake the fields."

Addie groaned. *Rake the fields? That'll take days!*

"Come along, Miss Pearson," Mr. Carson replied mischievously. "Before you pass out from shock."

Mrs. Carson swatted her husband's backside as he led Billy and Addie down the porch steps. When the trio disappeared around the corner of the house she began clearing the table with a self-satisfied expression on her face. *Breakfast together had been a very good idea.*

*

Ranger was a tired, happy dog. The girl and boy from down the hill had visited him day after day, and when they traveled around the wide fields with his master, he happily chased the wagon wherever it went. But what Ranger did more than anything else was look to the girl for her approval, some sign that she was happy to see him too.

The dog rested under the shade of a tall pine as his master approached, followed closely by the boy. The girl, her eyes squinting with some unknown resentment, lingered behind. Ranger's head tilted in confusion when she failed to greet him.

When they reached the edge of the upper field, Mr. Carson grabbed a garden rake that was leaning against the shed. "You didn't think I was going to make you use one of these, did you?"

"Maybe," Addie replied sheepishly. Billy laughed, but Addie cut him off. "You did too, Shorty."

What could have descended into another name-calling argument was nimbly avoided by Mr. Carson. He didn't give Billy a chance to get angry. Instead, he told them each to open one of the shed's double doors.

"This is the hay rake," Mr. Carson said, pointing inside. "And that is a tedder."

Billy and Addie circled both contraptions as Mr. Carson wandered off to the barn. A few minutes later he returned with the tractor, backing it up to within inches of the tedder's hitch. He explained how the tedder's job was to spread the hay, allowing it to dry more quickly than if it were left where it lay. "Time's important. The sooner you two go over the fields with the rake and tedder, the sooner we get the hay baled so the second crop can start growing."

Billy and Addie looked at each other in confusion, but said nothing. Mr. Carson described how the rake's spoked wheels would spin the scattered hay back into rows for the baler to scoop up.

"So who's driving first?" he asked. Both were sure they had misheard him. "Nobody? Okay, how about this—Addie drives a lap, then it's your turn, Billy. Back and forth. Go over the fields with the tedder today and rake it tomorrow. Then we'll bale again Monday. Sound fair?"

Addie's wide smile told Mr. Carson everything he needed to know. Like the bales in the rapidly filling barn, she was hooked. Addie was no farm girl, he knew that much. *But she likes being treated like an adult, given adult responsibilities.* Having survived three bitter years in the Bog, Mr. Carson could appreciate that.

Ranger remained in the cool shade throughout the humans' jabbering. But after seeing the girl's changed expression, he trotted over to her. She obliged him with a scratch beneath his chin. Her attention was brief, however. After giving Ranger a quick pat on the head, the girl climbed onto his master's noisy, metal . . . whatever it was.

✳

The next two days—July 16th and 17th—played out just as Mr. Carson said they would. Back and forth, Addie and Billy took turns driving in ever-shrinking circles around the upper and lower fields. They pulled the tedder Saturday, the hay rake on Sunday.

During their first half-dozen laps, Mr. Carson stood on the running board while whoever wasn't driving sat on one of the broad metal flaps crowning each tire. Neither had mastered driving the tractor right away, but Mr. Carson never gave them a chance to give up. He simply said, "Try again."

His patience and their persistence paid off. After just one demonstration lap Sunday morning Mr. Carson told Billy and Addie that they were on their own. "You'll be fine," he said without a trace of concern. "Let's make it three laps in a row today, then switch."

They took his confidence to heart. Few words passed between them as they focused on the work. Hours later, after the raking was complete, Addie's simple statement—*"You were right, Shorty! It's not so bad up here!"*—spoke volumes. Her words came out much louder than she intended, their ears still ringing from a long weekend spent on the noisy Farmall.

Maybe that's why they didn't hear or see the truck come up the Carsons' long driveway. But when the front porch and two waiting glasses of lemonade came into view, Billy and Addie both saw a large man shake hands with Mr. Carson. The man waved nervously in their direction before hopping into his truck and driving away.

"Why was Jake here?!" Addie snarled.

Mr. Carson looked past her to the screen porch. His wounded eyes locked onto Helen's. She shrugged sympathetically. *It's your decision, Virgil,* her expression communicated. *I'll support you either way.*

"He was looking for work, Addie."

"Yeah, right," she snorted derisively. "Like that would ever happen."

Mr. Carson thought about the long-rusting wreck in the corner of his upper field, then looked back and forth from Billy to Addie, two people he had grown so fond of—come to love, even. He knew his next words could change everything.

"I'm going to give Jake a chance, Addie. I have to."

Sunday, July 17th

Hi Dad,

It's me, Addie.

Our trip to Minneapolis turned out even better than I imagined. I felt so free there. Sara showed me places she knew I'd like, even if I didn't know it yet myself. But regardless of how close we were that day, things haven't felt the same since.

Maybe that's not fair to say. I've been busy on the farm and Sara and her family have been coming and going all week. But whenever I call her she seems like she's in a hurry to get off the phone. I hope giving her that poem wasn't a mistake. Maybe I'll go over to her house tomorrow. That's better than making another phone call.

You're not going to believe it, Dad, but Mom got what she wanted. She got me on the farm! I understand now what Shorty was trying to tell me last month, though. Mr. and Mrs. Carson are nice people. And there's something about that farm. I feel calm up there.

Correction: I used to feel calm. For some reason Mr. Carson is going to let Jake work with us tomorrow. With me! I understand what he said, wishing he would have talked to his father before he punched him that night in the Junction a long time ago. But what's that got to do with me and Shorty? Jake's not our Dad and he's not our problem! All Mr. Carson said was that everyone deserves a second chance. Second chance?! Jake's had a million of them!

We didn't stick around the farm for long after Jake left. Mrs. Carson had a snack waiting for us on the porch, but I just sat there while Mr. Carson explained his decision. I could see that Shorty wanted to understand, but even he looked disappointed.

Mom wasn't too happy either. She was on the phone with Mr. Carson when we got home, but he did most of the talking. The only thing I heard her tell him was that she understood why he was letting Jake work there, though his reasons couldn't change what they had agreed to last Christmas. When I asked Mom, "What agreement?" she just said she wants us to keep working, Jake or no Jake.

179

Jake and I can't be in the same room together for more than five minutes. How are we going to make it through an entire day on the same hay wagon?

It's late, Dad. I've got to get to bed if I'm going make it through tomorrow. It's supposed to be another hot one. I told Shorty I'm skipping breakfast with the Carsons so I can sleep in, but honestly I just don't feel like it.

I still miss you all the time.

Love,
Your daughter, Addie

17

FORGIVENESS, FOR STARTERS

Jake's painting of Lost Elm's water tower turned out better than he could have hoped. Hour after hour for a day and a half he ran back and forth from the basement to the yard observing how the sunlight and shadows played across the water tower's tank and supporting framework. Finally finished, he lugged the painting into the kitchen and promptly fell fast asleep on the couch. Even an overnight downpour couldn't rouse him. Flashes of lightning passed unseen, cracks of thunder went unheard. But when Jake woke the next day, he was met by a ravenous hunger.

There was hardly any food left in the house to quell his appetite. He found a sleeve of stale crackers in the cupboard and numbly nibbled on them while gazing intently at his creation. *It's like a Hopper painting,* he thought.

Edward Hopper, an artist Jake had admired as a teenager, was known for works that expressed a certain solitary loneliness often present in American life. But what Jake didn't appreciate was that, in a sense, he had really painted himself. His two versions of the water tower—the half-finished painting from his youth and this completed one—had bookended a sad, solitary life. The fiery red top of the tower represented his anger and resentment while the hazy shades of gray were the shadows of everyone and everything he'd ever lost.

Hunger wasn't Jake's only problem. He was broke and, with the painting now finished, dangerously bored. It was this unforgiving reality that compelled him to drive out to the Carsons' Sunday afternoon and ask for a job. He knew Billy and Addie might be there, but that didn't discourage him. He had nothing to lose.

Showered and dressed, Jake looked around the house for anything to soothe his rising anxiety. Nothing was out of place except his sketchbook, but rather than return it to the basement, he placed it in the dining room hutch for safe-keeping.

All the drawers were crammed full save one—a drawer that held pictures of Betty Pearson, photographs taken from every stage of her life. One, a black and white photo taken by the shore of a lake, drew Jake's particular attention. In it she was smiling faintly, her face partially covered by strands of long, dark hair. Jake turned it over. *Betty, July 1933* was written in faded black ink. His mother couldn't have been more than fifteen or sixteen at the time, but there was something about her expression that seemed familiar to him. He tucked the photo in his back pocket and returned the other pictures, along with his sketchbook, to the hutch. Jake had stalled long enough. Carson Farm was waiting.

*

Virgil Carson woke up with the sun the next day, Monday, July 18th. Ranger too, roused himself from Jimmy's old bedroom and they crept downstairs together. The dog waited patiently next to his stainless steel bowl until food tumbled into it. The familiar metallic sound was met with his tail-waving approval.

While Ranger wolfed down his breakfast, Virgil sipped black coffee and looked through the kitchen window down to the Pearsons' trailer in the distance. *I doubt they slept any better than I did,* he guessed as the coffee fortified him. *Gosh, I hope I'm doing the right thing.*

"I hope you're doing the right thing, Virgil," Helen said from the top of the stairs.

"Me too," he replied glumly, never taking his eyes off the Loop. Helen came up behind him and wrapped her arms around his chest.

"I understand why you did it, Virgil," Helen murmured. "But aren't you being a little selfish? How is having Jake here going to help in the long run?"

"What would you have me do, Helen? Say no? Jake came to me this time. How can I ignore that?"

"I can give you three very good reasons."

Virgil turned and put his hands on her shoulders. "I know," he sighed. "I haven't forgotten what's at stake."

"I saw how happy you were last week," Helen reminded him. "You love having the kids here. Why risk that now with the end . . ."

"So near?" Virgil acknowledged, reaching over to the coffee pot for a refill. "I couldn't just turn my back on Jake. He needs this. Look on the bright side. One more set of hands means I can take it easy all week."

"Just don't forget what Anna wants, Virgil. What we agreed to."

182

"I won't," he replied. "But second chances, Helen. Everyone deserves 'em, even Jake."

"So did your father. But would he have changed? Will Jake?"

Virgil caressed Helen's cheek. "I'm being selfish, I know," he confessed. "I just couldn't say no."

She placed her hand over his. "Should I get breakfast started?"

"You might want to wait," Virgil replied as he headed for the front door. "We might be eating alone this morning."

"Where are you going?"

"Just a quick trip to my dad's wreck."

As his master walked out the squeaky screen door, Ranger stepped lightly across the kitchen floor and sat next to the woman. He could always count on her for plenty of attention, but this time she only sighed.

*

They trickled in one by one. Billy arrived on time and ate the bowl of Malt-O-Meal Mrs. Carson had prepared for him. Addie came in a little before 9am, just as her brother was clearing the table. She joined him at the sink, but Mrs. Carson insisted she eat something first. Mr. Carson was reading the newspaper on the porch when she sat down next to him.

"Thank you for coming today, Addie," he said from behind the sports page. "I wasn't sure you'd make it."

"I said I would," she muttered as Mr. Carson lowered the paper. "So I'm here."

"Yes you are," he quietly agreed. "But for how long?"

Ranger came out from the kitchen and approached Addie hopefully. Stone-faced, she stroked his head and fed him a scrap of toast. Content, he flopped down next to her.

"That dog sure likes. . ."

"Why did you have to say yes?! We don't need Jake here! He'll just get in the way!"

"Addie, like I told you yesterday, I . . ."

"Why didn't you just say NO?!"

The dishwashing stopped during Addie's outburst, but quickly resumed as a difficult silence settled over the porch. Mr. Carson searched for the right words that would keep Addie on the farm. Ranger nuzzled the girl's hand, afraid she might leave.

"I heard what you said," she conceded. "But this is Jake we're talking about. What makes you think he's changed?"

Ranger circled the table and set his front legs on Mr. Carson's lap. "I assume you know what rock bottom is, Miss Pearson. Mine was the 4th of July, 32 years ago. I'm sure Billy told you about it."

"He did."

"Life seemed pretty dark then. But when I stopped numbing the pain, I started to feel things again. Good things."

"Like what?"

"Forgiveness, for starters."

"Are you saying I should forgive Jake?"

"Not at all. Besides, I doubt he'd ask for it—from either of you." Billy and Mrs. Carson stood in the kitchen doorway.

"Then what are you asking?" Addie repeated.

"That you give him some room to forgive himself." Mr. Carson nudged Ranger off his lap and leaned forward. "Jake hit rock bottom that night in front of the billboard. You both saw it."

"Don't be mad at your mom," Mrs. Carson chimed in. "She thought it was important that we know what happened." Addie was about to ask why when Mr. Carson returned to his point.

"No one can stay down there forever. So when Jake asked for help I couldn't say no. Besides, he said he hasn't had a drink since."

"And you believed him?!" Addie asked incredulously.

"If I'm giving him this chance," Mr. Carson replied, "I have to."

"So that's it?" Billy said. "Jake's back?"

"No," Mrs. Carson interjected. "Your mother said Jake won't be moving back home. Ever. You can both trust her on that."

"And as far as work is concerned," Mr. Carson promised, "Jake is on a very short leash. If I think he's been drinking, he's gone. If he argues with either of you, he's done. You get the benefit of the doubt, Jake doesn't. He said he won't start any fights, but that means you can't either."

Billy and Addie looked at one another. Neither was happy about the prospect of working with Jake, but both were satisfied with the conditions Mr. Carson had set for him. Their silent agreement came just in time. A truck turned off the road and began its long climb up the driveway.

184

"That wasn't so bad, was it?" Mr. Carson asked Addie and Billy when they gathered on the porch after Jake's first full day of haying with them.

Addie shrugged. *He'll do something stupid,* she figured. *He can't keep it together forever.*

But somehow Jake did. From that first day all the way through Thursday, July 21ˢᵗ, he was a model farmhand—arriving on time, working hard, avoiding Addie. And rather than join everyone for lunch on the porch, he ate by himself each day under the shade of a pine tree. His only company during these meals was the photograph of his mother, which he studied closely. Every quitting time he politely declined Mrs. Carson's offer of lemonade and dessert, choosing instead to collect his daily wages and leave.

"How come you pay Jake every day?"

"Because he needs to eat, Billy," Mr. Carson answered, biting into a ginger snap.

"He needs to drink too," Addie retorted. "Did you ever think of that?"

"If Jake wants a drink bad enough, Addie, he'll get his hands on something—money or no money."

Addie grunted, surrendering to Mr. Carson's logic. "How much longer is he going to be working here? He's not coming back at the end of the summer for the second cut, is he?"

The Carsons had discussed little else all week. So much could change, they knew, between mid-July and Labor Day. But by Thursday afternoon Mr. Carson decided that hiring Jake had been a smart move. He was able to take it slow, spend the better part of each day with Helen on their backyard swing monitoring his workers' progress *and* their behavior.

"I don't know yet," he told Addie. With his hands tied by Anna's demand for secrecy, Mr. Carson appealed to the girl's sense of fairness instead. "It hasn't been that bad though, has it? You and Jake are never on the wagon together. If anyone should be mad, it's your brother."

Billy's tanned face reddened further. "I don't mind," he replied. "But maybe we won't need Jake next month. He might find another job by then."

"Do you really believe that, Shorty?"

185

Billy didn't. As relatively trouble-free working with Jake had been for him, it hadn't been easy. Jake had tried to initiate plenty of small talk, but *"Yups"* and *"Sures"* were about all Billy offered him in return.

Jake didn't mind the quiet. His discomfort around his step-children had lessened considerably by the time his alarm rang Friday morning—so much so that he was almost impatient to get to work. Until he did, Jake feared, each morning was a struggle to keep his cravings at bay.

The time between workdays was a different story, as Jake spent every evening in his basement painting. Like the repetitious farm work, he knew he was safe with a brush in his hands. But nothing Jake painted after the water tower held his attention for long. That painting, he vaguely understood, had been like therapy. But every attempt since was nothing more than one distraction after another to get him safely from night to day again. By Friday, however, what had been poking at Jake's subconscious since Monday finally revealed itself.

He looked at is mother again—but not yet his mother—unable to shake the feeling that he knew her somehow. *How can that be?* he asked himself. *This picture is more than 40 years old.* Then an idea came to him, something he thought might help him finally put the past where it belonged. *I'll paint her.*

Jake left the photo on the kitchen table. He didn't want to take any chances that it might get lost or damaged while he was at work. Then he hurried out the door, got into his dad's truck and drove out to Carson Farm. But his thoughts never left her face.

*

"You okay, Jake?" Mr. Carson asked him after Helen waved them in for lunch. "You missed some hay on that last pass."

"Huh?"

"I said you missed some hay out there. Just make sure you bale it up after lunch."

"I can go back over it now if you'd like."

"No rush. Is everything alright?"

"I'm fine. The heat's just getting to me."

186

Billy and Addie heard Mr. Carson's question but they couldn't believe Jake's answer. Friday's weather was turning out to be the mildest of the week. Something else had to be going on.

Something else was, but what that might have been didn't affect Mr. Carson's decision later that day—a decision that had seemed more and more unlikely with each passing day. Mr. Carson didn't want to do it, but he had given Billy and Addie his word.

He fired Jake.

18
WINDBLOWN HAIR

Jake's excuse to leave the farm over Friday's lunch break, *"I gotta run to the bank,"* seemed pretty flimsy. Mr. Carson had paid him in cash all week. Nonetheless, his promise to return had been sincere, even if where he said he was going was not.

From the moment Jake decided to paint the photograph of his mother, he knew he wanted a real canvas to work on. The idea had grown larger in his mind with every lap the tractor made around the field that morning. But while neck-deep in a fight with alcohol, leaving the farm to steal a clean canvas from the high school was a lie made worse by the theft, even if it was a petty one.

None of this crossed Jake's mind, however, when he brought his sketchbook down to the basement and taped the photo of young Betty Pearson to the top of his easel. *Ready to paint after work,* he thought. But then he opened his sketchbook. Fifteen minutes later a form took shape. Jake studied the drawing, then tore it out and started over. His second attempt joined the first. By the time he was satisfied with a sketch he could paint from, the floor was littered with paper. *One more,* Jake told himself, but his growling stomach drove him back upstairs.

The first thing he noticed when he took at a seat at the kitchen table with a bologna sandwich and a glass of milk was the time—2:20pm. *That can't be right?!* Jake rushed to the guest room and checked his alarm clock—2:21.

"Dammit!"

He hurried back into the kitchen and grabbed the phone off the wall but there was still no dial tone, so he snatched his keys off the table and raced out the door. He backed the truck into the street as its radio blared out a hypnotic song.

> *Mama always told me not to look into the eyes of the sun,*
> *But mama, that's where the fun is!*

Jake leaned on the steering wheel and considered his options. *I'll explain everything tomorrow. Carson will understand.* Kidding himself

189

was the hardest part. The rest would come easier. He pulled the truck back into the driveway as the song repeated itself over and over:

Blinded by the light,
Revved up like a deuce,
Another runner in the night,
Blinded by the light . . .

When the song faded into nothingness, Jake shut off the engine and returned to the basement—to the girl with the windblown hair.

＊

Without a word, Mr. Carson climbed up onto the tractor after lunch and pulled the wagon around the field all afternoon as if nothing and no one was amiss.

"Is Jake coming back to tomorrow?" Addie asked him after she and Billy unloaded and stacked the last bales for the day.

"I doubt any of us will, Addie." Mr. Carson pointed to a darkening sky north of the upper field. "The forecast is calling for heavy rain. I'll have to run the rake over the fields again."

"I can do that, Mr. Carson," Billy offered. "I haven't driven the tractor all week."

"How about Sunday, son? There's something else I'd like you to do for me tomorrow."

"What about Jake?" Addie repeated.

Mr. Carson ignored her question for the time being. "Are you and your friend going into town tomorrow, Billy?"

"I think so. Why?"

"Would you mind dropping off Jake's pay for me? I'll put some money in an envelope for you. Just slide it into his mail slot."

Addie's eyes narrowed. "Does that mean he's done?"

"I said he'd get a short leash, Addie. And a promise is a promise. Jake won't be coming back."

＊

190

A warm, steady rain fell all night, but by morning the clouds had moved on and were replaced by a dazzling, sapphire blue sky. Billy and Addie woke to find a note their mother had left for them on the kitchen table:

> *Mr. Carson came by—said you both have the day off. Billy, here's the envelope he wants you to deliver. Just drop it off and leave, okay? Addie, Sara called. She wants you to come over after you wake up. I had to run into town for a meeting at the bank. I'll be home by 2.*
>
> *Love, Mom.*

An hour later, Billy and Addie were standing at the Farelli's front door. Renny opened it, chattering on about some movie that was coming to the theater in Wood City.

"*Star Wars*, Billy! We were gonna see it yesterday in Minneapolis, but the lines were so long!" He spun around and swung an imaginary sword against some unseen enemy. The movie had been gaining momentum all summer. By July 23rd, it was a national obsession, which suited Renny just fine.

"I don't wanna know too much before I see it," he babbled. "I just know it's about a kid named Luke and some bad guy called Dark Vader."

"You were in Minneapolis again?" Addie asked.

"Yeah, we were looking at . . ."

"Renny, did you make your bed like Mom told you?!" Sara hollered as she ran upstairs from her bedroom. "Wow, am I glad to see you, Addie! I feel like I've been stuck in a car with this little twerp all week."

Addie blushed. "Gone again, huh?"

"Yes, *Mr. Important* had a bunch of meetings. He's decided to turn each trip to the Cities into a little family vacation."

"Should we tell 'em now, Sara?" Renny asked her hopefully.

"Tell us what?"

Sara's hands dug, unnoticed, into Renny's shoulders. "My dad's getting us tickets to *Star Wars,*" she said. "Do you want to come? It's in a week or so."

191

"Okay," Addie replied, though Sara's invitation didn't seemed to fit Renny's question. But her suspicions were quickly forgotten by the prospect of spending the whole day with Sara.

*

"Who d'ya think did this, Billy?" Renny had slowed to a stop in front of the Northern Pacific billboard on the way to Ervin's and was sifting through the broken glass.

"How would I know?"

"Hey, look at this—maybe it's a clue!" Renny dangled a piece of black plastic shaped like the letter C between his thumb and forefinger. Attached to each end of the plastic were small metal loops with torn pieces of orange fabric. He gave it to Billy for inspection, though none was necessary.

"Can you keep a secret, Ren?"

"This must be part of that bag the cops found," Renny deduced. "Didja see the ad in *The Journal*? The sheriff's offering a $100 for any clues to what happened that night. Don'tcha think this is a clue, Billy?"

"Can you keep a secret or not, Ren?"

"Sara says I can't," Renny pouted. "But she doesn't know everything."

That was good enough for Billy. They got back on their bikes and pedaled on toward Lost Elm. Along the way he told Renny everything— how he and Addie had dug up Jake's bottles, their battle with him at the billboard, even Sara's appearance and the chase back to Halverson Road. By the time Billy finished they had reached the outskirts of town, where Renny paused to catch his breath. Throughout the re-telling he had listened closely, his gaze turning inward as Billy's words made a movie in his mind.

"I didn't know dads could be like that."

"Things are better," Billy assured him. "It's just me and Mom and Addie now. Besides, Jake's not my real dad. He never was."

"I forget that sometimes," Renny admitted. "Didja ever know your dad?"

"No. Wish I had though."

"Me too," Renny agreed. He took the black handle from Billy and threw it into the ditch. "I'll keep your secret, Billy. Promise."

Soon after Billy and Renny had pedaled off to Lost Elm, Sara and Addie went for a walk on Halverson Road. Sara did her best to sound supremely bored when she talked about her trips to Minneapolis, but Addie knew better. She hadn't forgotten Sara's plans for the future—about making a life of her own.

"How do you like the farm?" Sara asked when they had reached the far end of Halverson Road.

"It's not exactly Uptown."

"Don't I know it," Sara laughed. "That's not what I mean, though. Something's different. What changed?" Addie ran her fingers over the palms of her hands. They had grown tough and calloused, but her heart hadn't—the change Sara was referring to.

"Over Christmas vacation last year, Billy and I tried to make my Mom's chocolate chip cookies," Addie began. "They were awful. But when Mom made them the next day they were perfect. *'You've got to have the right ingredients,'* she said. That's how I feel right now—like I've finally got the right ingredients in my life. Oh God, that sounds so corny." She covered her face, but Sara wouldn't let her.

"No it doesn't, Addie. Normal, remember? It's okay to want things."

"Thanks to you."

Sara's mind flashed back to Addie's poem—*None can rival you, Sara.* "I can't take all the credit," she said with playful conceit. "But I'd like to thank the Academy, my fans." Addie broke into a fit of giggles as Sara gave a mock acceptance speech. She ended with a flourishing bow, blowing kisses to an imaginary audience in the upper field.

After her performance the girls turned and headed for home, only to be met by the county road grader. Its long, wide blade was lowered onto Halverson Road and began leveling the gravel. Sara stepped in front of the machine and waved her arms.

"Let's hitch a ride!" she yelled over the rumbling engine. The grader braked and Sara climbed up to the cab, talking to the driver in her most endearing fashion. He listened skeptically, but eventually shrugged his shoulders as if to say, *Fine by me.*

The grader was a stroke of luck. Sara knew she couldn't put off telling Addie her news forever. She had stopped Renny in the nick of time an hour ago, but Sara knew that sooner or later he would spill the beans. *But it can wait 'til tomorrow,* she decided after seeing the rare carefree expression on Addie's face, partially hidden behind strands of her straw-blonde hair. *One more day won't make a difference.*

*

Billy and Renny sat under the awning of Ervin's, wax-paper wrappers littered in front of them, along with two stacks of baseball cards and pink bubblegum. Billy took a long drink from his can of orange pop and belched loudly. Renny laughed, bits of chocolate dribbling down his chin. He wiped it on his bare arm, creating a dark brown smudge from his wrist to his elbow. Still unblemished in his hand, however, was a 1977 Topps Rod Carew baseball card from the last pack he had opened.

"So how's he doing?" Billy asked, pointing to the card. The Twins 1st baseman was reaching out his glove to receive an infielder's throw.

Renny's expression soured. ".387."

Billy slapped the envelope Mr. Carson had given him across his thigh and changed the subject. "I have to drop this off at Jake's. It's for working on the farm Thursday morning. You wanna come with?"

"Sure." Renny took the envelope and sifted through four $5 bills. "That's a lot of money for one morning, isn't it?"

Billy thought so too. He had a sneaking suspicion Mr. Carson had been overly generous all week. "Probably, but I think Jake needs it."

Mr. Ervin waved goodbye as the boys pedaled into Lost Elm, watching them until they crossed Otter Creek. Once they faded from his poor eyesight, he took a seat in his usual spot on slow summer days—an old tree stump outside the store's entrance.

"There's Jake," Renny yelled, pumping furiously to catch up to Billy.

They coasted into town on the shoulder of 3rd Street, but when Billy saw Jake he braked hard and skidded sideways in the dirt.

"Follow me, Ren." They dropped their bikes and ran through a narrow alley between the bank and the two-story brick municipal building. Billy looked left when they came upon the sidewalk next to Chestnut Avenue. Jake was a block away, standing in front of Paulette's. They moved toward him, finding cover in the bank's side entrance alcove.

194

"What are you doing, Billy? Jake's right there. Why don't you just give him his money?"

"Better not cross the street, Jake," Billy muttered to himself.

Jake was looking across Chestnut Avenue at the Junction, clenching and unclenching his fists, when a waitress came out of the café and handed him a small container. He gave her a few dollars then doubled back across 3rd Street, heading straight towards them.

Billy tugged on the bank's side door but it was locked. *Closed on Saturday*, he remembered with a grimace, pulling Renny into the corner of the alcove as Jake rushed past them.

"Let's get our bikes," he said without waiting for Renny to follow. They crept back into the alley as Jake continued down the street.

"Didja see?!" Renny said excitedly. "Jake's hands were covered with paint. Whaddya think that means?!"

"I think it means he's been painting." Billy laughed, grateful for a break in the tension. Renny didn't. He pouted as they got back on their bikes.

"Sorry, Ren. I didn't even see his hands. See, you'd make a better private eye than me."

"Like *Rockford*?" Renny suggested hopefully.

"Just like him," Billy agreed, glad to steer Renny back to the task at hand. He didn't want to snoop around Ron Pearson's house all by himself.

They coasted down Chestnut Avenue and turned onto 4th Street, but Jake was nowhere in sight. Billy ditched his bike again and clambered fifteen feet up the slate ridge that ran for a block behind Ron Pearson's back yard. That's where Renny caught up to him.

"Is Jake home?" Renny asked breathlessly.

"Let's find out." Billy climbed down the side of the rock face and urged Renny to follow. When they reached the ground Billy pulled him across the yard, not stopping until their backs were against the side of the house. They circled it, looking discreetly in every window, but saw no evidence that Jake was home.

Billy was about to slide the envelope into the mail slot next to the kitchen door when he and Renny heard footsteps coming up from the basement. They hid behind a hedge, hearing water splash into the sink. Moments later, those same feet pounded back downstairs. Billy ran around to the front of the house and dropped to the ground. Renny, pretending to be "on the case," did the same. They crawled forward to a basement window beneath the living room and peered in.

What Billy saw didn't make any sense. Jake was standing in front of a painting of a brown-haired girl, dabbing his brush on the canvas.

"Jake's painting," Renny whispered.

"I can see that," Billy replied, looking around the basement for any bottles of beer or Swamp Rot. There were none.

"It's pretty good, don'tcha think?"

"Let's go, Ren." Billy scrambled away from the window, walked back to the side of the house and dropped the envelope in the slot. After retrieving their bikes, the boys rode in silence for ten minutes until the blackened billboard was visible in the distance.

"Maybe Mr. Carson was right," Billy finally said. "Maybe Jake has changed."

"Beats me, but I'd say we solved the mystery," Renny replied.

"What mystery?"

"Why his hands were covered with paint."

"See? I told ya, Ren," Billy smiled. "Just like *The Rockford Files*."

"Yeah, but there's still one thing I don't get." Renny paused before asking the one question he assumed Billy was wondering too. "How come was Jake painting a picture of Addie?"

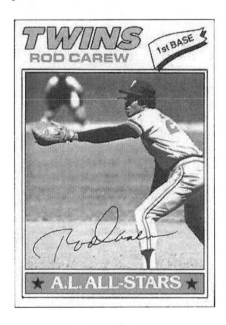

19
HE DOESN'T LOOK SICK

By the time the county grader reached the same dip in Halverson Road where Billy had been thrown from his bike, Sara and Addie had already sung a couple ABBA songs, though screaming them might be more accurate given the roar of the grader's engine. Nonetheless, the girls outdid even that, much to the annoyance of the driver who regretted picking up his two hitchhikers.

"What should we sing next, Addie?! *Life in the Fast Lane*?!" Sara laughed as the grader chugged slowly up a gentle incline to the corner of the Farelli's back yard. Addie hadn't heard her question. She was looking ahead at a man digging a hole near the corner of Halverson Road and Pine Drive. A second man lifted a post from the back of a truck and dropped it on the ground next to the hole.

"Sara! What's that all about?!"

The color drained from Sara's face. She made a slashing motion across her throat to the driver and the grader lurched to a stop. Both girls jumped down and stepped aside as the big machine rolled past them.

"I'm sorry, Addie. I didn't want you to find out like this."

"Like what?" A disembodied feeling washed over Addie as one of the men picked up the post and slid it into the hole while the other hung a sign on the post's crossbar. Eyes wide with shock, she looked back at Sara as the men tamped the earth down around the sign.

FOR SALE
Northland Realty
Brian Ferguson, Agent
(218) 384-4652

"You're moving?!"

"I told my dad to wait until I had a chance to talk to you," Sara explained, turning on the men. "What are you guys doing here?! My dad said Monday, didn't he?!"

The older of the two men pulled a work order from his back pocket. "Says here Monday, but no one ever complains when we're ahead of schedule." He nodded to his partner that they should get going.

"Addie, I didn't mean for . . ."

"How long have you known?!"

"Since the Twins game."

The gears in Addie's brain churned. "So the bank we dropped your dad off at, those men . . . was that a job interview?!"

"Not exactly, but yes."

Then why all the trips since?"

"We had a lot of fun that day didn't we, Addie? Just you and me."

"Why all the trips since, Sara?"

"We've been looking at houses. My parents thought we should have a say in where we live."

"*My parents thought we should have a say*," Addie repeated, shaking her head at words she'd never heard before. "When?"

"Two weeks."

"Two weeks?!" Sara's words had the force of a sledgehammer. Addie dropped to the ground in front of the sign, hot tears burning her cheeks.

"I'm sorry, Addie. I didn't know the right way to tell you."

"There isn't any," Addie whispered hoarsely, her throat constricted.

"I'm really going to miss you, you know," Sara insisted, taking her hand.

"What am I going to do without you?!" Addie desperately wondered.

"What are you talking about?!" Sara scoffed. "You're still going to be Adeline Pearson—braver than any person I've ever known."

"Is *braver* even a word," Addie replied, half crying, half smiling.

"Of course it is! Up *Lady Braver*!" Sara commanded. "Receive your new title!" She placed her hands on Addie's tear-stained cheeks. "Your name is Addie Braver. That's who you'll always be to me."

News of the Farelli's move, coupled with three straight days of sporadic rain, cast a pall over the Loop. Addie couldn't explain or express the feelings she had for Sara, so she tried not to feel anything. It was an easy switch for her to flip—after all, she'd been burying her feelings for years. Sara noticed immediately, but rather than let her friend dwell on endings, she spoke reassuringly about the future, to a time when their friendship would resume and they could live their lives freely, far from Lost Elm.

*

Jake, meanwhile, busied himself doing everything he could think of after he finished the painting of his mother. Meaningless yard work consumed most of his time, but he also re-painted his dad's kitchen and living room in a vain attempt to outrun a return to normalcy. Whether he could or not, only time would tell.

"Normal" suddenly looked a lot different for Jake after a thick envelope arrived in the mail from his sister the last week of July. It was a signed copy of their father's will. Her curt letter explained everything. "You can have the house. I've enclosed a check for your half of Dad's pension." His eyes widened when he saw the amount. Ron Pearson had taken care of his children after all, though Jake's sobriety just got a lot harder.

Such good fortune escaped Anna. She dutifully went to work, but Tuesday afternoon she asked Michael Farelli for a favor. "Is it okay if I take a couple days off? I'm making chocolate chip cookies for the bake sale this Sunday and if I don't get started tomorrow, I'll never finish." After promising to set aside a couple dozen for the Farellis, Anna gathered her things and left.

She hadn't lied—not exactly. But what Michael Farelli didn't know, what no one knew, was that Anna was in almost constant pain. Her appetite was gone again, she was tired all the time and even her vision blurred from time to time. Worse still, Anna didn't know how much longer she could hide the truth from Billy and Addie. Nonetheless, she joined them for breakfast on the farm when haying resumed Wednesday, July 27th. Her reason was simple. She needed Mrs. Carson's help.

"Aren'tcha gonna go to work, Mom?" Billy asked when he saw the assembled measuring cups and mixing bowls on the Carson's kitchen counter.

"Your mom and I are making cookies for the Railway Days bake sale," Mrs. Carson announced.

"But you never let anyone help you," Addie complained. She put a finger to her lips. "It's a secret, remember?"

"Helen and I are teaming up this year," Anna told them. "Besides, who do you think gave me this recipe in the first place?"

Billy and Addie had completely forgotten about Railway Days. Everything else that summer—from Ron Pearson's death to stories of Will Travers, then broken bottles and now the Farelli's move—had driven it from their minds. They simply had no room for one more thing.

One more thing was the reason Billy wasn't as preoccupied with the Farellis' fast-approaching move as he might have otherwise been. His thoughts dwelled on Renny's belief that Jake had painted a picture of Addie. He stubbornly maintained that Renny was wrong, but it didn't stop him from stealing glances at his sister all week. A growing doubt soon gnawed at him—he had to know for sure.

*

"Hey, Mom, I'm gonna bike to Ervin's," Billy announced as he came down the hallway Friday morning.

"Is Renny going with you?"

"No, but I still wanna . . ." he stopped in mid-sentence when he saw his mother. It was 8am and she was still in her bathrobe. Strewn across the kitchen countertops and table were all the cookies she and Mrs. Carson had baked over the last two days.

"Wow. Looks like you're ready for Sunday."

"Almost," Anna replied wearily. "I've got a few more batches to go."

"Why so many?"

"Just giving the people what they want," she joked, puffing herself up.

"Is Mrs. Carson coming over to help?"

"No, she has to work. The library is setting up for the book swap tomorrow."

"Can I help?"

"What about Ervin's?"

"I can go later. Please?"

Anna looked at her son's hopeful face and called Addie into the kitchen. She came out of the bathroom a minute later, her hair lightly curled and her freckles masked beneath a thin layer of blush.

"How would you two like to learn how to make my chocolate chip cookies?"

Addie's expression betrayed a mixture of surprise and disappointment. "Sara and I are going shopping in Wood City."

"This won't take long, honey. I'll have you out the door by ten o'clock."

"Come on, Ad—this is what we've been waiting for!"

The last pan didn't come out of the oven until 11, but Addie didn't mind. Their mother's recipe was now theirs. Anna wrote down all of the ingredients and instructions for safe-keeping. "Yours to make whenever you want, for the rest of your lives," she proudly announced, holding up an index card.

"Being a little dramatic aren't you, Mom?" Addie teased.

"I'd say this is a dramatic moment, wouldn't you? The cat's out of the bag."

"Speaking of, do you want us to bag these up for you?" Billy asked her.

"They need to cool first. You two go ahead. Have fun."

"Thanks, Mom," they replied, both unable to shake the feeling that their mother was leaving something unsaid.

Billy did go to Ervin's, but the trip was just an excuse to bike to Ron Pearson's house and take a longer look at Jake's painting. Asking Renny to join him wasn't an option this time—Renny would only slow him down. But first, Billy bought five packs of cards and found a patch of shade where he could open them.

All the cards in the first pack were commons and duplicates, cards of average ballplayers Billy already had. The next three packs yielded mostly the same. He chewed on two sticks of bubblegum, each piece so sweet his back molars tingled, then slapped the last pack across his knee for luck. The face on the first card stared back at him solemnly. Billy didn't whoop or holler, but he grinned broadly. There he was—the late Danny Thompson. His smile quickly faded, however, as he studied Thompson in his pale blue Texas Rangers jersey, knowing that the man was no longer alive. *He doesn't look sick,* Billy thought. Instead, Thompson stood poised and focused, swinging his bat expertly. "Things can happen pretty fast, Billy," Anna had explained to him after he heard the news of the ballplayer's death the previous December. Billy didn't bother going through the rest of the pack. The picture he had biked into town to see was still waiting for him.

Lost Elm was buzzing with activity. Railway Days hadn't started yet— it wouldn't officially kick off until 5pm with a siren blast from the water tower—but most businesses had already closed for the day. One of the few exceptions was the Junction. Along with the local VFW Post a few blocks west down Chestnut Avenue, the two bars would bookend most of the weekend's festivities. Year after year the Junction and VFW put out all the stops, sponsoring volleyball and softball tournaments, calling countless bingo games and selling food and beer well past midnight. All that, plus live music, didn't end until Railway Days concluded with a huge parade Sunday afternoon.

Jake loved Railway Days. The carnival atmosphere had always legitimized his binge drinking, at least for three days. People who usually looked the other way when they saw Jake, laughed with him instead. Not this year. This year Jake knew he had to escape Railway Days, and fast.

His plan was simple—row his dad's old boat out to the small island in the middle of the Gap Lake reservoir Saturday morning and stay there until Monday, August 1st. July and Railway Days would be over. But first Jake needed to buy food and supplies from Isaacson's Market, located one block from the Junction and the bank.

That's where Billy nearly plowed into him on his way into town from Ervin's. For a second he barely recognized his step-father. Jake was his usual careworn self, but something—perhaps his wolfish, predatory nature—was missing.

"Hi, Billy. Sorry, I didn't see you there."

"That's okay. I probably shouldn't bike on the sidewalk."

"Thanks for dropping off that envelope last week. That was you, right?"

Billy nodded. He wanted to mention the painting, ask Jake who it really was and why he'd never painted in all the years he lived on Halverson Road, but Billy bit his tongue.

"How's your Mom? I was in the bank the other day but she wasn't there. Everything okay?"

"She's fine."

Good," Jake replied, averting his gaze. He waved a grocery list in his hand. "I should get going. I'm going camping this weekend." He wanted

Billy to notice that he was trying to stay out of trouble, but the boy had pedaled off.

Billy rode hard for School Avenue. He leaned his bike against the far side of Ron Pearson's house and hurried down to the basement. A shaft of light from the same window he and Renny had looked through penetrated the gloom. The easel and canvas were still there, covered by a sheet, but the sketchbook was gone and Jake's palette was scraped clean.

A sick feeling rose from the pit of Billy's stomach. After going to all the trouble of lying to his mom and sneaking into the house, he wasn't sure he wanted to know who Jake had painted. Looking around for some distraction, his eyes were drawn to a tall door leaning in a corner of the basement. He pulled on the chain of an overhead light, illuminating the painting of Lost Elm's old water tower.

Billy stared at the painting for what he thought had only been a minute or two, but it must have been longer. Upstairs, the screen door creaked open and slammed shut. He looked around for somewhere to hide, but Jake's frantic cleaning weeks earlier left Billy with few options. As footsteps lumbered down the basement steps, he slipped behind the water tower door.

"Thought I turned that off," Jake mumbled. He was about to tug on the chain, but instead removed the cloth from the painting and studied the girl again. Sighing heavily, he snapped the light off and left.

Billy didn't come out from behind the door and face the girl until he heard Jake drive away. The eyes, the shape of her face, even the thin, sad smile were all Addie's. The only things missing were his sister's freckles and her straw-blonde hair. Why this girl had dark brown hair, Billy didn't know. But Renny was right—Jake had painted Addie.

Do I tell her? he wondered, pedaling furiously through town. Upsetting Addie now, especially with the Farellis moving so soon, seemed cruel. He decided to tell his Mom instead. *But after Railway Days. Jake's in the middle of Gap Lake. He can't hurt us there.*

Halfway home, Billy coasted to a stop and fished the baseball cards from his back pocket, thumbing through them until he came to Danny Thompson. After finding his date of birth on the back of the card, Billy did a quick calculation.

"29?! How's that even possible? How could someone so young die so suddenly?"

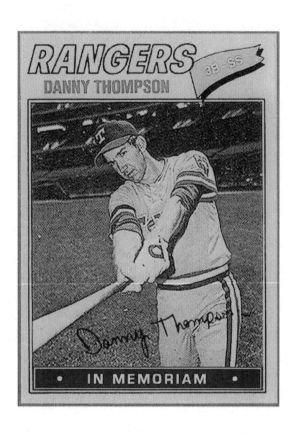

RANGERS
DANNY THOMPSON
3B-SS

IN MEMORIAM

204

Hi Dad,

It's me, Addie. It's almost midnight but I can't sleep so I thought I would write to you.

I wasn't sure Mr. Carson would keep his promise, but he fired Jake after Jake left the farm and didn't come back. Probably off doing his usual bullcrap at the Junction.

Before Jake started working on the farm, Mr. Carson talked to us about forgiveness and fresh starts, but how many fresh starts does one person get? Jake will never change and who cares if he does? He's not a part of our lives anymore.

But Jake or no Jake, I'm glad haying is over until September. With Sara leaving, I'd rather spend my time with her. That's right, the Farellis are moving. I can still hardly believe it. Sara's dad got a job with some bank in Minneapolis. They leave this Saturday, August 6th.

I guess that's why Sara was acting strange. She knew she was moving and was afraid to tell me. We had a great weekend together, though. We went shopping in Wood City on Friday and played on a volleyball team in the Railway Days tournament Saturday. Neither of us are very good but we still had fun.

That's why this is going to be so hard, Dad. Everything is more fun with Sara. I don't know what I'm going to do without her. I want to do something nice for her before she goes, let her know just how important she is to me, maybe tell her how I really feel.

Mom was sick this weekend, said she overdid it getting ready for the bake sale. She went home before it began and left me and Shorty in charge. We sold out of cookies before the parade even started and when we showed her the money we made, she let us keep it. $30 each!

It's now after midnight, Dad. I've got to get to bed. I have to make every minute with Sara count. Our time is running out.

I miss you all the time.

Love,
Your daughter, Addie

20
THOSE PLEADING EYES

Ranger's joyful summer continued even after the hay was cut and gathered from his master's fields. Every morning he woke to the puttering sound of a contraption he quickly associated with the girl and boy—a small, rounded object that rolled up to the farmhouse nearly every morning. He scampered down the porch steps to meet his young friends, knowing they would greet him affectionately. A third person, gentler and frailer, was always with them. Ranger sniffed her cautiously, sensing something about the woman that was just outside his understanding.

But now with their work done, the girl and boy never stayed long on the farm. Every day Ranger watched the pair race down the hill to the home of the other girl and boy, the ones with the dark hair.

"What's wrong, fella?" Addie asked him as they started off for the Farelli's for the fourth day in a row. The dog barked twice, the second time louder than the first.

"He wants to come with, Ad."

She looked at Ranger and patted her legs. He approached her and stood, placing his front paws on her belly. Addie stroked each side of the dog's face. "You wanna come and play?"

For the next two days the old dog felt young again. He chased the boys as they raced around the dirt path on their bikes. When he grew tired, the slower pace of the girls suited him. But wherever he was on the Loop, whoever he was with, Ranger was happy.

✳

Anna was not. She told Billy and Addie that breakfast with the Carsons would continue after haying ended, but it was all just a ruse. Every morning after they went off to spend their last days with Renny and Sara, Helen drove Anna into Wood City for her scheduled treatments at Memorial Hospital.

She stubbornly insisted that she felt fine but Virgil wasn't fooled. "Why are you fighting us on this, Anna? It's not like we don't know what's going on. Besides, you have the time off and the kids are with the Farelli's. They won't find out."

Michael Farelli, already distracted by his family's impending move, hadn't given Anna's request a second thought. "You've saved up more than two months of vacation days in the last ten years. You could take the rest of the summer off and no one here would look at you sideways." That Anna's request was sudden and made over the phone Sunday evening seemed unusual, but Michael had other things on his mind. "Enjoy your time off. I'm just sorry you won't be here on my last day."

Last days were very much on Anna's mind when she and Helen drove into Wood City on Thursday, August 4th. After four straight mornings in waiting rooms and receiving treatments, she was worn out. Doctors told her this would happen, citing all the ways she was going to feel a whole lot worse. "Normal for this kind of treatment," they said. "So don't be surprised."

Anna was certain nothing would ever surprise her again. She spent each afternoon after her hospital visits in the Carson's first floor guest room, grateful to be near a bathroom. What little food she ate she couldn't keep down for long. Between the nausea and the developing sores in her mouth, Anna grimly thought it made more sense if Virgil simply lugged her mattress into the bathroom.

"I'll bring you home this afternoon, Anna," he said Friday morning. "But what about tomorrow? How are you going to drive up here for breakfast? You can barely walk." Virgil and Helen stood in the doorway of the guest room, concern apparent on their faces.

"Is this *The Talk*?"

"Shouldn't it be, dear?" Helen replied. "How much longer do you think you can fool Billy and Addie?" At the mention of her children, Anna turned away. Helen pulled a chair over to the side of the bed and took her hand.

"Just a little longer," Anna pleaded. "Their friends are moving. I want them to say goodbye without any distractions."

"Distractions?!" Virgil said in disbelief. "Is that what you think this is?!"

Anna closed her eyes, in too much pain to think too far ahead. When she opened them, Virgil was looking at her like a father who couldn't bear to lose another child.

208

"Don't worry about tomorrow," she said, reaching her hand out to him. "Everything's going to work out."

Virgil and Helen wanted to believe that Anna's months of planning—from the December morning when she knocked on their door and asked for help—would turn out exactly as she hoped. But in all of that time they never discussed the one thing Anna couldn't control—Jake. They didn't see any reason to burden her with thoughts of him now.

"You rest for a few more hours," Helen told her. "Virgil will bring you home at 5."

"Is there anything else you need, Anna?" he asked.

"After I talk to the kids, would it be okay if we stayed here with you?"

"Of course, dear," Helen said. "We were planning on it. That's what families are for."

*

Billy and Addie were never fooled. They had wondered what was wrong with their mother long before she hatched her plan with the Carsons, but their private worries were always overshadowed by Jake's volatile presence in their lives.

Then when their concerns were finally voiced in late June—*"Are you okay, Mom?"*—Anna got lucky. Jake was gone and she enjoyed two weeks of renewed energy and optimism. In return, Billy and Addie spent time with a version of their mother they hadn't seen in years. Why spoil it with more questions? Fooled, they weren't. Happy to ignore reality for a few untroubled summer days, they gladly were.

As August gained steam, Billy and Addie's attention was diverted again—this time to the Farellis' move. Anna knew those friendships had served as crucial buffers for her children. She wasn't going to rob them of a proper goodbye on her account.

And as far as Jake was concerned, Anna simply had no more energy to give the man. The last ten years had drained her dry. Marrying him, supporting him, enabling him—she had justified those choices for one reason, hoping it might redeem Jake somehow. But how could it? Anna had never told him where his redemption could be found.

To Anna's everlasting surprise, Jake never asked her why she had married him in the first place. What her answer might have been, she didn't know—but the truth would have torn her family apart. And telling him now was simply out of the question.

*

Anna rolled over and looked at the alarm clock on the nightstand—4:30pm. Sunlight filled a corner of the guest room, striking the hardwood floor beneath a tall bay window. In the distance, Anna saw two specks racing around the Loop—Billy and Renny. She searched further for some sign of Addie, but when her vision blurred, she gave up. *I have to drive myself home today,* she realized. *If the kids see Virgil drop me off they'll ask questions.* She'd gotten lucky the last three days. Billy and Addie had been nowhere in sight each time Mr. Carson parked next to the trailer and helped her inside. Now, as Anna walked unsteadily out of the guest room, Mr. Carson was waiting on the porch with her car keys on the table next to him.

"Can't risk it today, Virgil," Anna said, swiping the keys before he could object. "Billy and Renny are down there right now." Mr. Carson didn't say a word, just raised his hands in mock surrender before helping her into the car.

"Call if you need anything." He patted the roof of the Volkswagen. "We can be there in five minutes." Anna nodded, released the clutch and coasted down the driveway.

"Is that girl trying to kill herself?!" Helen wondered as she met Virgil in the front yard. "A few hours ago I thought we were going to have to call an ambulance. Why does she have to be so stubborn?"

"I guess we know where Addie gets it," he replied. "But she hasn't been wrong yet, has she? Anna means to do exactly what she told us last Christmas—save those kids."

"It's been pretty bumpy along the way."

Virgil thought about those bumps as Ranger rounded the top of the hill. His tail wagged happily at the sight of them, but the dog flopped to the ground, too tired to go any further.

"There'll be a few more, Helen. We better brace ourselves." They watched Anna far below step out of the car and wave to Billy and Addie—both high in the Pines with Renny and Sara—before disappearing inside the trailer.

210

The Carsons walked back to the house arm in arm. "Come on, boy," Mr. Carson called out to Ranger. "Let's get your supper." The dog's eyes perked up but he didn't move. "First Anna and now you too?" He put two fingers to his mouth and blew. The sharp whistle communicated to Ranger that his master meant business.

*

Billy and Addie skipped breakfast the next morning in order to help Renny and Sara pack up their things. Mr. Farelli sent Billy off to Renny's bedroom with the simple instruction: "Renny can get pretty pokey, Billy. Keep him on task." Addie went straight downstairs. She and Sara boxed up books, notebooks and sketchpads. By noon a large moving van parked in the driveway was nearly full.

Anna was relieved that her children had passed on breakfast. She doubted she could have joined them if she tried. She woke slowly, only minutes before Virgil knocked on the door at 10am. They slipped out of the Loop unnoticed and were soon zooming north on I-35 into neighboring Wood City.

While Virgil waited for Anna in the hospital's visitor center, he was overcome by the same feeling he'd had when he learned of his son's death years earlier—utter helplessness. Virgil Carson had done his best to live a life of integrity—setting a good example, treating others fairly, telling the people he cared about just how much he cared—and yet he couldn't help Anna now any more than he could have saved Jimmy then. He exhaled slowly in an attempt to force the frustration from his body, but it just wouldn't leave.

An hour and a half later an exhausted Anna was rolled out to him in a wheelchair. Hat in hand, Virgil rose and took over from the attendant. As he maneuvered her outside, his hand dropped onto Anna's shoulder and she began to cry. By the time they got to his truck, her shoulders convulsed rhythmically, her entire body expressing its pain and grief. With supreme effort, Anna stood and faced him.

"Thank you. For everything."

"Helen and I love you, you know," Virgil replied hoarsely.

Anna smiled and put her hand on his cheek. "Promise me one more thing?"

"What's that?"

"Don't make me come here again."

Mr. Carson understood what she was asking. His mind drifted back to his son again. *We had to accept Jimmy's death,* Virgil remembered. *But this is different.* He looked at her pale face and those pleading eyes.

"Okay," he finally nodded.

"Good. Now let's go home."

As she had all week, Anna spent Friday afternoon at the Carson's. Perhaps because she knew she would never return to the hospital for another treatment, she slept soundly, free from any nausea or pain. Sneaking back to the trailer wouldn't be necessary, either—Billy, Addie had left early with Farelli's for the 6 o'clock screening of *Star Wars*. Instead, Anna spent a quiet evening on the Carson's screen porch. Helen and Virgil joined her there but said little. There was, after all, nothing more to say. Helen crocheted while Virgil tuned in the Twins game, keeping the volume low enough so that the play-by-play mingled with the peaceful twilight sounds of summer all around Halverson Road.

*

When the moviegoers returned from Wood City, they lingered outside for a long time. Billy and Renny recited lines they could remember while the girls strolled around the Loop. Sara narrated the end of *The Call of the Wild* for Addie, describing each tragedy Buck overcame in his short life. "His will to survive only got stronger," she said. "No matter who he lost. Even near the very end, Buck sang *'a song of the younger world'*."

By 9am the next morning the van was gone, the movers having left for Minneapolis at daybreak. There was nothing to do now but say goodbye. Anna followed Billy and Addie to the Farelli's driveway. She hugged Michael and Sharon, whispering small "thank yous" to them and giving Michael a container full of her chocolate chip cookies. "A deal's a deal," she said with a warm smile.

The boys weren't sure how to say goodbye until Billy took Danny Thompson's card out of his pocket. "I told you," he said, handing it to Renny. "If I ever got one, it would be yours."

Renny's eyes widened as he cradled the card in his hands. "I didn't think Topps made one for Thompson this year."

"They didn't—not exactly. Look at the other side." Renny flipped the card over. Thompson's biographical information was there, but his statistics weren't.

"Thanks, Billy, but I didn't get you anything."

Billy smiled faintly, wondering what the Twin Cities would be like for his friend. Would Renny find someone there who could look past his quirks and awkwardness, learn what Billy had long ago—that Renny was a true and loyal friend? He wasn't so sure. People could be awfully cruel to a boy like Renny.

"Yeah you did, Ren."

"You were right all along," Renny said, his eyes downcast. "Carew's not gonna do it this year. He's hitting .383 and we both know how he fades in the fall." Billy smiled at the irony, the idea of Renny being pessimistic about the slugger's chances of reaching .400. He wasn't going to let his friend leave that way.

"Are you kidding? Seventeen points in two months? Carew can do that in a week! Rod's gonna do it this year, Renny—I guarantee it!"

Renny looked up, hearing his own words spoken back to him. Billy's thoughts on Rod Carew usually triggered some statistical soliloquy, but not this time. This time Renny didn't know what else to say. He tried to smile but his face betrayed a mixture of emotions he struggled to express. Overwhelmed, his eyes fell back to the ground. He murmured a hasty, "Bye, Billy," then disappeared into the backseat of his father's car.

Mr. Farelli backed the Caprice out of the driveway and onto the Loop. Before the car pulled away Renny looked out at Billy. His momentary sadness was gone, replaced by an innocent smile Billy knew well. They exchanged small waves and, just like that, Renny Farelli was gone.

Anna and Billy said a brief goodbye to Sara and walked back to the trailer. The girls were suddenly aware that it was just the two of them and the idling El Camino. Addie patted the car's hood affectionately.

"I'll never forget the night you pulled up next to us in this thing."

"And I'll never forget when I knocked Jake on his ass," Sara added with unmistakable pride. She swung her fists at an imaginary foe and soon both girls were giggling uncontrollably. When their laughter subsided, Sara retrieved a small package from the car and handed it to Addie.

"It's not much but I know you liked the other one."

Addie tore off the wrapping paper and opened a small box. Inside it was a new bracelet to replace the one she'd lost at the billboard. This one had a piece of curved gray metal two and a half inches long and half an inch wide. It was connected on both ends by a thick strand of leather.

"Read it."

Addie studied the metal strip and saw the words *Addie & Sara* inscribed on the band's inward curve. Her heart skipped a beat and she looked hopefully into Sara's eyes.

"Turn it over."

Addie did, realizing that their names were meant to be worn against her wrist, not facing out for the whole world to see. The world would see Sara's simple, heartfelt inscription: *Once There Was a Summer*.

"The engraver said he couldn't fit that," Sara explained. "But I told him he had to. Do you like it?"

Addie loved it. But they were connected on one side of the bracelet and torn apart on the other. One short summer—just two months—and now it was over. *Do I tell her?* Addie wondered.

"This one won't break." Sara gestured for Addie to hold out her wrist.

"I love it, Sara," she murmured. "I love . . ."

"Those words say it all, don't they? As long as I live I'll never forget the summer of 1977, or you, Addie."

The lump in Addie's throat made more words impossible. She took a folded piece of paper out of her back pocket, hoping the words she'd written the night before would say everything she couldn't.

"Someday I'm going to tell my kids about this girl I knew, how she wasn't afraid of anything. When they ask me who she was, I'll tell them her name was *Addie Braver*." Sara laughed at the thought of having children one day. "Isn't that crazy?"

Addie understood the meaning behind Sara's words. She tucked the poem away, ungiven and unread. It said:

Only you, Sara, saw the real me,
Somehow, someway, with you I was free.
What I do now, I can't really say,
But dream of seeing you again,
Somewhere, someday.

Addie tried to say something, but her words were drowned in fresh tears that wouldn't stop. Sara hugged her, whispering softly that everything would be okay.

"You are exactly who you're supposed to be, Addie. Do you know what I'm saying? Don't let anyone ever tell you different. Promise?"

Addie pulled away and looked into Sara's eyes. *She knows*, Addie realized. *Sara knows.* Suddenly the thought of never fitting in—of always feeling different—didn't matter. Someone she loved was saying there was nothing wrong with her.

"I promise."

"Good," Sara said, wiping away Addie's tears. "There's one more thing we have to do before I go." She took a cassette out of the El Camino's glove compartment and slid it into the tape deck. Her fingers raced across an imaginary keyboard and kicked off a familiar song— ABBA's *Dancing Queen*.

Sara refused to let Addie's self-consciousness win the day. She danced in the Farelli's driveway until Addie joined her. "See?! I told you!" Sara yelled over the blaring music. "You didn't have a choice, Addie! You never did! Aren'tcha glad?!"

A final question, but this time Addie left it unanswered. Instead, she let herself feel as free and alive as the friend she loved. They danced and sang like they were the only two people in the world. And for one song, that's exactly what they were.

21
HER SEVEN MONTH SECRET

Jake wasn't sure what to do next. Railway Days was over and his dead father's house no longer held any appeal for him. His paintbrushes were there, but what other reason did he have to leave his rocky island in the middle of Gap Lake?

Camping, however, had served its purpose. Jake managed to notch three more sober days, fighting off a terrible thirst the first night. Whether it was the music drifting across the lake from Lost Elm or just another craving, he stumbled from his tent to search the island for a red bandana. When his flashlight found one tied to the branch of a small pine tree, he dug furiously.

Swamp Rot in hand, Jake lay on his back and stared at the night sky. A faint glow from the Milky Way dazzled overhead. He held the bottle up to the light, stretching and distorting the stars.

You're stalling, he muttered to himself and pulled the cork free. For a split-second Jake was filled with regret as he upended the bottle, but his hand didn't flinch until all of its contents splattered on the ground around his feet. A minute later he was back in his tent sound asleep, his thirst conquered.

Without anything to drink or a clean canvas to work on, Jake had little choice but to face the future. For starters, he knew he couldn't go on living in the house he'd grown up in—too many memories. So while he collapsed his tent and extinguishing the campfire on Monday morning, August 1st—the day of Anna's first treatment in Wood City—Jake decided to sell his dad's house. He knew he'd have to say goodbye to more than just the house, but what had holding on too tightly to anything ever gotten him?

Jake wasn't exactly relieved when he returned to Lost Elm, but the frantic feeling that had chased him since he left Miller-Dwan was gone. After brewing a much-needed pot of coffee, he took his sketchbook out of the hutch and turned to a clean sheet of paper.

Two cups of coffee later, his list was complete. Jake had started it in his head on the island, but actually putting his future on paper took longer than expected. Satisfied, he taped it to the fridge.

1. *Sell the house*
2. *Get rid of everything*
3. *Give Anna the trailer*
4. *Let her go*
5. *Close bank account*
6. *Leave Lost Elm*
7. ~~*See Mom*~~

Still without a working phone, Jake walked to the Northland Realty office next to Paulette's and put the house on the market. A day later it was gone. "Some banker from Two Harbors," he was told. "He's taking over First National. Can you be out in a couple weeks?"

By Saturday morning—when Anna, Billy and Addie were saying goodbye to the Farellis—half of Jake's list was finished. He sat in the kitchen sipping more coffee, a little dazed by the events he'd set in motion. Townspeople had stopped by all week, lured by the yard sale signs Jake had put up all over Lost Elm. He took whatever he could get for almost everything left in the house.

Stuck to the fridge next to his shrinking list was a photocopied document embossed with official letterhead that read, "𝕿𝖗𝖆𝖓𝖘𝖋𝖊𝖗 𝖔𝖋 𝕿𝖎𝖙𝖑𝖊 𝖆𝖓𝖉 𝕯𝖊𝖊𝖉." Turning over ownership of the trailer to Anna, including all the land inside the Loop, went much smoother than Jake expected. "You fill it out, I'll notarize it, we'll file it," the clerk at the Abstract Office had instructed him. Stunned, Jake wondered if the rest of his life would have been as easy if he had only stayed sober.

Handing over the title to Anna gave Jake the excuse he needed to say goodbye, and the sooner the better. In a few days Ron Pearson's house would belong to someone else. Leaving Lost Elm after that wouldn't be a problem. But where would he go?

Jake tapped a pencil on the kitchen table, his eyes fixed on number 7, written then crossed out, much like Betty Pearson's existence. "Parents make us," he recalled the Miller-Dwan staff telling him. "And sometimes they break us. But no one has to stay broken forever." He took the list off the fridge and carefully re-wrote, *See Mom*.

*

As Jake wrapped up his affairs in Lost Elm, Billy and Addie moped around Halverson Road. With the Farellis gone, they spent the rest of that same Saturday by themselves—Billy on his bike, Addie in the Bog. Neither returned to the trailer until after supper, each driven inside by a steady downpour. A note from Anna—*I went to bed, there's tuna casserole in the fridge*—greeted them when they got home.

Sunday, August 7th dawned clear and bright, as if the gods had tapped Billy and Addie on the shoulder and announced, "See? Life's not so bad." Determined to make the best of a beautiful day, Billy persuaded Addie to go blueberry picking with him in Pete's Woods.

"Hey, Mom," he asked, knocking on her bedroom door. "Where are the empty ice cream pails? Me and Addie are gonna pick some blueberries."

The door opened a crack. "There should be a couple under the sink," she replied, her eyes no more than thin slits.

"You okay, Mom? Do you need anything?"

"Can you make me a pot of coffee?"

Billy smiled and nodded. "Comin' right up."

Anna reached her arm through the narrow opening and caressed Billy's cheek. "Where's your sister?"

"She's outside."

"How are you doing? You okay?"

"Sort of. It's gonna be weird not seeing Renny every day. Like someone died, ya know?"

Anna said she knew. "Go on, honey—have fun."

Billy and Addie found a ripe patch of blueberries and were soon talking about everything that had happened that summer—a search for some kind of meaning they hoped would help them make sense of it all.

"Maybe that's not how it works," Billy suggested.

"Not how *what* works?" Addie asked, tossing a blueberry in the air and catching it in her mouth.

"Maybe random stuff just happens."

"Like Dad dying?! How was that random?"

"You heard what Mr. Hopp told us last Christmas. What if Dad hadn't picked up that flower when he jumped outta the helicopter? Seems pretty random to me."

"You're nuts, Shorty."

219

But as their pails, filled Addie couldn't push Billy's words from her mind. Eventually her thoughts were interrupted by the sound of a dog's familiar bark.

"Come on," she said, pouring her blueberries into his pail. "We've got plenty."

They walked past the slate outcropping Addie had carved into two months earlier and saw Ranger waiting for them on the trailer's small porch. He was barking with a persistence they hadn't heard from him before.

"C'mere, boy!" Addie shouted. She patted her legs but Ranger wouldn't budge. Instead, he began pawing the mudroom door.

"What's his problem?"

"Who knows?" she replied, jogging ahead of Billy. The dog stopped barking, but his frantic excitement continued. Billy popped a few blueberries in his mouth as Addie and Ranger disappeared inside the trailer.

Hours later—when Billy replayed what happened next—he knew it hadn't been the urgency in his sister's voice that had caused him to drop his pail of blueberries. It wasn't her volume either. It was a rare desperation he heard from Addie, combined with a name she had never used before.

"BILLY!!!"

His first hurried steps toward the trailer squished through the blueberries scattered on the ground in front of him. Finding his footing, Billy leapt onto the porch and burst into the kitchen. He found Addie kneeling over the prone figure of their mother, who was lying face down on the floor. Ranger sat next to her, nuzzling Anna's face for some sign of life.

"What happened?!"

"I don't know! I just found her like this!"

Billy took a deep breath and forgot to exhale. When he finally did, he knelt down and pressed his fingers on his mother's wrist. "We've gotta turn her over!" he said, struggling to fight off a terror that had begun to grip him.

"Do you even know what you're doing, Shorty?!"

Billy didn't answer. He rolled his mother onto her back, revealing a welt on her temple, presumably from the fall she had just taken. He leaned over her face and turned his ear to her mouth and nose.

"She's breathing," Billy said, his face flooded with relief.

"Should we call the Carsons?!" Without waiting for an answer, Addie grabbed the phone and dialed. Busy. She tried two more times—same response. "Come on," she decided, putting her arms under her Mom's shoulders. "We have to get her to the hospital."

"You can't drive!"

"Sure I can. I've got my permit."

"But the car's a stick shift!"

"So?! It can't be much different than driving the tractor!"

It was a lot different. Addie didn't get the hang of the clutch and gears until they had reached the outskirts of Wood City. Even then it was another grinding three miles to the emergency room doors of Memorial Hospital.

Billy raced inside and returned with a nurse and young orderly in tow. The nurse, an older heavy-set woman whose name tag read *Maggie, R.N.*, calmly issued instructions. The orderly spun a gurney around to the back seat, transferred Anna onto it and whisked her into a trauma room. Dazed and scared, Billy and Addie followed.

"Come with me please," the nurse said as she closed the room's curtain behind her.

"Are you kidding?!" Addie nearly screamed. "I'm staying here!"

Maggie, R.N. dropped her business-like attitude and studied the two frightened faces. "Don't worry," she said gently, looking from Billy to Addie. "Your mother is in good hands." She guided them to a small office around the corner labeled *Intake*.

They answered a few obligatory questions—their mother's name, age, height and weight, as well as what had happened. Neither Billy nor Addie felt like they were much help, but the nurse nodded and smiled, writing down everything they told her. She was about to see if there was any news she could give them when a second nurse—tall, thin and nameless— walked in carrying a thick manila folder.

"Are you Anna Pearson's children?" She handed the folder to Maggie, R.N., who began leafing through it.

221

"Is our Mom gonna be okay?" Billy asked her. He chewed on his lower lip, hoping the nurse would tell them something, anything.

"She's resting," the woman replied coldly. "We'll let you see her soon."

Addie eyed the nurse suspiciously. "What's that?" she said, pointing to the folder.

"I'm sure Maggie has asked you a lot of questions," *Nurse Nameless* said. "But I'm going to need to ask you a few more."

Her questions were different than Maggie, R.N.'s. *"How has your mom been sleeping? Has she been lethargic, listless? For how long? Has she been eating? How much? Have you noticed any weight loss recently? What about hair loss?"*

As Billy and Addie fumbled to answer each new question, the veil that had concealed Anna's deteriorating health from them finally lifted. Nurse Nameless did nothing to ease their worries, never making eye contact as she clicked the end of her ballpoint pen and tucked it into a tightly wound bun in the back of her head.

"What you've told me is consistent with the information Mrs. Pearson has already given us."

"Then she's awake?" Billy said hopefully.

"Like I said, Mrs. Pearson is resting. As you know, your mother has been here before." She indicated the charts Maggie, R.N. was still looking at.

"What are you talking about?!" Addie demanded. "When?!"

Before the woman could say another word, Maggie, R.N. slapped the manila folder shut and pulled Nurse Nameless out of the room and down an adjacent hallway. Billy and Addie heard them arguing in low, harsh tones. A minute later, Maggie, R.N. returned wearing a pleasant but strained smile.

"Would you like to see your Mom now?"

They felt like they were at a stranger's bedside, next to some unknown woman with an IV in her arm and an oxygen mask over her face. Their mother's appearance—ghost-like skin and dull hair, along with the swelling on her forehead—shocked them.

"Your mom was dehydrated and her vital signs were low when you brought her here," Maggie R.N. explained. "But that tube in her arm is giving her the fluids she needs. The oxygen is just a precaution. We do

222

that for everyone who loses consciousness. You were smart to get her here as quickly as you did," she added, putting her hand on Addie's shoulder.

"When will she wake up?" Billy asked, taking a seat next to the bed.

"We added a mild sedative to the IV to stabilize her vitals, but she should wake up soon." Maggie, R.N. drew another seat over to the bed and motioned for Addie to sit. "Stay as long as you like. I have to make a call." She scanned the front cover of Anna's folder for a phone number, then hurried from the room.

Billy and Addie sat quietly next to their mother for ten minutes. He watched the hypnotic drip, drip, drip of the IV bag and followed the tube from her mask to the metal canister next to the bed. Under different circumstances these things might have fascinated Billy, but knowing they were attached to his mother frightened him.

"Was she like this all summer and we just didn't see it?" Addie wondered aloud.

"Didn't see what?"

"You heard that nurse. Think about it—Mom always says she's fine even when she's not."

"What about 4th of July weekend?" Billy said. "She was fine then."

"Was she? Come on, Shorty. You've seen the same things I have."

"Knock it off, Addie." Billy was ready to challenge his sister for the millionth time but was interrupted by a low moan.

"I must still be alive," a voice whispered. "Because I can hear my children bickering." Anna's eyelids fluttered open. She looked around the room, unsure how much Billy and Addie had been told.

"Mom!" Tears pooled in their eyes as Anna reached out to them. Billy told her everything that happened—minus their wild ride—since they found her on the kitchen floor.

"And now you're awake!" he said, flinging aside the curtain, determined to find Maggie, R.N. He needn't have bothered. She was striding toward them with the Carsons by her side. Helen murmured her relief as Virgil stood behind his wife with a grave expression on his face.

"The nurse said you gave Billy and Addie quite a scare."

"I'm just glad you and Helen were home when they called," Anna replied.

223

Mr. Carson shook his head. "We didn't drive you here, Anna." He looked at Addie. "Did you call us? Helen was on the phone with our daughter Trudy, trying to pick a date for our grand-daughter's baptism."

"We didn't hear a siren," Helen said. "Did the ambulance come right away, Addie?"

Maggie, R.N. adjusted Anna's IV and spoke up. "Your daughter drove you here, Mrs. Pearson. And it's lucky for you that she did."

All eyes except Billy's turned to Addie. "What was I supposed to do?" she shrugged. "Besides, it wasn't much different than driving the tractor."

"Is that true, Billy?" Mr. Carson asked him with arched eyebrows.

"Mostly," Billy replied after a quick glance at his sister.

"Addie, honey—come here," Anna said, reaching out her hand. "Thank you. Both of you."

"Okay, folks," Maggie, R.N. said with unmistakable authority. "Mrs. Pearson needs to rest. If you'd like, ma'am, I can bring your kids to the cafeteria. You two," she pointed at Billy and Addie, "Are probably hungry."

"That's a good idea," Mr. Carson seconded. "Helen and I will catch up with you in a bit." He looked knowingly at Maggie, R.N. before she led Billy and Addie to the elevator.

An emotional exhaustion settled over them as they absent-mindedly chewed their food. Twenty minutes later and only slightly revived, Addie hoped they could go home soon.

"A couple more hours, maybe," Billy guessed. "So do you think you'll get in trouble?"

"For what? Driving? I'd say that's the least of our problems."

"What do you mean?"

"Mom's not just tired, Shorty. And you know it."

Billy wanted tell Addie she was wrong, but that Billy was long gone. He had disappeared the same night the Northern Pacific Railroad sign went up in flames. He wasn't coming back.

"Aren't you supposed to be yelling *bullcrap* right about now?"

"Probably, but what's the use?" They picked at their food again as the Carsons entered the cafeteria.

"We're going to bring your mom to the farm in a few hours," Mr. Carson told them. "I'll bring her car back to the trailer then meet you up there." He held his hand out to Addie for the car keys. "You can ride back with me if you'd like."

"Why do you need to go to the trailer?"

"To pack, dear," Mrs. Carson said. "You're going to stay with us. I'm going to take some time off from the library to help out."

"Help out with what?!" Addie stood but Mrs. Carson's hand drew her back down.

"How sick is she?" Billy asked, surrendering to reality.

Mr. Carson looked from the boy to the girl. He and Helen had given Anna their word the previous Christmas, but that seven month secret had expired when she collapsed in her kitchen. He knew he should be relieved, but he wasn't. The worst, after all, was right in front of him in Billy and Addie's anxious eyes. They were waiting for him to say that everything was going to be alright. But that would be a lie, and Mr. Carson wasn't going to hide the truth from them any longer. Not one more day.

"Billy, Addie—I'm sorry. Your mom has cancer."

Sunday, August 14ᵗʰ

Dear Dad,

    Sara's gone and Mom's almost gone, too. Doctors told us she has pancreatic cancer. They said it was terminal. Shorty asked what terminal meant but I already knew. Mr. Carson said that after Mom got her diagnosis last December, she made a plan with them that if the cancer got worse, we would live with the Carsons. That's why Mom wanted us to work on the farm. She was hoping it would eventually come to feel like a second home to us. Mr. Carson said he was sorry, he thought Mom should have told us right away. "But your Mom had her reasons," he said. The only reason I can think of is Jake.

    What's going to happen when he finds out? No one has seen Jake in weeks, but Mr. Carson still thinks he should be told. I don't know, maybe he's right. What's the point of keeping secrets anymore?

    Shorty hasn't left the Carson's house since we moved here. I guess he's doing for Mom what he did for me that night in the Bog. Helping any way he can. I wish I was like that because I don't know what to do.

    I don't know what to feel either, Dad. The doctors told us Mom is dying, but if that's true how come she's not scared? She said, "See Addie, everything is working out for the best." How is her dying for the best?!

    Shorty and Mrs. Carson come and go from her room with glasses of water that Mom can barely drink and plates of food that she can't keep down while I read to her and try to ignore the fact that her sheets have to be changed three times a day. "Keep reading, honey," she tells me while our whole world is falling apart. And when night comes I can't stop hearing her cry out in pain.

    I know you didn't see death coming, Dad, but Mom can and she still insists, "No more doctors, no more hospitals." Why won't she fight? How can she think just letting go is everything working out for the best?!

    It's almost dawn. Mom will be awake soon, if she even slept at all. Last night she asked if Shorty and I could get her photo albums from the trailer today. I'll try, but I doubt he'll budge.

    I miss you all the time, Dad. Now more than ever.

Love,
Your daughter, Addie

22
WISHFUL THINKING

Jake wasn't sleeping well, though not for the usual reasons. The urge to drink still came and went, but the constant compulsion had faded. For weeks he'd been a damp dishrag, continually wrung dry by cravings that threatened to overwhelm him. But somehow Jake had found a way out—enough peace to turn towards a life after Lost Elm. But he had to finish his list first. So as Addie wrote her pre-dawn diary entry, Jake considered the last four moves he had to make.

Numbers 5 and 6 on the list would take care of themselves. There was no reason to stay in town after he closed his bank account, and the house keys would be handed over to the buyers on Friday morning, August 19th. But then what? As Jake fretted over his future, the answer literally landed on his doorstep.

Before the summer of 1977, Current events had never much interested Jake. He'd always been too busy thrashing in his own quicksand to care about what was going on in the wider world. But one state and national issue had caught his eye—the political fight over one million acres of unspoiled land in northern Minnesota known as the *Boundary Waters Canoe Area*.

At stake was the future of a great swath of the state north of the Mesabi Range. Lumber and mining interests were poised to advance to the Canadian border whenever Congress gave the word. But conservationists believed just as ardently in saving the Boundary Waters in its pristine condition—a refuge for nature and nature-lovers alike.

Jake poured over stories in the *Duluth Herald* about the looming showdown in Washington. He understood the position of the mining and lumber companies—he'd been out of work too often not to. Open up the B.W.C.A. to both, they argued, and employ hundreds of people, maybe thousands. But with each new story, Jake found himself siding with the conservationists.

Like most days since he left Miller-Dwan, Jake brought a cup of coffee out to the porch and turned to the editorial page of the Herald. An article, *"Why We Need the Boundary Waters,"* laid out a hopeful future not only for northern Minnesota, but for Jake as well.

People were disillusioned and dissatisfied, the article began. Modernity, for all its gadgets, wasn't making anyone any happier. The answer, the writer believed, was obvious. Seek solitude and freedom in nature. Jake didn't need to read another word. He rushed inside, stuffed a few items into an overnight bag and promptly sped out of town.

Jake wouldn't be gone for good. Ely, Minnesota, at the southern edge of the Boundary Waters, was only a two-hour drive north of Lost Elm. He figured he would return in a day or two, give Anna the title and deed, stick around long enough to hand over his dad's keys, then leave town and never look back.

With every passing mile Jake expected roadblocks or detours or some other delay—the universe's way of telling him to give up and go home, be the aimless failure he'd always been. But none appeared except for an old bull moose who stood his ground in the middle of Highway 1. It eyed Jake suspiciously for a minute before disappearing into the forest.

Flush with outdoor adventurers, Ely was bustling on a Sunday afternoon. Everywhere Jake looked, cars and trucks brimmed with camping gear. A few bars were sandwiched between storefronts promoting fishing and guide services, but Jake didn't notice any of them. His eyes were fixed on the largest building in town—*Boundary Outfitters*. Taped to the window in front of a faceless mannequin dressed in a flannel shirt and cargo pants was a sign advertising what Jake had driven over a 100 miles to find. *Help Wanted*.

The owner, an older man behind the cash register, quickly sized him up and said bluntly, "We can probably use you." The rest of Jake's day was a pleasant blur. He helped outfit fishing parties and tagged along with guides and groups going in and out of the Boundary Waters. He made mistakes and struggled to keep up, but the owner offered only encouraging words. "You can stay at my cabin on Miners' Lake tonight. Longer if you want the job." The cabin wasn't more than a crude shack, but Jake didn't care. It gave him the solitude he needed.

Thirty hours later Jake returned to Lost Elm. Coasting in on Chestnut Avenue, he couldn't help noticing that the town seemed smaller than it had the day before. But Jake didn't waste any time or energy wondering why, he only knew that home didn't feel like home anymore.

Exhausted, Jake collapsed on his bare mattress, anxious and afraid. The job he was promised would be his when he returned to Ely, but when had anything ever gone his way? Jake had a nagging feeling that the next five days were going to be hard ones, the past's way of testing his resolve and desire for a newfound future.

When sleep finally claimed him, Jake was wondering why the owner had hired him in the first place. What he didn't know was that the man had recognized at a glance Jake's shaky grip on sobriety, the same one he had struggled through years earlier. Turning Jake away was never really an option. *If someone like me asks for help,* the older man reasoned, *How can I say no?*

✻

Addie woke the next morning knowing she couldn't take no for an answer. A full week had passed since they moved in with the Carsons, and yet Billy hadn't been outside even once. Addie's efforts the day before had failed, even when Anna weakly insisted that she wanted Billy to help his sister bring some keepsakes back from the trailer. "Tomorrow," he assured her, though no one believed him.

Addie tiptoed downstairs and found Billy already at the stove scrambling a few eggs, something bland he knew his mom could eat. As he dished them onto a plate, a piece of bread sprang up from the toaster. He buttered it, then turned toward the first floor guest room. Addie was blocking his way.

"Tomorrow's today, Shorty. You promised."

"Knock it off, Addie," Billy snapped as he tried to move around her.

"You heard Mom. She wants us to get her photo albums."

"Get 'em yourself!" Billy yelled. He charged forward and collided with Addie, the plate slipping from his hands and crashing onto the hardwood floor. It didn't break but made enough noise to wake everyone in the house. Ranger greedily gobbled up the food before Billy could shoo him away.

"Now look what you did!" he hissed. "Do you wanna wake up Mom?!"

"Kind of, yeah!" Addie shot back. "What are you so afraid of?"

"That I won't be here when he gets back," a small voice behind them answered. Anna stood in the doorway of her bedroom, a blanket draped over her shoulders.

At the sound of their mother's voice and the truth in her words, Billy's shoulders shook as he vainly fought back tears. Although Anna had withered even more in the past week, it was Billy who disappeared into her arms.

She kissed his forehead and whispered, "I'll be waiting for you on the porch when you get back, okay? We can look at the pictures together."

Billy struggled to compose himself as Mr. and Mrs. Carson came downstairs, though neither acted as if anything was amiss. Helen busied herself with the coffee maker while Virgil scanned a list of chores he'd written down the night before.

"Did you sleep well, Anna?" he asked.

Anna nodded and smiled. For the first time since they brought her home from the hospital, she had slept through the night. No painful cries, no fevered dreams.

"Addie," Mr. Carson said. "I think now would be a good time to run down to the trailer. In the meantime we'll get your mom set up on the porch. It shouldn't take you more than a few minutes."

Billy frowned. "It'll take longer than that just to walk there."

"Not if she drives."

"But I only have my permit."

"You've driven under worse circumstances, honey," Anna reminded her.

"Come on, Shorty," Addie said, fishing the keys out of a kitchen drawer. "Let's go."

*

Jake crossed his fingers and lifted the phone off its cradle. A Bell Telephone repairman had restored service, but Jake hadn't used the phone yet. The receiver crackled for a second then emitted a steady dial tone.

He called the trailer repeatedly but there was no answer. The bank wouldn't open for another half hour. Jake dropped into a chair at the kitchen table and slapped a thick envelope against his open palm. The same envelope the county abstract office had given him, he would give Anna. Her freedom.

Jake stood and paced, then sat down again. When he did, he saw his reflection in the tarnished chrome of an old breadbox on the kitchen counter. A beleaguered man stared back at him, but one whose eyes were no longer haunted. And the skin on Jake's cheeks was now colored by the sun rather than alcohol. He looked up at the clock—8:40am—and rubbed the stubble on his chin before disappearing into the bathroom.

When Jake stepped out into the morning sunshine twenty minutes later, he was freshly scrubbed and shaved. He drove over to Chestnut Avenue and idled next to the post office, half a block down from the bank. Twenty more minutes passed. Familiar employees pulled into the parking lot across from First National Bank but Anna wasn't one of them. At 9:30 Jake got out of his truck and walked to the intersection. He looked up and down Chestnut and 3rd but didn't see her green Volkswagen anywhere, noticing instead a *Come in, We're Open* sign hanging in the window of Ginny's Mop Shop. *The trailer can wait a few more minutes,* he decided. *I could use a haircut.*

✳

Billy and Addie beat Jake to the Loop by five minutes. He parked the truck next to the driveway and surveyed the property. The lawn looked like it needed mowing, but nothing else seemed out of the ordinary. When he stepped onto the trailer's narrow porch, the door suddenly burst open, knocking him off the porch and to the ground.

"Mom said it was under her bed!" Billy yelled. "Check again!" He had backed out of the mudroom with his arms full, forcing the outer door open with a hip check.

"Hi, Billy," Jake murmured as he rose to his feet.

Billy hadn't seen Jake in weeks. The grubby, disheveled man of his memory had been replaced by a stranger—neat, clean, bordering on respectable.

"Hi," Billy replied, barely audible.

"Is your Mom home? I have something for her." He waved the envelope.

"She's not here. I can take it."

"I was hoping to talk to her," Jake said uncertainly. "But I guess everything she needs is in here." He handed Billy the envelope.

"You look different."

"Yeah, I thought I should . . ." Jake's voice trailed off as he rubbed his smooth chin. "I gotta new job, figured I should clean up a little."

Billy hoped Jake would leave before Addie came out of the trailer. Still, he had to ask. "What job?"

"Is Anna gonna be home soon?" Jake said. "I stopped by the bank but she wasn't there. Is everything alright?"

"Everything's fine, Jake," a voice behind him answered. Addie stood in the doorway with a box in her arms.

"Where are you taking that?"

"Mrs. Carson got some bad news from the doctor a few weeks ago," she replied. "Mr. Carson asked Mom if we could move in with them for a while and help out."

"Is she gonna be okay?"

Addie shrugged. "The doctor doesn't know."

"Really?" Jake said, stunned. "She seemed fine last month."

"Things change."

"Geez, I'm sorry. Mrs. Carson was a real nice lady."

"She still is," Billy maintained. Embarrassed, Jake only nodded.

"Let's go, Shorty." Addie came down the porch and strode past her brother, done giving Jake answers he didn't deserve, even if they were half-truths.

"If Anna's not here, who drove?"

Addie set the box in the back seat of the Volkswagen and flashed him the car keys. "I had to learn how to drive sometime, Jake. You coming, Shorty?"

"Tell Mom I'll be there in a few minutes. I wanna get my baseball cards."

"Suit yourself." She backed out of the driveway, sped around the Loop and turned onto the highway as fast as her inexperienced hands and feet could drive her.

"When did Addie learn how to drive a stick shift?"

"Last week."

Jake didn't press Billy for more answers. He was just trying to find a way to say goodbye.

"So this job, is it real?"

"They all were, Billy." Humiliation crept into Jake's pale cheeks. "I just couldn't . . ."

"Keep one?"

"It's different this time. I found somewhere I think I can fit in, let a lot of things go."

"Like what?"

"Like your mom, for starters," Jake replied. "I was never her first choice."

"Were you and my dad really friends?"

"Since first grade."

"Mom said that changed. How come?"

"I blamed Will for something that wasn't his fault. I wish I hadn't, but I did," Jake admitted. "Happened a long time ago."

"I should get going, Jake. Mom probably needs me."

"Can you do me a favor, Billy? Can you wait 'til Saturday to give her that envelope? And this," he removed a key from his key chain. "Stick this in there too."

"Anything else?"

"Yeah," Jake asked, a little timidly. "Can you wish me luck?"

A faint smile crossed Billy's face, but what had bothered him before he learned of his mother's cancer—Jake's painting of Addie—resurfaced. But before asked, Billy came clean about sneaking into Ron Pearson's house.

"What did ya think of it?" Jake inquired, not at all mad about Billy's trespassing.

"You've never liked her," Billy accused him. "Why paint a picture of her?"

"I dunno . . . I guess I just needed to. That's how painting works sometimes."

"Whaddya mean, you needed to?!" Billy dropped his box of cards and balled up his fists. "That's Addie you're talking about!"

"What?!" Jake looked genuinely surprised. "That's not Addie. It doesn't look a thing like her." He pulled the photograph from his pocket. "This is who I painted. This is my mom." He pointed to the caption on the back—*Betty, July 1933*.

"Renny was positive it was Addie," Billy said, visibly relieved. "I guess he wasn't always right."

"Not this time," Jake replied, returning the picture to his pocket. "I should get going too, Billy," he said with an air of finality. "Tell your

Mom to take care of herself. Tell her I'm sorry." He gave the trailer a long last look and offered Billy a small wave before he drove off.

Billy didn't linger inside the Loop. Home was somewhere else now, where people who loved him were waiting. He crossed into the lower field and whispered, "Good luck, Jake."

*

The hours after Jake left the trailer blurred together. An uneasy, dangerous fog hovered over him that he couldn't wave away. At dusk he sat in the kitchen, a road atlas lying across his lap open to a map of Minnesota. In one hand he held the photograph of his mother, in the other was his list from the fridge. He stared back and forth from young Betty to number 7. *See Mom* seemed like an impossibility, but deep down Jake knew that if his list went unfinished it would eat away at him, and eventually he would scratch old, destructive itches. *You wrote this for a reason,* he decided. *Finish it.*

A twinge skipped across Jake's chest like a flat rock on water as he crossed out Talk to Anna. *Billy will explain everything. So will the envelope.*

"I guess that's it then."

The words echoed into the basement. Jake followed his voice downstairs until he was again face to face with the painting of his mother.

"This doesn't look a thing like . . ." Addie's name died on the tip of his tongue as a dim, dormant thread of memory wound its way into his consciousness.

For years Jake never gave the memory a first thought, much less a second. He had simply chalked it up to wishful thinking and heavy drinking. But his sobriety uncovered more than he had bargained for in the last six weeks. Why not more memories too?

Jake unscrewed the caps off a few tubes of paint and squeezed them onto his palette. Using a wide brush, he mixed them together until he was certain he'd gotten the colors right. Satisfied, Jake began painting over his mother's dark-brown hair.

An hour later he seemed to snap out of a trance. After gulping down a large glass of water, Jake examined the picture anew, his clothes spattered with shades of pale orange and yellow. Billy's little friend had been right all along. Jake wasn't looking at his mother anymore. The girl with the windblown hair looked just like . . .

"Addie."

He hadn't imagined it. The long-buried memory was real. "It's true," Jake realized. "She's mine."

23
WHEREVER SHE IS, FIND HER

Adulthood hit Will and Anna hard after high school graduation in May 1960. Judy Travers, a fading shadow of herself after her husband's death four years earlier, died of tuberculosis in July at the age of forty-five. Faced with the prospect of losing his parents' house, Will postponed college and got a job at the paper mill in Wood City.

Anna's dreams of college wouldn't wait. Always a whiz with numbers, she majored in accounting at the University of Minnesota-Duluth, joining classes full of young men who scoffed at "the girl" in their midst. Nonetheless, *the girl* proved that she belonged, quickly rising to the top of her class.

Anna's rise ended on Election Day—November 8, 1960. She hurried home after classes to watch the TV coverage with her parents, but was met by Will instead. "They were killed by a drunk driver out on Highway 61," he whispered. A note on the kitchen table explained everything:

> *Anna,*
> *Your father and I went to vote, then out for a drive.*
> *Don't spoil your appetite. I'm making pot roast.*
> > *Love, Mom.*

Will and Anna did what any 19 year-olds would do in the same situation, they found solace and support in each other. She dropped out of school and began waitressing at Paulette's, but her meager wages weren't enough to prevent the bank from taking her parents' house. An only child like Will, Anna rented a small apartment in town for the sake of appearances, but spent most of her nights with him.

Jake, meanwhile, had mounted a serious campaign for the position of town drunk. His father got him work at the feed mill after graduation, but like so many other jobs to come, he couldn't make this one stick. To make matters worse, Jake knew his dad wouldn't fire him and he was unfazed by the fact that he had alienated his co-workers in the process.

Will didn't struggle with sudden adulthood like Jake, at least not at first. Though he chafed at the routine of his job, he did what came naturally—he led. The paper mill was in a dispute with its union workers and Will found his way right into the middle of it. He joined a bargaining team and helped draft editorials for the local newspapers. But as soon as labor and management reached an agreement in mid-November, the mill's ownership fired every new employee who'd been active in negotiations. Suddenly out of work and labeled a troublemaker, Will's bright future dimmed to a flicker.

Imprisoned in her own grief, Anna accepted his brooding as best she could. With the Christmas season in full swing—their first without their parents—Will weighed his narrowing options. Over supper he mentioned the idea of military service.

"You signed up already, didn't you, Will?" she said, his betrayal obvious in her accusation. He stabbed at a few peas and nodded. "Were you even going to tell me?!"

"I'm telling you now."

"So that's it then?!" Anna rose from the table and grabbed her coat. "You know there aren't any unions to organize in the Army!" she seethed.

"The Navy."

"What?!" Anna's face reddened as she punched each arm through the sleeves of her coat.

"I joined the Navy."

"Any other bombs you want to drop?!" she fumed, reaching for the front door. "Or whatever the Navy does—fire torpedoes?"

"It's not like that, Anna. I'm going to be helping people, not hurting them," Will tried to explain. "After basic training I'm going to be a medic."

The question Anna was afraid to ask loomed between them. "For how long?"

"What do you mean?"

"You know what I mean! How long?!"

"Six years."

"You signed up for six years?!"

"What choice did I have?!" he replied, his own voice rising. "I lost my job, the house is next. Where does that leave us?"

"It leaves us together, Will! What you're doing won't!"

"It's something I had to do, Anna," he said, taking a step toward her. "I didn't have a choice."

"Oh please! We all have choices. You didn't have to tell Jake what you saw at his house two summers ago. You didn't have to ask me to prom either. And you could have just done your job instead of getting involved in all that union business."

"I'm sorry."

"That you signed up or that you didn't tell me?"

"What can I do?" Will begged her.

"You already did it, Will, and you didn't say a word." She unclasped the necklace that was threaded through his class ring and handed it to him.

"Just like that?" Will said in stunned disbelief. He wanted to hold her tight, propel them back to that day on the bridge a year ago when he showed her *WILL AND ANNA*. He held out his hand, but this time she didn't take it.

"When do you leave?"

"Next week—the 15th."

Will's looming departure was the last straw, the final act in a months-long tragedy—he would be leaving her before Christmas. To Anna, locked out from Will's thoughts and his choices, it seemed unforgivably cruel.

*

From his first push-up at the *Great Lakes Naval Station* an hour north of Chicago, Will knew he'd made a terrible mistake. He didn't regret enlisting, but he knew he should have found a way to join the Navy *and* keep Anna. Letter after letter to her followed, though she never wrote him back. Will wasn't discouraged. Each night before lights out he wrote about every aspect of boot camp, closing each letter the same way: *I'm sorry, Anna. I should have talked to you. Love, Will.*

She read and kept each one, but soldiered on believing she'd seen the last of Will Travers. Nevertheless, Anna's broken heart made space for him alongside the open wound of her parents' deaths. She plodded numbly through Christmas, picking up extra shifts at Paulette's from co-workers eager to spend time with their families.

Jake, on the other hand, rolled merrily through the holidays and into January as if he didn't have a care in the world. The Junction was his home most nights, but he also made frequent visits to a certain house on the east side of Duluth. Each trip there was never more than a drive-by, though whenever Jake glimpsed his mother inside, harder drinking usually followed.

His outlook didn't brighten when he found out Will had joined the Navy. The news was just one more reminder of all he had lost since the summer of '59—a best friend, his mother, any chance with Anna. He assumed two of those people were gone for good, but not the third. So as calendars across Lost Elm turned over to January 1961, Jake swiveled his attention—and his bar stool—to Paulette's Café.

What happened next was predictable. Loneliness has a mind of its own and Anna was trapped in a dark and lonely place. From the moment Jake took a seat at the café's lunch counter, she saw him as an easy way out of her misery.

They hardly spoke. He came in before work (when he worked), bracing himself with coffee and eggs. Hours later, if Anna worked the lunch rush, Jake returned. She didn't particularly look forward to seeing him, but always felt a little better when he appeared. Whatever it took to paper over her pain, she vaguely decided, was a soft place worth landing.

Anna wasn't the least bit bothered when Jake showed up outside Paulette's on a late Friday night in mid-January waving a six-pack of beer in the café window. With no more customers, she closed up and led him to a booth in the back. They said little—mostly small talk about President-elect Kennedy's inauguration the next week. Anna nursed two beers while Jake chugged the other four.

When he emptied his last can, she offered to walk him home, guessing that Jake had probably been to the Junction earlier that evening. When he didn't object, they bundled up and crossed the deserted intersection. Ron Pearson's house wasn't far, but Jake leaned heavily on Anna the entire way. She wasn't sure if he needed her help, but was glad for the warmth and closeness of his body. They stumbled noisily through the dark kitchen, though Jake wasn't worried about waking his father. "My dad won't hear a thing," he mumbled. "He's probably been passed out for hours."

Anna knew she should have left right after helping Jake into bed—slip out before doing something she'd regret—but she didn't. Instead, they fumbled together in the dark—two desperate people trying to feel anything but alone, if only for a little while.

A chorus of drunken snoring from Jake and his father drowned out whatever noise Anna made on her way out of the house. Her apartment was on the far side of the water tower but she turned toward Jay Cooke Park instead, along the same tracks Will and Jake had wandered over the previous summer.

Anna found their carved names on the bridge, faintly visible in the moonlight. She stared at them, then down to the icy river far below. A small headache wormed its way into her brain— payback for the choice she'd made a few hours ago. Now that choice left her feeling emptier than ever.

By the time she turned back toward Lost Elm, the western sky had begun to lighten, though her mood had not. Will was no longer hers, yet Anna knew she had betrayed him just the same. Numb to everything since he left, the wound of his absence tore open with a vengeance, reminding her that she was still alive and still loved him. With the stars overhead rapidly twinkling out, Anna realized that she had no idea what she was doing, though there was one thing she promised herself she would never do again.

Jake made that promise easy. He trickled in and out of the café over the next few weeks, but the lonely space he had briefly filled in her was gone. There was no confrontation, no falling out. In fact, they both acted as if nothing had passed between them. By Inauguration Day—Friday, January 20th—Jake stopped coming into Paulette's altogether.

Not surprisingly, he picked up right where he'd left off, but this time the trips to Duluth ended. Instead, Jake slipped easily into the skin he wouldn't shed until he rolled the Comet into the ditch next to Halverson Road. The cement on that façade would have years to harden; years in which Jake was nothing more than a bystander in his own life. At his best, he was sullen and irresponsible—at his worst, destructive and dangerous. Ironically, the same day a new President asked his fellow Americans what they could do for their country, Jake returned to a life he knew all too well—one where he could only do for himself.

*

Back at Great Lakes Naval Station, Will's unit assembled in their barracks to watch the young President's swearing-in and inaugural speech

243

on television. A former Navy veteran himself, Kennedy's address was tempered with realism and hope, a call for vigilance in a world full peril and promise.

Like many other Americans who heard the new President's speech that day, Will was deeply moved. The soaring rhetoric made an indelible mark. "Let every nation know," Kennedy proclaimed, "Whether it wishes us well or ill, that we shall pay any price, bear any burden, meet any hardship, support any friend, oppose any foe, to assure the survival and the success of liberty."

Kennedy's sentiments were why Will had joined the Navy in the first place, what he hadn't been able to express to Anna a month ago. But face them without her? Unthinkable. Which is why Will—weekend pass in hand—boarded a Greyhound bus ten hours later. It was bound for Duluth, with a convenient stop in Lost Elm.

Too anxious to sleep on the overnight ride, Will prepared an inaugural address of his own. Always methodical, he jotted down some notes on an old brochure he found jammed between the seats. It didn't dawn on him until the bus passed a road sign—*Lost Elm: 5 miles*—that Anna might not want to hear any of it, rehearsed or not.

"Home to see a girl?" a dignified voice next to him asked.

Will looked over to the window seat. An older woman, asleep for most of the trip, pointed to the paper in his hand.

"A girl," she repeated. "Is that what this is all about?"

Feeling a little ridiculous, Will folded the brochure in half and was about to stuff it in his coat pocket when the woman snatched it out of his hand. A few seconds passed before she clucked and shook her head.

"You're going to have to do better than this if you want to get her back. *'We make a good team?'* I don't know a woman alive who wants to hear that. And this part, *'You're my best friend?'* Young man, if you need a best friend, buy a dog." She handed back his notes. "If you're headed to Duluth, you better work fast, otherwise you came a long way for nothing."

"Lost Elm," he mumbled.

"Oh, Lord. You have a roundtrip ticket right?"

Will sized her up. She had eyes that burned with an uncommon intensity.

"I'm just teasing," she said, patting his hand. "Forty-three years ago a boy a lot more scared than you did the same thing for me. He was off to

France with General Pershing. *Over There*, and all that nonsense. He went A.W.O.L. from Fort Snelling, hopped a train to Duluth and begged me to marry him. All in one day. Can you believe that?"

"Did you say yes?"

"I did. But yours won't if you repeat any of that dreck."

"What would you want to hear?"

"What's in your heart. You do have a heart, don't you?"

Will laughed at her bluntness as the bus pulled into Lost Elm. She smiled reassuringly as they came to a stop in the courthouse parking lot. It was 7am. Paulette's had just opened.

"Is this your stop too?" he asked, retrieving his pack from an overhead compartment.

"Yes, that's my daughter right there." She pointed to a striking woman standing next to a car. Add twenty more years and the two women might have been twins. Will grabbed the lady's suitcase and followed her off the bus.

"Are you just visiting?" Will asked as the bus pulled away.

"You're stalling, young man. Go. Wherever she is, this girl of yours, find her. Say what you came to say."

"What if she says no?"

"Then she said no to a question you had the courage to ask." The woman's expression suddenly grew serious. She took a step toward Will and put her gloved hand on his cheek. "Don't wait, and don't take anything for granted. There is only now. Now may be all the time you have."

Will looked past the woman to her daughter. *Early 40's,* he guessed. "Did your soldier make it home?"

She shook her head.

"Was it worth it?"

"Every day since," she said as her daughter approached them. "Now go. Tell her what's in your heart. Time's a-wasting."

*

Even if Will had known what to say when he walked into Paulette's, Anna didn't give him a chance. Instead, her sleepy eyes opened wide and she ran into his arms. Customers beamed at them then quickly looked away, their Midwestern reserve re-asserting itself. Anna held Will for a long time, afraid he might melt away if she let go.

"Is it really you?" she whispered.

Will held her face in his hands and kissed her. She looked into his eyes. Their fire—missing when he left—had returned.

"Can we go somewhere?"

"I can't, Will. My shift just started."

"Go on, honey," Paulette hollered from behind the counter. "You're not going to be worth a nickel today. I'll see you bright and early Monday morning."

Will led Anna across the street to a bench below the water tower. She was so overwhelmed that she almost forgot she was still mad at him.

"How have you been?" he asked after they sat down.

Anna's quiet anger returned. "You left me here to pick up the pieces, Will."

"Have you?"

"In a month?" she bristled. "You know it doesn't work that way."

"I'm so sorry, Anna."

"You don't have to apologize anymore, Will. I read all your letters. I know you meant what you said." Anna exhaled slowly, her breath thick in the cold morning air. "I just don't understand why you didn't let me in. Weren't we a good team?"

Will's face pinched at her description. "I don't want to be a good team, Anna."

A familiar dent formed between her eyebrows. "Then why are you here?"

He took her hands and thought about telling her how inspired he was by the President's speech but nixed the idea, remembering the woman's advice, *"Tell her what's in your heart."*

"There's a tree right outside our barracks that I pass by every day. About ten feet up there's a slit in the trunk where two birds have made a nest. When my squad leaves the barracks in the morning, one of the birds flies off. When we come back after evening chow, the bird does too."

"So?"

"So that's what I want, Anna. I want us to go out into the world, do all the things we have to do, then come home to each other. I don't care if every day is different as long as it begins and ends with you."

Anna withdrew her hands. "You had that, Will," she reminded him. "And you still left."

"Nothing matters like it should without you, Anna."

She knew the feeling. She didn't want to know the feeling again. "So now what?"

Like everything else he told Anna, Will didn't plan his next move. In fact it wasn't until he heard her say, *"Yes!"* three or four times that he realized he had dropped to one knee and asked her to marry him. Stunned, they both rose from the bench and looked at each other—their person to come home to.

They didn't have much time. Will's weekend pass meant that he had to leave for Chicago by noon the next day. Neither wanted to wait until basic training was over to get married, but there wasn't much they could do on a Saturday—the courthouse was closed.

They hurried across town to the one person Will knew might be able to help them—Mr. Erickson. Charmed by their story, his wife thumbed through the phone book for the local judge's number.

"Don't worry," Mr. Erickson said, winking as he dialed. "Judge Fox is a lousy poker player. He owes me fifty bucks."

The judge, still in his bathrobe, was waiting for them on the courthouse steps thirty minutes later. With the Ericksons as witnesses, Will and Anna signed a marriage license and said their *"I do's."* Kisses, handshakes and hugs all around followed. Even the judge joined in, though he reminded Mr. Erickson, "That makes us even, Jim."

Will and Anna clung to each other in her tiny apartment for most of the next twenty-four hours. As they did, their future began to take shape. One more month of boot camp, Will said, and they would be together. Wherever he went after that, Anna promised, she would follow.

But when Anna joined Will in San Diego ten weeks later, it wouldn't be just the two of them for long. Addie was on her way.

*

Almost sixteen years later, in the wee hours of Thursday, August 18th, Jake stared at the painting and did the math. Mid-January of 1961 to September 30th—almost nine months. He climbed the basement steps and staggered into the blackness of his father's back yard. Fragments of every fight he'd ever had with the girl—his failures and his cruelty—flashed before his eyes. Jake collapsed to the ground, drenched in defeat and disgrace, one question hammering over and over in his brain.

If it was true, if Addie really was his daughter . . . *Why didn't Anna ever tell me?!*

24
TEN YEARS OF CHANCES

Ghosts alive and dead haunted Jake after he finished painting his mother's dark-brown hair to Addie's straw blonde. He didn't know how he could face any of them for long without the numbing relief of alcohol.

Thankfully, the sale of his dad's house at the Woodland Realty office Friday morning went smoothly. The buyers signed and initialed the purchase agreement while Jake stared blankly across the street at the Junction. Once the sale was complete he quickly endorsed the check they gave him, stuck it in his back pocket and walked out the door. *That's it,* he thought. *There's nothing left to keep me here.* But if Jake wanted real peace—and the truth—he had two more stops to make before he left town for good.

He almost drove past the first one. The gravel road was pocked with divots that shifted the few possessions he had already loaded in the back of his truck. After checking them for damage, he walked across the freshly cut grass. No one seemed to be anywhere on the property.

Jake was careful to walk between the headstones, a superstition left over from childhood. He didn't have to zigzag for long—the grave wasn't far away. It was glossier and newer than its neighbors, but said much less:

Ronald J. Pearson
1917 – 1977

Further down the hill was another grave, but Jake didn't visit it this time. Two long months ago he vowed he would never come back, blaming Will Travers for every bad turn his life had taken since their friendship ended. But in that time, Jake accepted that his parents had made their own choices—Will was just the messenger. Betty Pearson had sought out her own happiness, something Jake should have done too. Instead, he took the job she abandoned—caretaking for his alcoholic father. Now Ely, Minnesota and his own happiness were waiting for him. But Will Travers was standing in his way again, this time in the form of a girl who would soon turn sixteen.

Jake spent the rest of the afternoon and evening wandering the shores of Gap Lake. It wasn't until sunset before he remembered that he didn't have a place to sleep. But Jake had slept in cars and trucks plenty of times. One more night wouldn't make a difference.

For one untroubled moment the next morning, Jake woke up and had forgotten his past. But when he rose from the bench seat and saw himself in the rearview mirror, reality rushed back in, as well as a powerful hunger. *Paulette's—then I'll figure out what to do next.*

Paulette's Café, like so many other places in Lost Elm, was unchanged since Jake and Anna split a six-pack of beer on that cold January night in 1961. The booths, the lunch counter, even the sign hanging above the men's urinals—*We Aim To Please, You Aim Too, Please*—were all the same. Jake had never given the place much thought before, but he did now as he stared at the empty booth in the back of the restaurant, imagining his younger self sitting next to the demure Anna Olson.

Jake sat there most of the morning trying to recall details from that night, but the more he tried the more elusive they became. He was consoled by the fact that he had all the proof he needed in the back of his truck—the painting. His mind made up, Jake threw a few bills on the counter and drove out to Carson Farm.

*

Addie woke up early on Saturday, August 20th. Each morning since moving to the farm had been the same—sneaking downstairs, peeking into her mother's room, sitting with Ranger in the screen porch and watching the sunrise. Despite the cruel waiting game playing out in the Carsons' guest room, Addie's thoughts were clear during these solitary moments. She opened her small notepad and wrote:

> *He went first. Now you too, soon.*
> *At peace, at home, from fear, immune.*
> *Perhaps then I will understand,*
> *What is slowly sinking in now,*
> *That every tomorrow without you,*
> *Will be impossible somehow.*

"Promise me something, Addie?" Mr. Carson leaned against the doorway to the kitchen, two cups of coffee in his hands.

"Depends," she replied. Mr. Carson took that as an invitation to sit down. He set a cup in front of her.

"Whatever you're writing," he said. "Don't stop."

Addie reflexively snatched the small notepad from the table, then set it back down. She took a sip, grimacing at the coffee's bitter taste. Mr. Carson chuckled before disappearing into the kitchen. He returned with a bowl of sugar and a small container of cream.

"I mean it," he insisted, stirring in plenty of both. "I've got Helen and the farm and my dad's old Ford to help me. You're going to need those words of yours more than ever."

"What about Billy?"

"He'll find something, but for now he's got your mom. Looking after her is what he needs to do."

"What's it gonna be like?" Addie whispered. "At the end."

"Your mom will pass the same way she lived. With dignity. We'll make sure of that."

Addie's eyes became liquid. The next ten minutes passed silently between them as a few scattered vehicles headed east and west on the highway below. Mr. Carson refilled her cup, then headed into the kitchen to make breakfast.

"I could use a hand. Helen and Billy will be up soon." Addie gave Ranger's belly a quick rub and followed Mr. Carson inside.

Anna felt better that morning than she had all week, good enough to sit in the rocker by the big bay window in her bedroom. Mrs. Carson suggested they all join her there for breakfast. Anna ate sparingly, smiling contentedly at everyone in turn and remarking softly, "I feel good today."

*

After the initial shock of their mother's diagnosis wore off, Billy and Addie did what they had always done—they found ways to survive their grim reality. But coping skills honed under Jake's roof weren't foolproof. They both wandered off daily to some far corner of the farm to grieve what was coming. Saturday was no different.

Addie left first, walking the length of Halverson Road over the same ground she and Sara had covered weeks earlier. By the time she reached the road's intersection with the state highway, she was so consumed by thoughts of her friend that she didn't hear Harold Hinkum's tow truck pull up behind her.

"Whaddya doin', Addie? Try'na get yourself killed?!" His frown quickly turned into a broad smile. "Hop in. I was just on my way to visit your mom. I wanna see how the Volkswagen's been runnin'."

"We're staying at the Carsons' right now," she said, unsure how much Harold knew.

"Perfect. I can give Virgil some grief. He wasn't at our VFW meeting last week. Wonder what excuse he'll give me this time?"

Mr. Carson came out from behind the barn as the tow truck appeared. The two men greeted each other warmly.

"Pick up a hitch-hiker, Harold?"

"Nearly hit her. It was like she didn't even hear me coming." He looked around for Addie, but she had already gone inside.

"I doubt she did," Virgil said. They eased down onto the porch steps and he explained Anna's condition.

"Geez, she seemed fine a month ago," Harold replied, his face stricken. "A little tired maybe, but no worse for wear. Gosh, those poor kids."

"Would you like to see her, Harold? She's having a good day. You'll make it better."

Harold put on a brave face and stood in Anna's bedroom doorway. She waved him forward. He slid a chair next to her bed.

"Harold, I'm so glad you're here. How are you?"

"Oh, same as usual, ma'am. You look prettier than ever though. Maybe if you're feeling better next week, we can take your car out for a spin."

She smiled and squeezed his hand. "Thank you, Harold."

"For what?"

"For giving me the best week I'd had in a long, long time."

"Just doing my job. So how's she running?"

"You'll have to ask Addie."

"But isn't she only . . ."

"Fifteen, I know," Anna said, her voice fading. "Her birthday is next month." She reached for a glass of water from the nightstand but it was empty. Harold filled it from a pitcher on a small table by the window.

"Can you help me, Harold?" Anna asked, her fingers pressing into his wrists. He brought the water to her lips and she drank slowly.

"I better let you rest. Virgil said just a few minutes."

"Harold?"

"Yes, ma'am?"

"I'll tell Sharon how much you miss her." Overcome, Harold bent down and kissed Anna's forehead.

"Goodnight, Anna. Sleep well." The big man lumbered from the room straight past Billy, Addie and the Carsons. Seconds later he slapped his oil-stained cap across his leg, climbed into his tow truck and was gone.

*

Anna slept for a few hours after Harold left, but was awake when Billy crept downstairs and heard hushed voices—hers and the Carsons'— coming from the guest room. He sat on the bottom step and listened.

"Maybe it'll be good for Jake to know, Anna. It might give him some peace," Mr. Carson said.

"Do you really believe that, Virgil?" Her voice was faint. "Don't forget what happened when he found out Ron died."

"Anna's right, dear," Mrs. Carson chimed in. "Can we risk it?"

The room fell silent. Billy heard footsteps pacing back and forth across the wood floor. He held his breath until Mr. Carson spoke.

"We'll do whatever you want, Anna. But this time might be different. Jake will have the chance to say goodbye."

Anna raised herself up in the bed. "I appreciate what you're trying to do, Virgil. But I can't worry about Jake anymore," she said, shaking her head. "It's too late for that."

"Jake's gone," Billy announced from the doorway, not wanting his mom and Mr. Carson to disagree any longer. "He left this morning." Billy told them about Jake's appearance at the trailer two days earlier, leaving out the part about receiving the envelope and key.

"Then it's over," Anna exhaled.

Mr. Carson nodded. "I'm sorry, Anna. I just thought . . ."

"It's okay," she whispered. "See? Everything is going to be fine."

They let her rest again. Like Addie had done after breakfast, it was Billy's turn to disappear. Gone for an hour, he took a long walk around the upper field. He thought the hay might be ready to cut in a few weeks, but the prospect of more work didn't excite him this time. When he and Addie hooked bales again their mother might be gone.

Shortly after Billy left, the Carsons had another visitor. Helen called for Virgil before she dared open the kitchen door. On the steps of the screen porch was a confused man who looked like he'd just seen a ghost.

"Mrs. Carson?"

"Can I help you?" she asked as Mr. Carson appeared behind her.

"I thought you were sick."

Mrs. Carson looked at her husband. He put his hands on her shoulders. They both stepped back from the doorway and waved their guest inside.

"You can come in, Jake, but Anna doesn't want to see you. She said so herself."

Jake looked around as he was led into the kitchen. "What's going on? Is she okay?"

Mr. Carson whispered something in his wife's ear. She nodded and slipped into the guest room.

"Anna's not well," Mr. Carson said, resting his hand on Jake's shoulder. Jake's entire body tensed from the gesture and the news.

"But Helen's okay?"

Mr. Carson's confusion confirmed what Jake had suspected when Mrs. Carson answered the door. *That's why Addie lied. She knew I'd come here.*

"Why are you here, Jake?" Mr. Carson asked him when Helen returned to the kitchen.

Jake spoke in a rush. He told them about the sale of his dad's house, his trip to Ely, the job waiting for him. A fresh start.

"For who?"

"Didn't Billy tell you? The trailer and the land. It's all Anna's now."

He's really leaving, they realized. Helen squeezed her husband's hand. "Jake, Anna just told me you can go in," she said. "But only for a minute."

"How sick is she?"

Mr. Carson told Jake everything, including how much time Anna had left. "Don't upset her. Just say your goodbyes and go."

Jake knocked softly. After a faint, "*Come in,*" he opened the door, revealing a large bedroom with a sitting area near the window. Anna was waiting for him there.

"We can talk over here, Jake. Close the door, okay?"

He understood immediately that Mr. Carson hadn't been exaggerating. Anna, wrapped in a heavy blanket, seemed no bigger than a child. Her hair was unwashed, her skin waxy and pale. But it was the expression on Anna's face that unnerved him the most. She looked untroubled, almost serene.

"How are you, Jake? You look good."

"Thanks. It's been, um . . . I've had a . . . I've figured some things out, Anna." He told her about his opportunity to start over.

"I'm glad. You deserve it."

"Are Billy and Addie gonna be okay?" he replied, shaken by her generosity.

"In time. They're going to live here with the Carsons."

"That's probably for the best."

"It is," she said with a quiet firmness. "Please don't make trouble for them. This is where I want my children to be."

It may have been her choice of words—*my* children—or perhaps Jake just needed a minute to find his courage. He pulled the old photograph from his back pocket and showed it to Anna.

"Do you know who this is?"

Anna took the picture and studied it. "Your mom. It says so on the back—*Betty, July 1933.*" She handed it back to him. "Mrs. Pearson was very pretty. I always thought so."

"Does she remind you of anyone?"

"No. Should she?"

Jake held up the photo. "What if she had blonde hair?" Whatever color was left in Anna's face drained away. She made a show of adjusting her blanket, but he had seen enough.

"I need to rest, Jake."

"Look again," he insisted. "My mom and Addie could almost be related, don'tcha think?"

"Why are you showing me this? What about Ely?"

"Ely's not going anywhere," he replied, leaning forward in his chair. "This can't wait."

"Yes it can!" Anna weakly shouted. She sank back in her chair, exhausted. Mr. Carson burst into the room.

"What did I say, Jake?!"

"It's okay, Virgil," Anna said, though the strain was written all over face.

"Wasn't I clear, Jake?! I told you not to upset her."

"He didn't. Jake will be leaving in a minute."

When the door closed, Jake pressed Anna again. "Well? Is she?"

"Is she what?"

"Is Addie my daughter?!" he asked, his voice climbing with each word.

There it was—the question Anna had feared for the past ten years. "You know who Addie's father was. He's buried a mile out of town and that girl has put him on a pedestal every day since. Do you really want to take that from her just because of some resemblance you think you saw in an old photograph?"

"Is Addie my daughter?" Jake repeated slowly.

"Would it make any difference if she was?! You had ten years of chances to be a father, Jake. You wasted every one of them."

"Why won't you answer the question?!"

Anna raised her head to the ceiling, closed her eyes and exhaled. "In every way that matters, Jake—*in every single way*—you are not Addie's father. She has never been more than an inconvenience to you. And rather than get to know her, you argued and you drank. I could go on, but why bother? You made your choices and now it's too late."

"Then why did you ever marry me?!" Jake hissed through clenched teeth.

Anna looked right through him. "Because I was alone and I was scared. And I thought you might change if you got to know . . ."

"My daughter?"

"But you didn't. And now you want me to tell you some big truth?! Why? The past is the past, Jake. You can't change it."

"Did you ever love me, Anna?! Did you ever give us a chance?!"

Anna didn't answer either question. Instead, she told Jake a much harder truth.

"I married you for one reason, and that reason was a mistake—just like that night sixteen years ago was a mistake." She strained to rise to her feet. The blanket fell to the ground around her feet. "I thought I'd get over Will in time. But when I didn't, I learned something. Time doesn't heal anything. We don't get over the people we truly love. We just get a little better, day by day, at living with the pain of their absence."

Jake's mouth opened but no words came. He put his mother's picture back in his pocket and slunk from the room. Mr. and Mrs. Carson sat silently at the kitchen table. The screen door creaked open and shut. Footsteps pounded across the porch.

"What the heck is Jake's truck doing here?!" Addie yelled.

Jake froze. He stared at her with a haunted, desolate expression. Addie wasn't having any of it as her hands went defiantly to her hips.

"What are you looking at?" she said, her eyes narrowing.

Jake didn't stick around for more. When he drove away, something inside him snapped. His future was gone, chased away by a past he couldn't rescue. If only he had told Anna years ago how he really felt. If only he had been a better husband. If only he had been a better father. If only . . .

The truck skidded to a stop at the bottom of the Carsons' long driveway. The freeway—with Ely to the north—was so close, just half a mile away. But Jake couldn't make that turn anymore. The only road he could take now carried him inescapably back to Lost Elm.

25
A BETTER DAD

Every barfly in the Junction was happy to see Jake. They didn't ask him where he'd been for two months—frankly, they didn't care. His return simply reassured them that he was okay and they were okay too. Bud didn't seem surprised. *They always come back,* the old bartender knew as he filled a beer mug for one of his lost sheep. *Always.*

"First one's on me, Jake."

He didn't stop at one. Sobriety may have turned Jake into a cheaper drunk, but he still knew how to get there. One beer quickly turned into another and another.

"What time you got, Bud?" he asked after his fourth.

"3:30, why? You gotta be somewhere?"

"The bank. I sold my dad's house yesterday." He slapped his check on the bar.

"It's Saturday, Jake. Bank's closed. And I'd put that away if I were you. Folks around here see that much money and you'll be buying drinks all night."

Jake looked at the amount on the check again, then quickly folded it around the picture of Betty Pearson and put them both in his back pocket.

"Another one?" Bud said, reaching for Jake's empty mug.

"Why not," he answered bitterly.

"Did Albert Lea work out like you hoped?"

The question rang in Jake's ears. "Plans changed. No big deal."

"Okay," Bud said with a practiced neutrality.

But it wasn't okay with Jake. As he brooded over another beer it dawned on him that Anna never had any intention of moving. *She lied to me again.*

Jake was kidding himself, of course. He never had a first chance with Anna, much less a second one in Albert Lea. But this was no longer the desperate, delusional Jake from earlier that summer. He had turned into someone much worse. Bud had sensed it when Jake walked in hours ago, something almost dangerous about his prodigal patron—he was a man with nothing to lose.

259

The bartender was right. In Jake's mind, Anna's sixteen-year deception had replaced Ron and Betty Pearson as the focal point for all of his suffering. *And now she's got the Loop too*, he fumed, conveniently forgetting Anna's death sentence and the duffel bag full of money in the back of the truck, his share of Ron Pearson's cashed out pension.

Jake didn't dare think of Addie for fear that his self-pity would smother him. But with every beer he drank the wound opened wider. Anna's harsh words, *"In every way that matters—in every single way—you are not Addie's father,"* goaded him. If she insisted on hurting him, Jake decided, the least he could do was hurt her right back.

"You good to drive?!" Bud asked after Jake slapped a twenty dollar bill on the bar.

"I'm fine. Don't worry about it."

"Just makin' sure my best customer gets home safe."

Jake had heard Bud say the same thing to every other regular in the Junction at one time or another. It never bothered him then, but now he saw Bud for what he was—a bloodsucker feeding off the misery and addiction of the poor souls he poured drinks for every day. And for most of his adult life, Jake had been one of them.

"What'd you say?"

"Just wanna see you home safe, Jake."

"Why? So you can take my money again tomorrow?! Here, let's cut to the chase." He crumpled another twenty and threw it at Bud.

"Go home, Jake. You've had enough."

"But you'd give me another if I asked, wouldn't you?"

Bud glanced uneasily around the bar. He needn't have worried. His regulars would never agree with Jake, even if they knew he was right. Besides, Jake came and went. Bud would always be there.

The two men stared at each other, but the fight had already gone out of both of them. Jake spit on the floor in disgust as Bud quietly wiped down the bar, hoping not to provoke anyone else if he could help it. When he looked up again, Jake was gone. *He'll be back tomorrow*, Bud scoffed. *Where else is he gonna go?*

Jake wasn't thinking that far ahead when he climbed into the truck and tossed his check and the picture of his mother on the dashboard. Tomorrow would have to wait.

*

Anna's confrontation with Jake had taken the fight out of her too. All she wanted to do was sleep, but even that was becoming impossible. Fresh pain, with all its humiliations, visited her throughout the afternoon and evening. Between applying cool washcloths and changing her mother's sheets, Addie asked why Jake had stopped by, but Anna waved her off.

"He just wanted to say goodbye, honey," she whispered hoarsely. "That's all."

"Was that all?" Addie asked the Carsons later at the supper table. "He's not coming around here anymore, is he?"

"Jake's gone," Mr. Carson said, looking from her to Billy. "He said so himself. He even gave you something. Right, Billy?"

Billy looked up from his plate and excused himself, returning with the envelope Jake had given him. "I was gonna give it to you," he explained, handing it to Mr. Carson. "I just wanted to wait 'til . . ."

"It's okay, son." Mr. Carson flipped through the paperwork and found the key to the trailer. "Ron Pearson owned all the land inside the Loop. When he died it passed to Jake. But according to this," Mr. Carson indicated, sliding a piece of paper over to Billy and Addie. "Jake gave it all to your Mom. Eventually it'll be yours."

"Why would he do that?" Addie asked, annoyed by Jake's generosity.

"Guilt," Billy said before Mr. Carson could hazard a guess. "I think Jake felt bad . . . about a lot of things."

A sarcastic reply was on the tip of Addie's tongue, but she let it die there. Mr. Carson was right, Jake was gone. Still, she had to say something.

"I don't want the trailer or anything else down there, do you?"

"Not really."

"I don't blame you," Mr. Carson said. "But the land is worth something. Selling it might be a nice way to pay for college."

"College?!" Addie exclaimed. "Can't we just get through the summer first?"

"Absolutely, dear," Mrs. Carson said, shaking her head at her husband.

"You're right, Addie. I'm sorry," Mr. Carson agreed. "I just want to make sure . . ." His words were cut off by a deep moan coming from

261

Anna's room. They fled the dining room and hurried to her side. Anna clutched her blankets, unable to find any relief.

"Virgil!"

"We're right here, Anna. What do you need?"

"I know I said I didn't want to take anything," she winced, gritting her teeth. "But . . ."

"Shush," Mr. Carson fussed. "I've got something right here." He opened a dresser drawer and retrieved a small plastic case. Inside it was a tourniquet, syringe, cotton swabs, isopropyl alcohol and a bottle of morphine. He deftly tied the tourniquet around Anna's upper arm and disinfected the crook of her elbow.

"Not too much, okay?" she whispered. "I want to know where I am." This was more than Addie could bear hearing. She ran from the room. Mrs. Carson followed close behind her.

"What does that even mean?!" Addie cried. "What's going to happen to her?!"

"Your Mom's going to feel better in a few minutes. The morphine just eases the pain."

"Does Mr. Carson know what he's doing?!"

"Your mom's in good hands, Addie," Mrs. Carson assured her.

Anna's cry for help and the appearance of a hidden needle brought a harsh new level of reality to Addie's world. The unswerving certainty of what lay ahead took on a frightening immediacy. She snatched the spare trailer key off the table and headed outside. Billy came out of the bedroom just in time to see her disappear into the dusk.

"Where's Addie going?"

"To find a little peace, I think," Mrs. Carson replied. "Don't worry. She won't be gone long."

He sat down on the porch steps, never taking his eyes off the Loop. Everything within it was dark—darker than he'd ever seen it before. With his mom clinging to life inside and Addie running from hers outside, Billy felt more alone than he had all summer.

*

Addie jiggled the key in the doorknob a few times before it opened. She flipped the light switch up and down, but no lights came on. *Mr.*

Carson turned the electricity off, Addie remembered. Though everything around her was unseen, the living room floor was bare and the kitchen sink and counters were empty.

That's fine, she thought. *I can find my way around here blindfolded if I have to.* But to make matters worse, Addie wasn't sure if what she was looking for still existed. She had lost track of it a long time ago.

*

As Addie began to search the trailer, Jake turned off the highway and onto Halverson Road. The short drive from Lost Elm hadn't been an easy one. He nearly hit an oncoming car, swerving sharply at the last second to avoid a head-on collision. In the process, some of the truck's load spilled onto the highway. Jake didn't care. Returning later to pick up what he'd lost never crossed his mind. Everything was lost already.

He parked across from the Farelli's driveway and sifted through what was left in the back of the truck until he found a t-shirt. Night was at hand as he stumbled on the path that led to the slate rock outcropping in the middle of Pete's Woods. Along the way, he grabbed a sturdy fallen branch and tied the t-shirt securely around it. The next thing he needed was buried at the base of the big rock.

When Jake got there, he dropped to his knees and began digging. In a matter of minutes, he held the last bottle of Swamp Rot. But rather than drink it, he poured it over the t-shirt instead, careful to soak every part of the cloth.

Jake was too far gone to contemplate the wisdom of what he was about to do. In the past, alcohol had always driven him to do the things he did. Not this time. This time twenty years of regret blinded him to everything that could go wrong in the next twenty minutes. *There's no way I'll get caught,* he thought as he dug a pack of matches out of his pocket. The Farellis were gone, the new owners hadn't moved in yet and the trailer was empty. The match was struck.

For a split-second after the shirt burst into flames, Pete's Woods was ablaze with light, illuminating something carved on the slate rock next to Jake. He leaned in close and read the words, *I HATE HIM*, still legible beneath countless slashing cuts. Whatever chance he wouldn't carry out his plan vanished. Those three words, no less damning than WILL AND ANNA, guaranteed it.

*

Addie never saw Jake's bright orange flame. She was on the far end of the trailer, tearing apart every inch of Billy's bedroom after hers had turned up nothing. Without electricity, the search seemed futile until her knee pressed into a small nail hidden beneath the carpet. The pain was sharp, but triggered a memory of the last time it had happened to her— years ago when Addie hid the same photograph she was looking for now.

She crawled into Billy's closet and pulled at a corner of the carpet. It gave way easily, uncovering the black and white Polaroid her father had asked her to keep safe so long ago. *"It's going to be your job to keep this safe, honey. . . Put it somewhere you won't forget, okay?"*

Addie held it up to the faint moonlight. Written on the back was a date—*April 8, 1965*. She studied the small, grainy faces. Anna, with Billy in her arms, tried to smile but the strain of the day showed in her eyes. Will held her close, one arm around her waist, the other resting on the shoulder of a little girl standing in front of him. The girl looked up at her father, her hands tightly clutching his pant legs. Minutes after the photo was taken, Will Travers would board an airplane bound for Vietnam and oblivion.

*

Jake's options narrowed with every step he took towards the trailer. The heat from the torch sobered him temporarily, sweat beading on his forehead. He had made up his mind in the Junction hours ago, but when he reached the mudroom steps, he remembered that he had given Billy his only spare key days earlier. Unsure what to do next, Jake was startled by a dog barking somewhere in the night.

*

A single bark snapped Addie back to the present. She set the photograph on the bed and opened the window. Despite the gloom, she

264

recognized Ranger instantly. "Hey there, boy. Did the Carsons send you here to bring me home?" But rather than acknowledge her, the old dog tore around the corner and out of sight.

Ranger leaped at a hulking figure in the dark, his tired legs summoning the strength that had left him years ago. His momentum wasn't enough to knock the man off his feet, but a burning stick the man held fell harmlessly to the ground. He picked it quickly, however, and waved it back and forth in the dog's face.

Ranger wouldn't budge. The man advanced on him, swinging the torch with all the force he could muster. It grazed the dog's whiskers and slipped from the man's grasp, crashing through a window and disappearing inside the trailer. Ranger jumped onto the porch and began barking furiously as the growing fire lit up the trailer's living room.

*

Hearing the sound of breaking glass, Addie peered down the hallway, half expecting to see Ranger wagging his tail at her. Instead, she saw a surreal fiery glow move swiftly across the living room. For ten endless seconds, Addie didn't move. She knew she was looking at a fire, *but in the trailer?* When her mind finally screamed *DANGER*, it was too late. Flames shot up the thin paneled walls and engulfed the living room. The kitchen was next. The linoleum floor bubbled under the onslaught. Addie's only way out was gone.

The fire roared on, curling around the countertops, setting the cupboards ablaze. The melting linoleum slowed its progress, but thick smoke moved steadily down the hallway. Wild with fear, Addie dropped to her knees. The heat and hiss of the blaze began to overwhelm her senses until she heard Ranger bark again. Rising to a crouch, she backed into Billy's bedroom and screamed for help even as she realized how hopeless her pleas were. *No one is going to hear me!*

Jake heard her. He'd been so mesmerized by the speed in which the fire was incinerating the trailer in one unrelenting wave, that the possibility someone might be inside never crossed his mind. He jumped onto the porch and opened the mud room door. Smoke wrapped around him as he threw his shoulder against the inner door, unaware that it was unlocked. It gave way on his second try and he found himself in the middle of a collapsing ceiling, his shoes sticking to a pool of liquid rubber that had been the kitchen floor just minutes earlier.

*

"I'm down here!" Addie shouted. Flames chased Jake down the hallway as the roof crumpled at his heels. When he reached her, half the trailer was already gone.

"What are you doing, Addie?!" he yelled over the fire's roar. "You're not supposed to be here!"

Addie couldn't answer. She fell to her knees again as smoke enveloped the bedroom. The fire wasn't far behind. Jake dragged her away from the surging flames and looked around the room for something heavy. The room was empty except for Billy's dresser.

Curled up in a corner, Addie coughed uncontrollably as Jake rammed a dresser drawer through the window at the end of the trailer. Not satisfied that the opening was big enough, he heaved another drawer through it with an inhuman howl.

Time was up—there was no air left to breathe. Jake lifted Addie in his arms even as the flames licked at his clothing. Fast losing consciousness—the smoke searing her lungs—she clearly heard the last words Jake spoke to her before the Polaroid slipped from her hand and she was thrown through the narrow window opening.

"I'm sorry, Addie! I'm sorry! I shoulda been a better dad!"

Addie had the momentary sensation of floating, then fell heavily to the ground. Unseen hands dragged her away from the blaze and Ranger was on top of her. She fought off the dog and crawled mindlessly back toward the intense heat. "Jake!" she screamed over and over. "Jake!" But Jake was gone. She called out his name a few more times, but the fire roared back at her as the walls and ceiling caved in.

"Addie?! What are you doing?! Are you trying to get yourself killed?!"

Billy had sprinted across the field the instant he saw a flame crash through one of the trailer's windows. By the time he reached the edge of their yard, Addie was lying in a heap outside his bedroom window.

"Come on! The trailer's gonna. . ." Before Billy could say *blow*, it did. Mr. Carson may have shut off the electricity, but the propane tank in the back yard was still hooked up to the kitchen stove. The explosion sent a

266

plume of fiery gas high in the air, igniting the dry needles and branches of their beloved Pines. All four trees began to crackle and burn.

The shockwave knocked them to the ground. Ranger was the first to regain his senses. He found the girl and curled up next to her, his head resting on her belly. Billy and Addie watched, unmoving, as their home became nothing more than a flickering, black smear.

She tried to stand but fell to her hands and knees, coughing and convulsing before vomiting into the grass. Billy knelt beside her and placed his hand on her back until her body was still.

"Why'd he do it?!" she sobbed. "Why?!"

"Why did *who* do *what*?!" Billy shouted, barely comprehending the scene he'd come upon. The trailer was gone and he had found Addie lying half-conscious next to it. "What happened here?!"

Addie sat up, her face streaked with tears and smoke and confusion. "I don't know why," she said. "But Jake just saved my life."

More questions would have to wait as chaos descended on the Loop. Mr. Carson's truck appeared out of nowhere, skidding to a stop in the yard. Lost Elm's lone fire engine wasn't far behind, its wailing siren drowning out every other sound around Halverson Road.

26
THE BEST VERSION

Morphine coursed through Anna's veins all the time now, every day. She still knew who she was and where, but a fog had settled over her fragile existence—just enough so Anna was oblivious to all the commotion swirling around the farmhouse in the days after Jake fled her bedside. She never learned that her children had been questioned by the police or that Addie was treated at the hospital for smoke inhalation.

Mr. Carson intended to keep it that way. Nothing would be gained, he reasoned, by telling Anna what had happened that night inside the Loop. Helen and the kids agreed without a second thought, but he had to argue long and loud with the sheriff and his deputies before they finally relented.

Anna remained in the dark while every subscriber to *The Wood City Journal* learned of the grisly details on Friday, August 26th. While Mr. Carson stayed ahead of her pain with ever-increasing doses of morphine, people studied the front page photograph of fire investigators sifting through the trailer's ruins. As Billy spooned broth past Anna's dry, cracked lips, they read that a local man's remains, identified as Jake Pearson, had been found in the collapsed trailer. And each time Addie and Mrs. Carson changed her sheets, readers learned that it was Pearson himself who started the fire, though the article never said why.

Billy and Addie didn't know why either, though the sheriff asked them repeatedly. Billy's statement—that he'd seen a torch in Pete's Woods move straight for the trailer before being thrown into it—was supported by Addie. Evidence at the scene—fragments of a charred tree branch found in the ruins of the living room—further pointed to Jake. And if that wasn't enough, his truck was found parked on the Loop. Case closed, the sheriff concluded, though the *why* of it was never discovered. Like the burnt billboard, some mysteries would remain unsolved.

With the investigation over, Mr. Carson arranged for the trailer's removal. A bulldozer and dump truck were on site the day after the story appeared in the paper, though plenty of gawkers drove around the Loop to see where one of their own had met his end. They didn't stay long, however. Mr. Carson stood in the empty driveway, shooing people away throughout the entire two hour clean-up. What was left of the scorched Pines was cut down the next day.

Billy and Addie saw it all from the Carson's screen porch, their childhoods being dismantled before their eyes. They'd never wished for Jake's death, though his frequent absences had always been welcome. Being gone was one thing, dead and gone was quite another.

Billy had been happy for Jake when he learned of his opportunity in Ely, hopeful that he might finally do something he'd never done before—keep his word. Now Billy would never know, and not knowing dwarfed seeing his life inside the Loop hauled away in pieces.

Addie, on the other hand, was distracted and adrift. Jake's last words to her, *"I'm sorry! I shoulda been a better dad!"* echoed in her brain all week. The more she replayed the fire in her mind, the more she was forced to accept that Jake had chosen her life over his own.

It was that realization that led Addie to join Billy and Mr. Carson at Jake's burial on Monday, August 29th. While Mrs. Carson stayed behind to care for Anna, the trio was met in the lawn by a truck that had towed Jake's impounded vehicle up the long driveway. With the investigation over, the driver explained, the truck and everything in it could be returned to the next of kin. "Sheriff said I'd find Anna Pearson here."

Mr. Carson signed for Jake's truck and parked it next to the barn. He found a piece of paper and a photograph wedged between the window and the dashboard that he guessed Jake had left behind. He tucked them in his shirt pocket, then they left for the cemetery.

Jake, whether he wanted to be or not, was laid to rest next to his father. The bier holding his coffin was in place and ready to be lowered into the ground when the attendees arrived. Including the local priest who recited a familiar dirge for the dead (ashes to ashes and so forth), as well as a stern warning to the living, only seven people stood around the freshly dug hole.

Bud was there but his eyes never left the ground. For days he'd heard nothing but gossip regarding the circumstances of Jake's death—so much that he threatened to cut off his regulars if they didn't "shut up about it." Graveside wasn't much better. He was certain plenty of judgment was being heaped on him by the Pearson kids and Virgil Carson, though he wasn't sure if some of that judgment was also his own.

Betty Pearson came too, accompanied by a friend, everyone presumed. She stood erect and dignified, though her face betrayed a tender anguish. Trance-like, Betty stared off into the distance for most of the service while her friend stood close by. Billy and Addie stole glances at her when they could, each curious to know what Jake's mother might be like. She looked their way only once, gazing at Addie with a quizzical expression that seemed to ask: *Do I know you?*

After the final benediction, "*May the Lord bless you and keep you; may the Lord make His face shine upon you and be gracious to you; may the Lord lift up His countenance upon you and give you peace*," Bud and the priest beat a hasty retreat. Billy and Addie waited by the car while Mr. Carson spoke to Betty Pearson. Soon they departed, Mr. Carson explaining that Jake's mother and her friend would follow them to the farm for a little lunch.

*

Just past noon, the impromptu meal was winding down on the screen porch. The conversation was muted for Anna's sake, though only small talk had passed between the six of them. Billy and Addie answered a few token questions, otherwise plates and utensils did most of the talking. Betty Pearson and her friend (introduced as a co-worker) said little and seemed anxious to leave.

"I think these belong to you, Betty," Virgil said. He produced the photograph and the check from the sale of Ron's house and slid them across the table to her.

"Where did you find this?!" she exclaimed, ignoring the check.

"In Jake's truck just sitting on the dashboard."

Betty stared at the photo. "This was taken at our cabin on Gull Lake. It must have been our last summer there," she said, flipping the picture over. "Banks were failing right and left that year. My father did everything he could to keep the place, but we had to let it go."

"I saw Jake painting a picture of that," Billy said.

"Jake was a very talented artist," Betty replied. "He kept it a secret from his dad, but I always knew."

"I never saw Jake paint a day in my life," Addie remarked, though her words lacked any of their usual bite. She abruptly stood and left the porch, walking around the corner of the house to the Carson's back yard.

"I'm sorry, Betty," Helen said after an uncomfortable silence. "Addie was used to Jake being a certain way. Saving her life wasn't something she expected him to do."

"I'm sorry too," Betty replied, her apology directed at Billy. "It sounds like Jake still had a lot of his father in him." She looked at her companion and nodded. "Lunch was wonderful, Helen. Virgil, thank you so much for taking care of the funeral arrangements. Please let me help with the cost."

"Don't thank me, Betty," he said, waving her off. "Turns out Ron took care of everything for Jake a few years ago. But why don't you see if there's anything in the truck you might want. It's parked next to the barn."

A cry from Anna broke up the gathering. Billy and Mrs. Carson hurried from the porch while Mr. Carson walked Betty and her friend out to the yard.

"I doubt there's anything of value in it," he said, pointing to the barn. "But you're welcome to look."

"Is she going to be okay?" Betty asked.

"Doctors say she might make it to Thanksgiving," Virgil replied, jamming his hands into his pockets. "But I'm not so sure Anna has that long. She's in a lot of pain. That's why I didn't tell her about Jake. It would have been just one more thing."

"That's probably for the best, but I was actually asking about Addie," Betty said, looking to the back yard where Addie was twirling aimlessly in an old tire swing.

"She's had a helluva summer. Billy too. Anna always said her daughter's the tough one, but I'm not so sure. Either way, they're both in for some hard times."

Betty opened her purse and took out a pen and the check Virgil had given her on the porch. Below Jake's signature she signed her own, adding the words, *Pay to the order of Virgil Carson on behalf of Addie and Billy Pearson.*

"Take this," she insisted. "Those kids deserve it."

"They do," he agreed, accepting the check without argument. "Thank you, Betty. And thanks for coming today. Both of you. Maybe we'll see you again sometime."

Addie saw Mr. Carson beat a hasty retreat inside, then watched Betty Pearson and her companion with growing curiosity. An easy familiarity passed between them, a certain intimacy Addie couldn't ignore or explain away.

"Addie?" Betty called to her. "Do you think there's anything in here I might want?" She poked her head inside the truck's cab while her friend lingered behind.

"I haven't looked," Addie said, slipping out of the tire and approaching the truck. "It was just towed here this morning." Betty circled it once before deciding she didn't want anything.

"You didn't like Jake much, did you?"

"No," Addie replied, too drained to be anything but honest. "I'm sorry, Mrs. Pearson, but everything Jake should have been he wasn't."

"Ron and I didn't make a very happy home for him and his sister," she murmured, placing her hand on her cheek, recalling a decades-old wound. "Was he an angry person?"

"Most of the time." Addie didn't want to make the woman feel worse, so she changed the subject. "Who's your friend *really*, Mrs. Pearson?"

Betty looked over her shoulder and smiled. "That is someone very dear to me," she said. "We've been together since I left Lost Elm in 1959."

"You mean you're . . . together?"

Betty watched Addie closely, saw her work out the answer for herself. Expecting some measure of disgust, Betty unconsciously took a step backward. Receiving none from the girl, she made a decision. After a lifetime of lying, she wouldn't lie to Addie Pearson.

"We are."

"Did Jake know?"

"Jake found out the hard way. I'll never know how, but there he was one day, staring at us through the dining room window."

"So you two . . ."

"Are in love, yes," Betty acknowledged, recalling the last words she had spoken to her son like it was only yesterday. *This is me, Jake. This is who I am and that's who I love. But you're my son. I love you too.* "There were so many times I wanted to explain myself to Jake, make him understand. But I told myself he'd never listen. And now it's too late."

"If it helps," Addie offered, "Jake told Billy that he was going to start a new life for himself somewhere up north. He said Jake sounded kind of hopeful."

"Thank you," Betty smiled. "But I'd like to remember my son by the last thing he ever did. Jake could have lived another fifty years but he'd never do anything better than save your life."

Addie's eyes widened and the shock and disbelief of the past week washed over her. She burst into tears and fell into Mrs. Pearson's arms.

"Is everything okay, girls?" Betty's companion asked, approaching them.

"I think so," Betty replied soothingly. "Sometimes us girls just have to have a good cry. Don't you think so, Addie?"

Three months earlier, Addie never would have agreed. *But yesterday's gone.* "I suppose so," she admitted.

"Good," Betty said. "Now before we go I want to properly introduce you to the person I share my life with, Addie, not work with. This is my partner—Janet Williams."

Addie knew she should have been shocked. Other people would be. But she wasn't, not after Betty answered her unspoken questions with a simple truth before she and Janet drove away. "We're not hurting anyone, Addie. We just want to be happy. Besides, the best version of me is when I'm with her. Isn't that what everyone wants?"

And yet Addie could almost understand Jake's pain. Someone he loved had left him to pick up the pieces with someone he hated, his father. Will Travers had unintentionally done the same thing to Addie. How can a person make peace with that and not destroy themselves in the process?

*

Half-formed, these competing thoughts rattled around Addie's brain as she wandered the Bog the next day. Thanks to Mr. Carson's morphine shots, Anna rested quietly, giving her children desperately needed breaks from their bedside vigil.

The sun hung low in the sky as Addie re-crossed the highway and made her way around the Loop. *We'll be haying again soon,* she thought, measuring the grass between her and the farm. Gone was Addie's usual resentment at the idea—her habit of rebelling against anything she hadn't thought of first.

Ranger met her halfway across the lower field and they walked home together in the approaching twilight. But rather than go inside, Addie went to Jake's truck. She understood why Betty Pearson hadn't wanted anything from it. There seemed to be nothing of value, sentimental or otherwise. Nevertheless, she climbed into the back, expecting to sift through hidden bottles or cases of beer. She discovered something else entirely.

It didn't look like much at first, just a large, flat rectangle covered with butcher paper. Addie unwrapped it and was held spellbound by the delicate smile of a young girl—the painting Billy had mentioned the day before at lunch—Betty Pearson more than forty years ago.

"Jake *could* paint," Addie whispered grudgingly. Her admission was drowned out by crickets chirping around the barn. Even Ranger, resting in the cool grass nearby, hadn't heard her. Never taking her eyes off the picture, Addie dropped to the ground, opened the driver's side door and turned on the truck's headlights. With the sun sinking fast, she wanted a better look.

The wrapping paper fell to the ground as she held the painting up to the headlights. The bright beams revealed details she'd hadn't seen in the back of the truck. The girl had straw-blonde hair, not young Betty's dark brown. Her complexion was altered too—pale skin dotted with freckles, just like . . .

"Me."

Confused, conflicting memories crashed in on Addie—the searching looks from Jake, the back and forth taunts, even their stubborn similarities, his painting and her poetry. She tried to let go of the picture but her clenched hands wouldn't open, nor could she stop staring at . . . herself?! *It can't be. How can it be?!* But it was. Addie knew her own face, her own eyes. They looked straight into her soul, asking, *"Don't you know me, Addie?"*

She did. Hair color and complexion aside, Addie and Betty Pearson could have been twins. She threw the painting back where she'd found it, but not before Jake's last words to her sank in. *"I'm sorry, Addie! I'm sorry! I shoulda been a better dad!"*

275

"NO!" Addie cried out. "NO! YOU CAN'T BE!" She looked at the canvas again. With almost no light to see by, the face flickered between hers and Betty's, light hair to dark, fair skin to tan—the same girl separated by four decades, yet connected by one man.

Addie fell to her knees, certain she was going to be sick. Hot saliva coursed down her throat and she swallowed hard as the truth sank in. Why her mom had married Jake, why she stayed with him through ten miserable years and why Jake had saved Addie's life.

"Because of me."

She tried to convince herself it wasn't true—a cruel coincidence to rob her of her real father, Will Travers. But with her own face staring at her in the fast-fading light, what else could she do? Addie's signature phrase had always been enough to combat any situation she thought unreasonable or unfair. But learning a truth too awful to bear, that word was no longer enough.

"THIS IS BULL . . . SHIT!!!"

No one saw Addie draw Billy's knife from her pocket and slash the canvas to ribbons. She stabbed the painting repeatedly until the blade stuck into something beneath it. Tossing the tattered portrait aside, Addie saw that the knife was caught in the zipper of a duffel bag. She twisted it free, prying the zipper apart in the process. The bag bulged with money. Addie lugged it over to the headlights and stared in astonishment at banded stacks of $5's, $10's and $20's—Ron Pearson's cashed out pension.

Dazed, Addie stumbled off toward the house with the money in tow. But somehow—despite the shock and pain of a revelation that might destroy her yet—a kernel of a plan crept into her subconscious. She veered over to the barn instead, stashing the bag behind a few bales of hay stacked in a corner. All of it would be waiting for her when she figured out what to do next, and when.

Did you know, Dad?! Did Mom tell you? Did you know the truth? Is that why you went to Vietnam?! Because of me? Did you hate me, Dad? Please don't hate me! You can't hate me! Oh God, I hope you never knew!

27
ADDIE BRAVER

Anna's final days unfolded in all the ways Mr. Carson had feared—sleepless nights, frightening bouts of delirium, and ever-increasing doses of morphine that couldn't chase away her pain. He and Helen did everything they could to spare Billy and Addie from this most cruel stage of their mother's cancer, but Anna's children refused to look away.

Tuesday morning, September 6th, the first day of school at Lost Elm High, was no different. Neither Billy nor Addie attended classes that day, but both woke before dawn, one following the other downstairs into their mother's bedroom. Anna's fingers twitched and fluttered, calling them over to chairs set up on either side of her bed. They sat, taking her hands in theirs. She wore a faint smile, her head moving slowly back and forth from Billy to Addie. In time the sun appeared, its rays crossing Halverson Road and warming the fields of Carson Farm. Anna lifted her head and looked at the glittering dew outside her window.

"It's so beautiful," she said, her voice cracked and hoarse.

"Do you want a glass of water, Mom?" Billy asked her. "Or a washcloth?" Drinking from a glass had become so difficult that Anna had resorted to sucking on soaked washcloths to stay even a little hydrated.

"You fill the pitcher, Shorty," Addie told him. "I'll get a fresh washcloth."

They started for the door but Anna managed to get their attention before they left the room. She looked at them with a shining smile and whispered, "Didn't I tell you? Everything worked out for the best. Just like I planned." Anna exhaled and her head turned on the pillow, revealing a long tear that curled down her cheek. Billy and Addie stood unmoving, their eyes never leaving their mother's face. The lines that had deepened in it with every new day softened as the tension in her body receded for the last time. Anna's struggle was over.

*

"Make sure you signal," Mr. Carson reminded Addie as she downshifted the Volkswagen on her approach to the Carsons' driveway.

"You're becoming such a good driver, dear," Mrs. Carson said encouragingly from the backseat. "Don't you think so, Billy?" Sitting next to her in a new black suit, Billy only nodded.

Addie sped to the top of the hill, shifted into neutral and coasted to a stop near the edge of the yard. Remembering Mr. Carson's earlier advice, she put the car into first gear then shut off the engine before releasing the clutch.

"You'll pass your driver's test on the first try for sure, Addie," Mr. Carson said. "Do you still want to take it on your birthday?"

Addie couldn't think that far ahead—the last two days had been a paralyzing blur. She knew Mr. Carson was just trying to take her mind off their mother's death and the funeral they'd just come home from, but even one question felt like one too many.

"I don't know, maybe."

"Would anyone like something to eat?" Mrs. Carson asked as they settled into chairs on the screen porch. "Lemonade? A dish of ice cream?"

"What about haying?" Billy blurted out. Mrs. Carson's lemonade reminded him of all the work they'd already done that summer. "Aren't we gonna hay again?"

"I'm going to hire out the second crop this year, Billy," Mr. Carson replied. "It's probably for the best."

"I'll hay if Shorty will," Addie chimed in as she smoothed out her dress. "I don't know about you, but I can't just sit around here doing nothing."

Mr. Carson understood what Addie meant. He had put his whole heart into the farm the fall after his father died, if only to erase a little of the pain. "What do you say, Billy?" he asked, patting Addie's hand. "Your sister might be on to something."

"Can we get it all done before Monday? We've gotta go to school sometime." Billy was right. In the grand scheme of things, missing the first week of school hardly mattered, but they had to start eventually.

"We'll have to put in long days," Mr. Carson calculated. "Is that really what you want to do all weekend?"

It was. Thanks to two weeks without a drop of rain, they began early and worked well into the evening. By Friday night both fields were cut and ready to bale Saturday morning.

The monotony of haying was a comfort to Billy. He slipped gladly back into it, taking pride in every wagonload—relieved not to have to think one second beyond the next twined bundle the baler spat out.

Addie wasn't so lucky. She couldn't outrun her thoughts, not this time. She did the work without complaint, but her mother's final words, *"Everything worked out for the best,"* haunted her. And now whenever Addie looked at Billy, she knew everything had changed. *I'm not a Travers anymore. I guess I never really was.*

School didn't bring much relief either—no welcome distraction from finding her face in Jake's painting. Addie's mind worked feverishly, but not on Math or English or Chemistry. Instead, she figured out why Jake had burned down the trailer in the first place. He must have learned the truth too.

And with Sara gone, Addie had no one to confide in as September lengthened, nowhere to lay her secret burden down. Whatever answers her mother might have given her were buried in Hillside Cemetery, next to her beloved Will. Mr. and Mrs. Carson weren't surprised by her withdrawal. They had grieved much the same way when their Jimmy died. Why should Addie be any different? But swirling amidst her grief was the awful realization that no one alive could tell her why Jake Pearson—not Will Travers—was her father. The evidence was only circumstantial, but deep down *that weird feeling* told Addie it was true. She had been a Pearson all along.

Billy had no mystery to solve. He missed his mother terribly and not a day went by that he wasn't moved to tears at the thought of her. But Billy had the Carsons, he had the farm and—despite her distance—he assumed he had his sister too. Addie, on the other hand, was trapped in a painting she couldn't unsee. For her, there was no way out.

*

"Happy Birthday to You! Happy Birthday to You! Happy Birthday Dear, Addie—Happy Birthday to You!"

Billy and the Carsons sang and clapped as Addie came down the stairs Friday morning, September 30th. Ranger met her halfway, barking happily at all the commotion.

"Sit down, dear," Mrs. Carson said, pulling out a chair for her. "I made your favorites—scrambled eggs and hash browns. But you have to eat fast. The bus will be here in fifteen minutes."

"She's not taking the bus today, Helen," Mr. Carson said with a grin. "Remember?"

"Why not?" Addie asked, swallowing a forkful of eggs.

"We're driving both vehicles into town," Mr. Carson replied. "Helen will take the truck and drop you and Billy off at school. I'll leave the Volkswagen in the lot across from the bank for your driver's test."

"But I didn't schedule my test."

"I scheduled it for you."

"Do you think I'm ready?"

"You were ready six weeks ago, Addie," he said, recalling her wild ride into Wood City with Anna and Billy. "This will be a breeze."

"I hope so."

"Are you sure you don't want to come with us, Addie?" Mrs. Carson interjected. "You can take the test next week." Billy and the Carsons were leaving for Fargo at noon. Their new granddaughter was being baptized that weekend and they wouldn't be home until Sunday night.

"We can trust Addie here by herself," Mr. Carson said. "Besides, Ranger will keep an eye on her—won'tcha boy?" He snuck a piece of toast into the dog's mouth. "But don't drive too much okay?"

"I won't," she said. "Thank you for breakfast. For everything."

"Of course, dear," Mrs. Carson said affectionately. "That's what family is for."

*

Addie skipped her last class—*American History: Reconstruction through World War II*—and went to the lot where the Volkswagen was parked. The keys were right where Mr. Carson said they'd be, under the passenger side floor mat. The bank clock flashed 2:30, its analog version having been switched out for a digital display two weeks earlier. With her test in half an hour, Addie had just enough time to guarantee herself a passing score.

She jogged two blocks down Chestnut Avenue, past the two-story municipal building and approached two orange traffic cones that were set up for the parallel parking portion of the test. It was the worst kept secret in town—test takers widened the distance between the cones another five to ten feet every test day. Addie did the same, then hurried back up the street and into the mostly empty municipal building. The woman at the *Vehicle and Driver Registration* counter barely looked up as Addie tried to check in.

"You're not Virgil Carson," she observed. "I have a Virgil Carson at three o'clock."

"He scheduled the test for me. My name is Addie."

The woman pointed to a chair. "Have a seat."

A large man huffed up the stairs five minutes later and looked at the test schedule. "Who's next?" he wheezed. The woman jerked her thumb toward Addie. "Name's Gary," he said. "Follow me."

Addie expertly navigated every maneuver the proctor put her through. With each success he merely grunted, but when she backed the Bug easily between the orange cones, she knew she'd passed the test.

"Ninety-two percent," he grumbled as the car came to a stop. He tore the test form out of his ledger and handed it to her. "Take this to the registration desk. They'll process your license."

Addie looked it over. "How come I only got a ninety-two? You didn't mark anything wrong."

"You think I don't know you kids move those cones?" he winked. "Nobody gets a hundred percent."

A different person—friendlier than the first—was manning the desk when Addie returned. He snatched the paper from her hand, administered a quick eye exam and then rolled a carbon copy license form into the typewriter. After plunking out her first name, he squinted at the test sheet.

"For Pete's sake! Gary smeared ink on another test. He's been told a million times not to use those fountain pens." Addie peeked over the desk. Sure enough, where her last name should have been there was only a long horizontal smudge.

"What's your last name?"

Addie stared past the man to an old door mounted on the wall behind his desk. Painted on it was Lost Elm's water tower. She studied it carefully, her eyes coming to rest on three letters in the lower right-hand corner—*JRP*.

"Where did you get that?" she asked.

"The painting? Beats me. I came back from lunch one day last month and there it was. Pretty good though, don'tcha think?"

"Yeah," Addie replied reluctantly. "It is."

"So . . . your last name?"

Addie looked at the painting's initials again, especially the last letter. "Braver."

"Can you spell that?" His hands hovered over the typewriter keys.

"B-r-a-v-e-r." His fingers obliged, thwacking out Addie's new last name.

Addie hadn't known she was going to say *Braver* until the word came out of her mouth. But with each higher gear she shifted into on her way out of town, the more sense it made. Addie wasn't a Travers and she couldn't be a Pearson, not one more day. Choosing the name Sara had given her was the only thing that made sense. She *was* Addie Braver.

*

Ranger heard the Volkswagen's puttering sound long before the car scooted up the Carsons' driveway. He rose from a patch of shade next to the house, intent on greeting whoever emerged from the odd little machine.

Addie left the car door ajar and brushed Ranger's face as she moved past him into the house and up the stairs. The dog followed, but his weary hind legs couldn't make the climb so he waited for her at the bottom. When she reappeared, she was carrying a large object down the stairs with her.

"Watch out, boy," Addie grunted. "I don't want you to get hurt." Ranger followed her outside again, but kept his distance from whatever she was dragging across the yard. He watched, head tilted, as she stowed it inside the car.

"Stay," Addie told him as she ran off to the barn. Ranger didn't need to be told twice, he'd been feeling his age lately. Having the girl and boy on the farm had been like a tonic for the old dog, but now the smells of autumn were in the air. And where there was autumn, instinct told him, change wasn't far behind.

Addie returned from the barn with Jake's duffel bag full of cash, glad to see that Ranger had disappeared. She opened the hood and dropped the bag next to her suitcase, peeling off a few twenty dollar bills and putting them in her pocket. *I'll count it all later,* she told herself. *But it should be more than enough.*

Addie looked down to the Loop. A moving van was backed into the Farelli's driveway, a station wagon parked next to it. Across the road, two small boys explored the stumps of the Pines while an older boy walked around the dirt outline where the trailer had once stood.

"Bark!"

Addie nearly leapt out of her skin to find Ranger curled up in the front seat of the car. He seemed to be waiting for her to join him.

"Bark!" His tail wagged happily, he wanted to go for a ride.

"Come on, fella—you can't come with me, not this time." A third bark, then a fourth. She tugged and pulled on his collar but the old dog's haunches were firmly planted on the passenger seat. "Are you sure, boy?" Ranger whimpered with excitement and put his paw on Addie's arm. She took a deep breath and exhaled. *I'm just Addie to him. Nothing more.*

The car rolled slowly down the driveway, then turned onto the highway. With the gas gauge nearly empty, Addie pulled into the truck stop by the interstate. She waited by the pump for a few minutes before noticing the big Sinclair sign overhead: *Now Offering Self-Service Fueling for your Convenience.*

"What'll they think of next?" she mumbled, recalling the day Harold had told Sara, *"You can pump the gas all by yourself now."*

When the tank was full and paid for, Addie pulled out of the truck stop and headed toward the freeway. To her right a sign read, *I-35 North*—to Wood City and Duluth and Ely. To the left, on the far side of the underpass, was the entrance to *I-35 South.* Addie wasn't sure where that road might take her, but hoped wherever it did the shadow of Lost Elm wouldn't follow.

She cleared the underpass and came to a stop at the bottom of the southbound on-ramp. Her head began to buzz and tingle as her throat constricted in fearful anticipation. Summoning a courage she didn't feel, Addie revved the engine and waited. *You're Addie Braver,* she told herself. *You can do this!*

She turned on the radio and spun the dial, smiling a little wistfully as Fleetwood Mac's latest hit began to play:

Loving you isn't the right thing to do.
How can I ever change things that I feel?
If I could, maybe I'd give you my world.
How can I when you won't take it from me?
You can go your own way,
Go your own way!
You can call it another lonely day.
You can go your own way,
Go your own way!

"Ready, boy?" she asked Ranger, her eyes glistening with tears. The dog licked her face. "Good. Let's go."

Addie shifted the Volkswagen again and again, accelerating up the ramp and merging smoothly onto the freeway. Soon she was out of sight, just one more car heading somewhere—anywhere—far from Lost Elm.

EPILOGUE
MAY 2, 1978

The search for Addie lasted months. Dozens of leads trickled in from people convinced they'd seen a girl in a metallic green Volkswagen Beetle, but the only real clue turned out to be a scrap of paper Billy found hidden under his bedroom pillow—a cryptic six-word short story he showed no one: *I'm sorry, Shorty. I couldn't stay.* Eventually, the investigation fizzled out. Billy and the Carsons mailed Addie's picture to post offices across Minnesota with the caption, *Have you seen me? Please call...*, but their phone didn't ring once over the long, bitter winter of 1977-78.

*

"*Excuse me,*" the classroom intercom squawked. "*Could Billy Travers please report to the office at the end of 8th period?*"

"Yes, ma'am," Mr. Meisner replied. He peered over his glasses at Billy. "Mr. Travers, you may leave now if you like, but don't forget to have chapter six read and outlined by tomorrow. Characters, settings, themes."

"Already done, Mr. M," Billy said as he grabbed his copy of *The Call of the Wild* and headed for the door. He walked into an empty hallway and stopped by his locker before going to the office. The school day—Monday, May 2, 1978—was nearly over.

Billy hadn't been called to the office in a long time—a quiet spring. Fall and winter were different stories. Rarely had a week passed when he wasn't summoned by the secretary or discreetly handed a note from a teacher to see the principal. The anxiety of all those meetings returned with a vengeance as he opened the office door to find Principal Hollman waiting for him.

"Hello, Billy. How are you doing today?"

"Pretty good. Just another Monday."

"I know what you mean," Mr. Hollman chuckled. "But only four Mondays left then school's out."

Billy got right to the point. "Let me guess, somebody somewhere thinks they saw Addie." Mr. Hollman opened his mouth to answer, but was interrupted by the dismissal bell. Seconds later, students filled the hallways and headed for the exits.

"This came in the mail today." He gestured to a small package on his secretary's desk. "I was hoping you could tell me who this is from." It was addressed to *Billy Pearson–Lost Elm High School: Lost Elm, Minnesota 55718.* Billy recognized the handwriting immediately.

"You look relieved," Mr. Hollman said.

"Every time I'm called out of class I brace myself for the worst. Some awful news about Addie."

"I'm sorry, Billy. I know how hard this year has been for you. But you haven't gone by *Pearson* since last fall. Addie couldn't have known about the name change. So I have to ask, is this from her?"

"No," Billy lied, turning the box over in his hands.

"Are you sure? Last fall the sheriff told me to keep an eye out for any mail that came to the school addressed to you. This is the first one."

"Do you remember the Farellis? They lived next door to us out on Halverson Road. They moved last August when my name was still Pearson. I'd know Renny's handwriting anywhere. This is from him."

"Why didn't he just mail it to your house?" Mr. Hollman pressed.

"They moved before we ever lived with the Carsons."

"That makes sense," Mr. Hollman nodded. "Thank you, Billy."

"No problem."

"Say, do you need a ride home?" Behind them, through Mr. Hollman's office window, the last bus had just pulled away from the curb.

"No, I biked to school. Thanks, though—see ya tomorrow."

Billy had put his haying money to good use, buying a red, 10-speed Schwinn as soon as the snow melted earlier that spring. He'd ridden back and forth to school ever since, but straight home wasn't his destination today. He pedaled south to Ervin's instead, clutching the package Mr. Hollman had given him.

"Good to see you again," Mr. Ervin greeted Billy. "Where's your friend?"

"Renny moved last summer, Mr. Ervin. It's just me now."

"Whatcha got there?" he asked, gesturing to the box in Billy's hand.

"I dunno, I haven't opened it yet. Probably just some old baseball cards."

"Speaking of." Mr. Ervin pointed to a display next to the cash register. "These just came in, the first packs of the season. How many should I put you down for?" Billy ran his hand over the cards. The texture of the wax paper and the scent of bubble gum filled him with an elusive nostalgia.

"I don't have any money today. I just stopped by to say hi."

The old man smiled broadly. "I can't have you go away empty-handed, Billy. Have one on the house."

"Thanks, Mr. Ervin. See you around."

"This Saturday?"

"Sure, but I don't know if I'm gonna collect cards anymore. It won't be the same without Renny."

"Well, until Saturday then."

Billy pedaled on to the entrance of Hillside Cemetery. He laid his bike in the grass and walked over to his mother and father's graves, then peeled open the pack of cards, making short work of the gum inside. Like he and Renny used to do at the beginning of every baseball season, Billy examined the first card's new design before skimming through the rest of the pack. The style of the 1978 cards didn't impress him much, though he wasn't sure if that didn't have more to do with Renny's absence than anything else. But when Billy came upon a particular card, he paused to admire it.

"Rod Carew."

The Twins first baseman had had a season for the ages. Even Renny's cherished hope, an MVP award, had been won by the slugger. But like every summer before 1977, hitting .400 was not meant to be. Rod Carew had finished with a batting average of .388 after a furious rush in the final week of the season.

"Last card," he decided.

Billy had put off opening the other package long enough. Why he hadn't told Mr. Hollman the truth—that it really was Addie's handwriting—Billy didn't know. But opening it in front of him had been out of the question.

Hands shaking, he tore the box open in a rush. Something wrapped in a piece of cloth fell to the ground, followed by a piece of paper with writing on it. Inside the cloth was Addie's knife—his knife. He withdrew the blade and threw the knife to the ground. It sliced through the paper and held fast in the grass. When Billy pulled it free, the paper came with it. But it wasn't paper at all. It was a Polaroid photograph with a piece of paper taped to the back. He gently removed the blade, put the knife in his pocket and read aloud:

The knife was never mine,
And neither was he.
But I miss you all the time,
Love Always, Addie

The words didn't make any sense. *Neither was he? Neither was who?* Billy turned the photograph over and there was Addie, standing on the sidewalk of some unknown street staring straight at him. Her hands were on her hips and Ranger was by her side. Billy knew that expression well. Addie looked determined, defiant, proud. *She's okay*, he told himself. *Addie's okay.* But that was all he knew. Somehow, it would have to be enough.

Billy looked at his sister for a long time, then down to his parents' graves. *Now what?* he wondered. *Where do I go from here?* But before the thought passed from his mind, he had the answer. Billy put the card and the poem and the Polaroid in his back pocket and rode hard for Lost Elm.

He slowed down only once, at the intersection in the center of town, but even then he barely braked. First National Bank and Paulette's Café and the Junction Bar and the water tower were nothing more than peripheral blurs as he raced past each of them, shifting his bike again and again until he reached tenth gear. Soon the old depot fell away as the Northern Pacific Railroad sign came up fast on his left. Billy gave it only the thinnest of glances, but his legs pedaled furiously at the memory of his and Addie's glory there.

He powered on, the new pavement of Halverson Road making his final push upward easier than it had been in years gone by. When Billy reached the top he made a wide turn across both lanes, remembering Addie's words to him the last time they were together on nearby Carson Hill. *"Halverson Road might be the only thing around here that lasts."*

Billy took a deep, jagged breath, unconsciously accepting what his mom had tried to tell Jake on her deathbed—that the bone-deep ache from the absence of people he truly loved would never fade. Time wasn't going to heal anything—Billy would go on missing his sister and his mother with a steadfast heart. One day, perhaps, he might get better at living without them. But not today.

Billy exhaled and looked down the road, half-expecting to see his sister waiting impatiently for him far below. Releasing the handbrake, he pushed off with both feet. The tires hummed on the blacktop as the bike quickly steadied itself and gained speed. He loosened his grip on the handlebars as a voice rose from some hidden place within him, imploring Billy to do what Addie always knew he could—*JUST LET GO!*

And so he did.

ACKNOWLEDGMENTS

I began ADDIE BRAVER with no clear idea where the book was going or how long it would take me to write it. I only knew that I liked Addie and Billy Pearson immediately and wanted to do their story justice. Soon they were on my mind all the time. I worried about them, wondered if they would be okay, but mostly felt fortunate to be able to tell their tale.

Not surprisingly, I bugged and bothered plenty of people along the way. *How does this sound? What do you think of that? Am I off track here?* It had to be maddening. But I was humored, listened to, and offered all kinds of helpful suggestions. Each person weathered my resistance to their constructive criticism patiently while I grudgingly came around to their points of view. To all those folks, I owe a huge debt and an even bigger thank you. ADDIE BRAVER wouldn't be the same book without you.

I dedicated this book to my kids, Maggie and Drew, who would be the first to admit they had no hand in its creation. But in a larger sense, they were seated next to me every time I wrote. After all, though parents rarely admit it, we want our kids to be as proud of us as we are of them. I'm no different.

Lastly, thank you, Dear Reader. I hope you found the heroic parts of yourself in this small story. Life, like Addie's world, has many.

About the Author

Eric T. Bergman grew up in the Lost Elm-like town of Carlton, Minnesota. After graduating from the University of Minnesota-Morris, he slogged through half a dozen years as a paralegal in Minneapolis before becoming a middle school social studies teacher in Osceola, Wisconsin in the late 90's, where he's been ever since.

In addition to writing his first novel, Eric authors a blog of musings, rants and personal stories called *The Cheap Seats*. Within those blog posts, in poetry and prose, the seeds of the story that grew into ADDIE BRAVER were planted.

Eric currently lives amicably in the Twin Cities with his cat Stella, though some days are better than others.

Made in the USA
San Bernardino, CA
29 June 2019